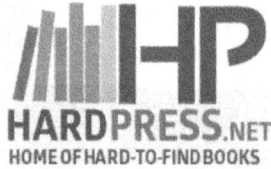

HARDPRESS.NET
HOME OF HARD-TO-FIND BOOKS

The Tourist in Spain
by Thomas Roscoe

Address:
HardPress
8345 NW 66TH ST #2561
MIAMI FL 33166-2626
USA
Email: info@hardpress.net

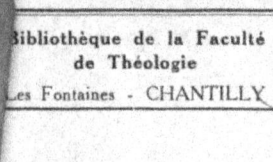

G 3

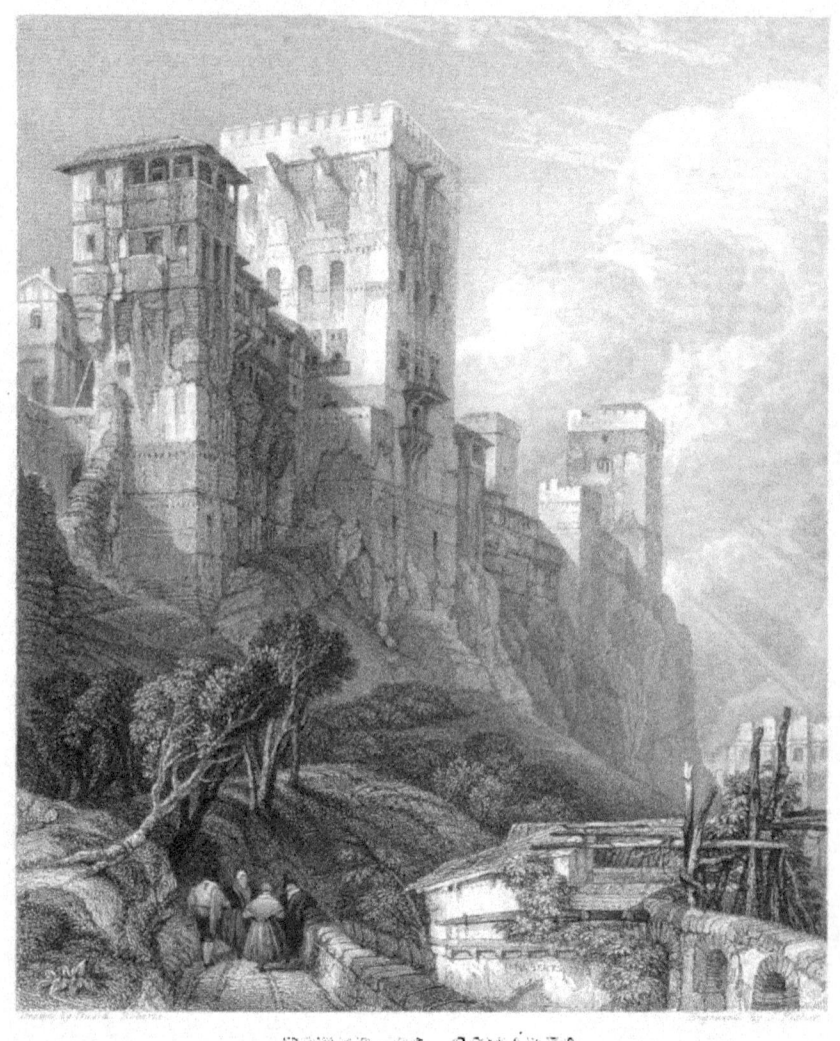

TOWER OF COMARES.

JENNINGS'
LANDSCAPE ANNUAL
FOR 1835.
TOURIST IN SPAIN.
GRANADA.

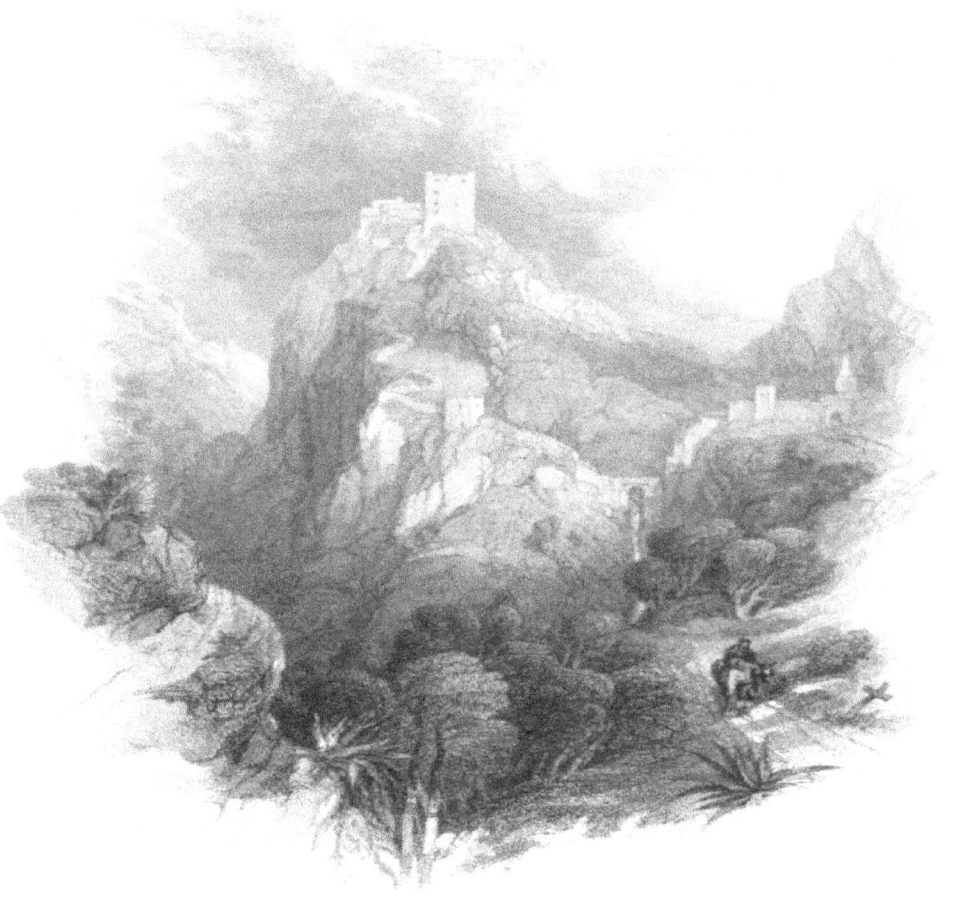

LUQUE

LONDON,
ROBERT JENNINGS AND CO.
62, CHEAPSIDE.

THE

TOURIST IN SPAIN.

GRANADA.

By THOMAS ROSCOE.

ILLUSTRATED FROM DRAWINGS

BY

DAVID ROBERTS.

As Death upon his hand turns o'er,
  The different gems the world displays,
He seizes first to swell his store,
  The brightest jewel he surveys.

Thy name, by every breath conveyed,
  Stretch'd o'er the globe its boundless flight ;
Alas ! in eve the length'ning shade,
  But lengthens to be lost in night !
                                KAMAL EDDIN

LONDON:
ROBERT JENNINGS AND CO. 62, CHEAPSIDE.

1835.

LONDON:
PRINTED BY MAURICE, CLARK, AND CO.,
FENCHURCH STREET.

TO THE

RIGHT HONOURABLE

LORD NORTHWICK, BARON OF NORTHWICK,

F.S.A., ETC. ETC.

AS A MARK OF THE ARTIST'S RESPECT,

THE FOLLOWING ILLUSTRATIONS

OF THE ANCIENT

MOORISH KINGDOM OF GRANADA

ARE

RESPECTFULLY INSCRIBED.

PREFACE.

THE Author of the LANDSCAPE ANNUAL has already conducted his readers to the fairest scenes of France and Italy. In traversing those lands, renowned alike in history and song, he endeavoured to gather from hoar antiquity,—from the page of the adventurous traveller, and the poet's lay, whatever he remembered as the bright source of his veneration for the genius of the south.

He pursues, in the present volume, a somewhat bolder flight. Spain—bold, ardent, melancholy Spain —the only land in Europe that the children of the East seem to have cared to make their home ;— the nurse of romance, after it left its cradle in the Arab desarts ;—the glowing mother of chivalry—the sovereign of an infant world, whose wondrous plains and forests, but for her, had been perhaps still unknown ;—

Spain——a land in itself bearing features expressive of all that can give interest to external nature, and possessing annals filled to overflowing with memorials of the great, the erring, and the ill-fated, furnishes themes on which the mind, looking either for lessons or for excitement, may brood long and well.

Old associations——the mingling surprise and admiration with which he traced these annals, placed the Author in a position midway between history and tradition——not far enough from reality to forget the truth, but still sufficiently excited to give credence to the whispers of his own opinions and sympathies. He presents the reader with the result of the inquiries and thoughts which have had their origin in this state of mind. That fiction may be made the handmaid of truth, is proved by many a memorable example, and he trusts that his attempt to combine the various consequences of a long succession of events in a narrative condensed by, rather than founded in fiction, will not fail in the principal object he has had in view. The Moors of Spain were a people marked by the strongest lineaments of human power and genius; their character, their glory, and their fall were alike distinguished by the mysterious energy which raised the founder of their nation into a conqueror; carried their tribes, first from desart to desart, and then from kingdom to kingdom, impelling them, when satiated with conquest, into the strange regions of philosophy, and in their desolation cast a glow of splendour, too deep, perhaps, ever to become evanescent.

But while thus endeavouring to develope the character of the Moors, and of Moorish history, by the aid of a slight fiction, he has not left the reader without the information he might naturally look for from the simple narrative of the traveller or the historian. Examining the best sources of intelligence, he has detailed the circumstances of the fall of the Moors, as they are recorded in the annals of the country; while in every instance the noble talent of the Artist has been brought into companionship with the knowledge and ability of enlightened travellers.

To combine, as far as his ability would enable him, the mild attractions of a descriptive tour with the more useful display of events and characters, has ever been the aim of the Author of the LANDSCAPE ANNUAL. The reception which has hitherto attended the work, affords him encouragement to believe, that he has, in some degree, succeeded in his efforts; and with the hopes thus inspired, he trusts that the present volume will be found not wholly unfaithful as a mirror of the noble scenes, and still nobler incidents which he has attempted to describe.

In the tone of language and style of imagery he has adopted, the author ought perhaps to add, in justice to his own views, that it was not done without mature reflection and deliberation. Had he continued to preserve, throughout, the calm and even tenour of the tourist's way, as in the narratives of Italy and France, he felt that he should have justly exposed himself to the charge of tameness and want of feeling on a subject like the downfal of the Spanish Moors. While the farthest possible from attempting to catch even the semblance of that fire and energy, combined with novelty and elegance of ideas, or that loftiness and magnificence of expression which displayed a genius at once refined and gigantic, the author's admiration of the noble theme on which he wrote of itself impelled him to a deeper and warmer tone, and to a more frequent use of that imagery and those epithets, resulting from the more impassioned interest which he felt. Whether he may be justified in this slight change, by what he has observed of the natural elevation and vigour of style whenever the passions are strongly roused, and by his reverence for the magnificently bold and sustained flow of mighty epic masterpieces, like the Iliad and Antar commemorating the fortunes and vicissitudes of rival nations, an enlightened public,——that great unerring critic,——will alone decide.

LIST OF THE PLATES.

* This Plate will be found at page 36,—not the Frontispiece, as there stated.

Description of Vignette-Title.

LUQUE is one of those strong mountain-forts, so often met with in the mountain passes that separate the kingdom of Granada from the other parts of Andalusia. It lies about two leagues to the south of an ancient Moorish city, with an extensive castle now in ruins, called CASTRO. This is situated in a line of country extending from Cordova to Granada, and is about one day's journey from the former. The aspect of the entire region is now wild and desolate, but still, in spots, retains marks of its former cultivation. Although almost totally neglected, the soil is so rich, that the tourist has the greatest difficulty in keeping his horse from sinking over the knees in the thick alluvial soil.

In crossing these wild hilly districts, stretching between the two cities, the country farther on appears covered with the richest verdure ; even the face of the loftiest cliffs is seen decorated with the most beautiful and variegated flowers. Notwithstanding the distance between these ancient capitals is not great, yet from there being no road whatever, the journey occupies a space of three days. Through the whole line of passage may be traced the remains of an ancient Roman road, which in many places continues in tolerable good condition, together with its bridges, which in some instances have a most singular appearance, the channels of the streams having long abandoned their original beds, leaving the bridges half buried and choked up by the soil around them ; and being only prevented from totally disappearing by the massy structure of the stones of which they are composed. It is not at all improbable, that this road may have been in active use during the reign of the Moors, inasmuch as a constant communication must have been kept up between the two great capitals of the Moorish empire. It has been allowed, like every thing connected with this unfortunate nation after their expulsion, to fall into decay. What farther renders this conjecture the more probable, is, the long line of Moorish watch-towers still in existence, connecting the intervening stations with each other, and following as nearly as possible the line of the great Roman road.

There is some allusion to this Tower of Luque in the very interesting Chronicle of Granada by Mr. Irving, when mentioning the battle in which Abu Abdallah was taken prisoner, and the brave alcayde of Loxa was slain.

List of the Wood Engravings;

WITH DESCRIPTIONS.

This gateway was erected on the northern side of the city, opening upon the beautiful and fertile plain, or *vega*, as that of the Xenil is situated to the south. It was in passing through this portal on his first campaign, that King Abu Abdallah broke his lance, as described in the course of the following narrative.

This far-famed and splendid portion of the Alhambra, called the *Quarto de los Leones*, or Apartment of the Lions, is an oblong court one hundred feet in length and fifty in breadth, environed with a colonnade seven feet broad on the sides, and ten at the end. The colonnade is paved with white marble, the square with coloured tiles, and the walls are covered for five feet from the ground with blue and yellow tiles in a chequered form. Both above and below these, are borders of small escutcheons in blue and gold enamel, with the motto, "No Conqueror but God." The columns that support the roof and gallery are of white marble, very slender and richly adorned with arabesques. The ceiling of the portico is finished in a still more elaborate and complicated manner, being frosted, and handled with astonishing delicacy; and the stucco laid on the walls with inimitable care and art. The capitals are of various designs, though each design is repeated several times in the circumference of the court.—*See the description of the Plate,* p. 245.

The Tower of the Bell, or as it is sometimes called *Torre de la Campana*, and *de la Vela*, is one of the loftiest in the whole fortress range of the Alhambra. It commands, with a perfect view of the city, the entire extent of the vega; and from this tower was the signal invariably given for the opening of the sluices, or floodgates, to distribute the waters, at fixed seasons, for the purpose of irrigating that fertile and magnificent plain. This was effected by intersecting it with canals, from which issued lesser streams, all which gave to the blooming vega the aspect of one spacious and delicious garden. On the top of this tower was raised an immense cross by the victorious Christians, when they took possession of the last grand strong-hold of the Moors. I may further mention some beautiful lines written on this very subject by Mr. Alaric Watts, which have much of the spirit and pathos worthy of so fine a theme.

The Torre de la Campana, or rather towers, have in later times been appropriated to the use of prisons. Below them, on the south side, on a slip of terrace, is the governor's garden, a very delightful walk, filled with fine orange and cypress trees and myrtle hedges, but wholly consigned to neglect. The view it commands is incomparable. Two large vases, enamelled with gold and azure foliages and characters, are the only ornaments left; these were taken out of the vaults under the royal apartments. On the right hand of the Plaza de los Algibes, is a solitary gateway, formerly the entrance into some of the outward quadrangles thrown down by Charles the Fifth, to make room for his superb palace, which stands facing the Torre de la Campana.

The *Plaza de los Algibes*, or Great Square of the Cisterns, lies contiguous to the palace of Charles the Fifth, and doubtless received its name from the circumstance of the great reservoirs for water having been constructed beneath its surface. These ancient cisterns are continually supplied with a running stream, fed by the neighbouring hills of the *Sierra Nevada*. So rapid and abundant was the flow as fully to suffice for the inhabitants and for the baths of that vast fortress. One of these, carried to a considerable depth, is one hundred and two feet in length by fifty-six feet in width, and is enclosed by a wall, over-arched, and six feet thick. The arch was forty-seven feet seven inches high in the centre, and seventeen feet five inches below the surface of the ground.

That quarter of the city of Granada called the Albaycin, must be familiar alike to the tourist and to the historical reader, as containing one of the oldest and most massive of those palace fortresses which decorated the great cities of the Spanish Moors. It was the chief scene of those ferocious civil conflicts of the people, such as they will be found described in the following narrative, towards the close of the Moorish monarchy, more eagerly contested in its decline and fall. It was the grand rallying point of the last Moorish king and of his mother, the Sultana Aixa, in their contest with the father and the uncle for the Moorish crown.

A considerable portion of the hill of the Albaycin is still enclosed by a thick massive wall, flanked by ponderous towers of equal strength, erected at short intervals along the ramparts. Like all other Moorish fortifications in Spain, they are formed of a strong composition called *tapia*, consisting of clay, mortar, and gravel. Time has rendered it more hard and durable than even stone itself, but though employed to such an extent, the art of producing it seems now totally lost. At Xeres, the city walls, which are of the same composition, were actually sawn into slabs for covering the drains and sewers of that comparatively rich and flourishing city. There is every reason to believe that this composition is of great antiquity, and the same so much in use among the Romans.

The entrance to the Albaycin is situated to the north, near the gate of Elvira, opening upon the beautiful plain.

The Gate of the Xenil, so named from its vicinity to the river so called, is situated on the south side of the town, opening to the part of the plain opposite to that of the Elvira. Not far from this gate, on the other side of the river Xenil, stands a small convent that marks the spot upon which the unhappy Abu Abdallah delivered up the keys of Granada to the conqueror.

El Tocador, or the Dressing room of the sultana, is a small square cabinet in the centre of an open gallery, from which it receives light by a door and three windows. It is surrounded by a balcony three feet broad, the roof of which is supported at intervals by columns of white marble. The look-out is perfectly charming. —the view of the Generalife with the embowered terraces, the flashing waters of the winding Darro, and the beautiful retreats along its banks—all combining to produce a species of fascination to the eye. The interior of the Toilet is exquisitely decorated; and subsequently, the Emperor Charles caused this pretty retreat to be painted with representations of his brilliant wars, and a great variety of grotesques, which appear to be copies, or at all events imitations of those in the *Loggie* of the Vatican. They are said to have been greatly defaced and injured by idle scribblers, although enough remains to show they were the productions of eminent artists. The tourist proceeds through a long passage, or antichamber, from the Tocador, and thence suddenly enters into the magnificent Hall of the Ambassadors; on the left hand it opens on the Comuna, or Great Baths, and on the right, into the large Hall of Audience in the tower of Comares.

From the inscriptions which adorn this charmingly secluded spot, some writers maintain that it was in old time the oratory of the palace, no doubt from the circumstance of the principal window having an eastern aspect. The inscription on the cornice, which runs round it, seems to tend further to corroborate the justness of such an opinion :—

" In the name of God, who is merciful ! God be with our Prophet Mohammed ! Health and happiness to his friends ! God is the light of heaven and of the earth, and his resplendence is like himself. It is a luminary with many branches and many lights, but producing only one general refulgence. It is the lamp of lamps, a brilliant constellation nourished with eternal oil. It is neither western nor eastern ; once illumined, it diffuses light for ever, without being touched, and with this light God guides those whom he loves ; and he gives proverbs to nations."

In the Hall of Comares, likewise, is situated the gallery which formed the prison of the sultanas, and is still termed the Queen's Prison, from the popular persuasion of Abu Abdallah's consort having been there confined on the charge of adultery. You ascend into it by a small modern staircase, the original and more beautiful one having been destroyed. A portion of this gallery is inclosed with an iron grating. Both the railing and the corridor have a modern appearance, when contrasted with the remaining portion of the palace. The gallery communicates with four apartments, built during the reign of Charles the Fifth, on a ground-work of Moorish construction.

The chapel of Ferdinand and Isabella constitutes the sole portion of the grand cathedral elevated upon the site of the ancient Moorish mosque, which was added to the original structure by these two illustrious princes, who reflect the same lustre on the annals of Spain, as do its Mohammedan conquerors themselves upon the genius and character of their native tribes. Adapted to the Gothic form of the cross, the modern cathedral presents an unwieldy mass destitute of real architectural beauty, consisting, as it does, of an assemblage of three churches in one. Of these, one is a rude-built parish church; the second, a large chapel erected by Ferdinand the Fifth during that unfavourable era of the arts, when the light, elegant style and ornamental beauty of the Saracenic was almost wholly abandoned to make way for the heavy, unmeaning, and sombre architecture which preceded the knowledge and introduction of the pure and noble Greek. Ferdinand and Isabella repose before the altar, under a large marble monument adorned with figures and grotesques, in a sufficiently improved style to show the progress which the arts had already made since the building of the edifice. Of the most costly materials, like most of the existing churches of Spain, it is overloaded with rich and lavish ornament, as totally destitute of taste as of simplicity. If the tourist will but be at the pains of comparing the modern Christian cathedral of Granada with the grand old mosque of Cordova, he will trace the grounds for the justness of this statement at once, with more pleasure and deeper conviction than any explanation could afford.

With the exception of the Zacatin, there are few places in Granada which have undergone less change than the square of the Viva Rambla. The houses and shops are as nearly as possible the same as when tenanted by the Moorish shopkeepers and artisans. It presents all those peculiar traits in its aspect and localities, which tend to impress the idea that it is still inhabited by the same active and ingenious people. Every where there is much to remind us of their former presence and useful possession, extending even to the Spanish dress and features; and we almost think we are conversing with the subjects of a Moorish monarch, as we note the swarthy complexion, large, dark, and full eye, and the roundness of countenance, still declaring their eastern origin. In regard to costume, it is true the modern Andalusian does not, like his Moslem ancestors, continue to shave the head; but, from the same cause, no Spaniard shaves *himself*, and consequently there are, perhaps, more barbers in Spain than any other country in Europe. Though he allows his hair to grow, he still envelopes his head in the folds of a handkerchief which has replaced the turban; his loins are still girded by an ample sash, and to this day the Spaniard wears his *capa*, or cloak, thrown over the left shoulder in the same graceful manner as the *haik* worn by the Moor, or his *manta*, a sort of coarse woollen cloth, by the peasant or muleteer. It is the same with the Arab of the present time, his dress is wide and open, principally to show the full embroidered cotton drawers underneath. " These and other things constantly remind you," says the ingenious and observant artist, who visited parts of Barbary as well as Spain, " that you are still walking amongst the descendants of the Prophet."

This tomb, intended as a monument rather to commemorate the triumph of the Christian sovereigns over the infidel, than of Spanish rulers who had united her scattered gems of empire in one grand symmetric crown,—is composed of the purest white marble, and is also of the most exquisite and elaborate workmanship. It is evidently the production of Italian artists, and has every appearance of having been constructed during the reign of the Emperor Charles the Fifth. Adjoining the two monarchs who lie side by side appear, on a similarly constructed tomb of still more admirable workmanship, the effigies of Philip the Fair, their son-in-law, and of their daughter Joan. Over the great door is the emblem of the united monarchies,—a bundle of arrows tied together, and clutched in the talons of a single-headed eagle. In the chapel is an altar-piece, on which appear some curious carvings in wood, apparently of the time of Ferdinand, representing the unfortunate Abu Abdallah surrendering the keys of Granada to Ferdinand and his court, whilst the wretched Moors are seen in the back-ground issuing from the Gate of Judgment with their hands bound and in an abject, despairing attitude.

In another compartment is shown the Moors, and also Moorish women with their faces concealed, receiving baptism; and they are the more interesting as being, perhaps, the only thing of the kind in existence giving an exact idea of the dresses worn by the Spanish Moors. That of the women, in particular, has been remarked for its precise similarity with the one borne by the women of Tetuan, and of these the artist in his costumes of Spain and Barbary has shown me several specimens. The veil, for instance, and the swathings round the legs are the same, and there are numerous other resemblances sufficient to establish the transcendent influence of the conquering Moor over the habits and character of his subject Goths. The cathedral is remarkably rich in sculpture and other remains, chiefly of Italian art, Charles the Fifth being known as a lavish patron of the leading artists of his age. Many of their best scholars, when they could not themselves attend, accepted his invitation to decorate the churches and other public buildings of Spain. Of these the most original and eccentric was Torrigiano, the rival of Michael Angelo, who in a sudden fit of anger struck the great Florentine and broke his nose, which ever afterwards appeared flattened. This irritable genius went to England, and was employed in the chapel of Henry the Seventh; but compelled by some fatal feud again to fly, he sought a refuge in Granada, and assisted to decorate the chapel of Ferdinand and Isabella. Having been employed by some Spanish cardinal to form a statue, he conceived himself inadequately rewarded, and broke it into pieces with his mallet. Soon after he was denounced before the Holy Inquisition, and condemned to expiate his temerity and his plain-dealing in the fires of the *auto-da-fé*.

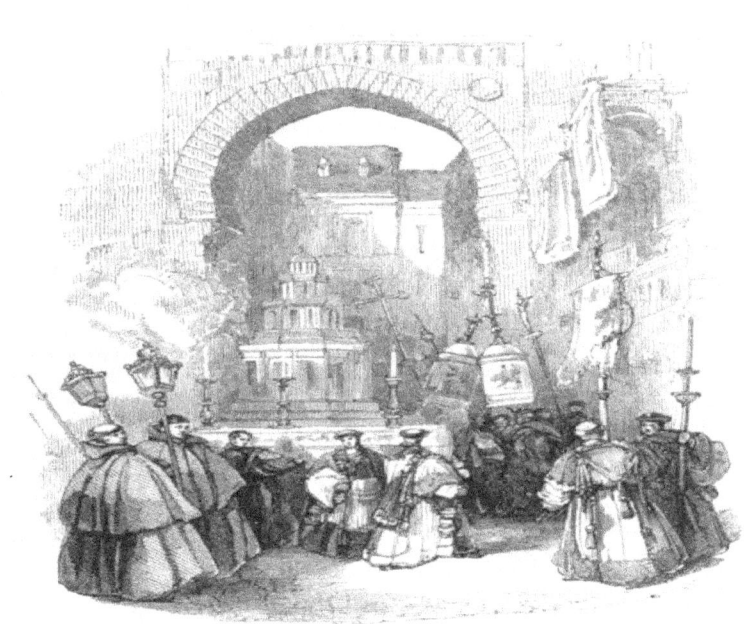

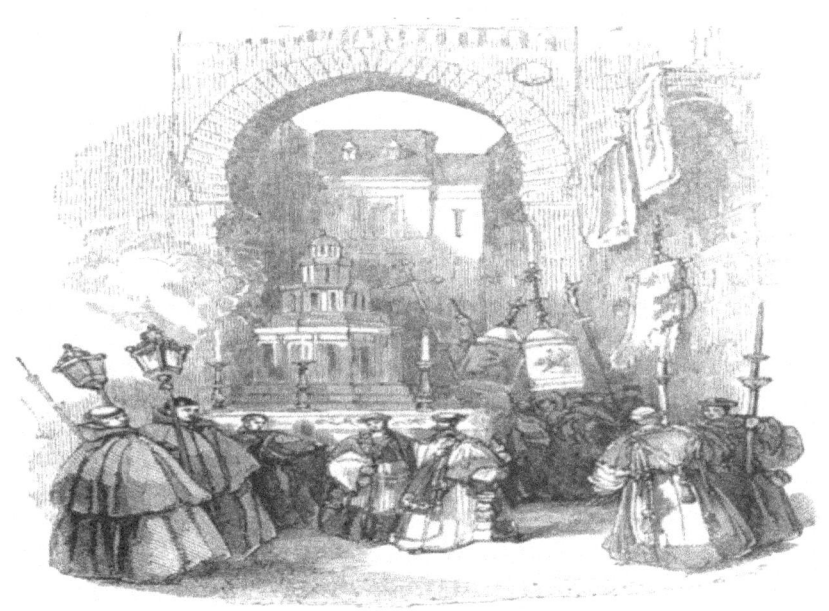

THE FALL OF GRANADA.

CHAPTER I.

Come Hope, with golden ray,
Beam through the gathering night;
Lo, the same sun that fades to-day
In the far main, ere dawn repairs his light.

ROMANCERO ANTIGUO

AT the close of that dread eventful day, when the
Moorish monarch beheld the Christian captives of the
fallen Zaharāh led in triumph through the gates of

B

Granada,* a noble and elder of his council, famed alike for eloquence and wisdom, left the evening banquet of the Alhambra to meditate in the cool delicious shades of its spreading gardens. The venerable yet still chivalrous Aben Kassim had been the companion of the ruling prince from the earliest period of his career; had shared in his victories, been the partner of his pleasures, and, in the most perilous moments, approved himself the chief stay and pillar of the state. But while the Moslem king continued, as in youth, fiery and impetuous, enamoured of power, but wild, dark, and involved in all the wanderings of passion, Aben Kassim had become mild, temperate, and thoughtful. The fervid zeal for the glory of his religion which had led him into the noblest scenes of Moorish conflict; the passion which had made him the hero of some of the tenderest lays of the poets, still exerted their power over his soul; but his motives were now wholly embued with the glowing spirit of his love of country, and of his friend.

The creed of the great prophet and reformer did not however teach him to gather wisdom from the internal warfare of self with self. It left him his passionate dreams of delight; he was too devout a Musulmān not to cherish them as anticipations of the bright and everlasting paradise. But Aben Kassim had too much mind to be kept in bondage by the rich and sensual visions of the heaven pictured to

* The city of Zaharāh, carried by storm, was the first blow struck by the king of Granada, which provoked this last and memorable campaign.

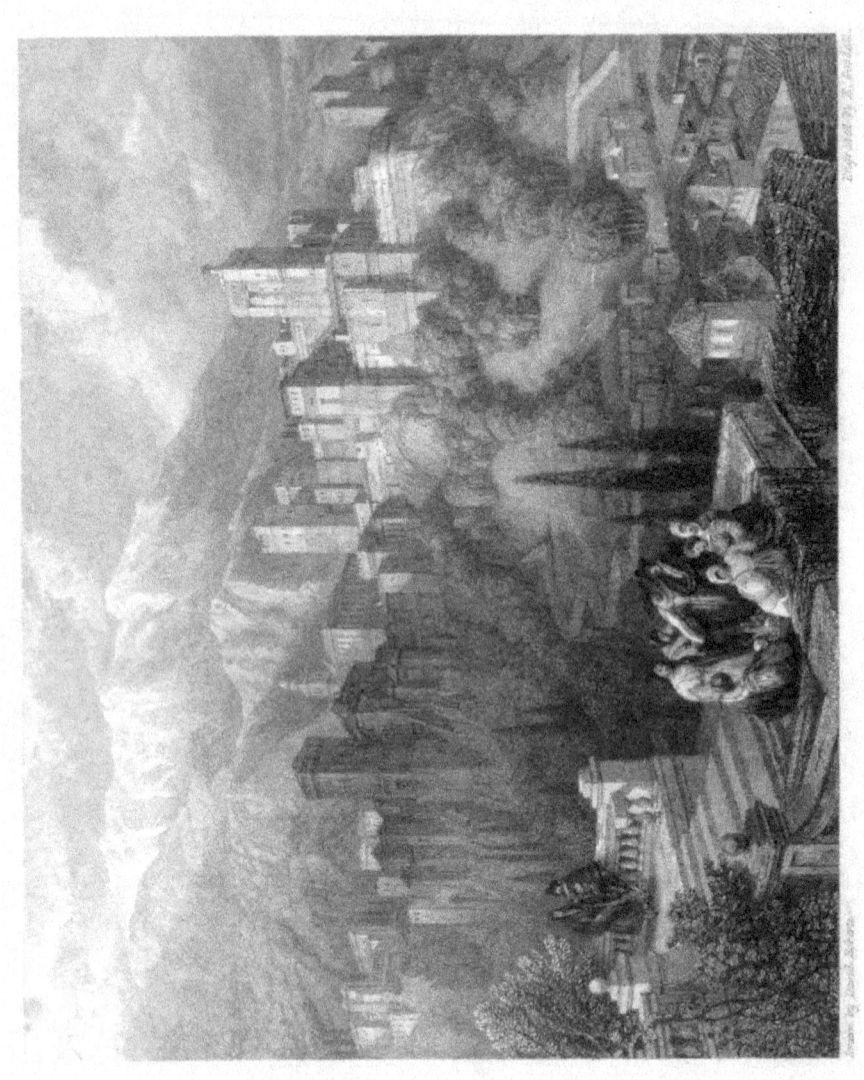

the eyes of the faithful in their bold career. Almost unconsciously rising beyond the highest circle of the visible domain of faith; disposed to that seriousness so revered by its loftiest disciples, he had by the mere force of thought, and by a rapid succession of changes, not unobserved, acquired a habit of attention to the signs of the age, and the shadowy aspect of coming events. Genius, combined with knowledge, gave him a power higher and truer in the study of destiny, than the oldest of the Islamite prophets, who held communion with their celestial chief.

The noble hajib* now entered the deep grove of mingled cypress and myrtles, which skirted the eastern towers of the Alhambra. Through the occasional vistas of these sequestered shades, the vast edifice presented itself to the eye in all its dim, undefined proportions; its gorgeous and sumptuous hues.† Its

---

* The prime minister, and presiding chief of the council.

† On emerging from the hills, into the spacious and blooming plain, the old Moorish capital is seen in the distance, and more conspicuously the ruddy light of its Vermilion Towers, (a) high overhung by the range of the snow-clad Sierra. The sight of the famed Alhambra, associated with the memory of the adventurous heroism, the strange romantic loves, the fearful fate, the now mouldering towers of its lordly masters, impresses the soul with deep and mournful feelings ere the traveller enters its deserted courts, its yet splendid but silent halls. A fortress of palaces, its walls bristling with castellated forts, embrace the entire crest of the hill which commands the city, forming part of the grand Sierra Nevada, a chain of mountains perpetually covered with snow. Thus spacious as splendid it would admit a garrison of forty thousand men, and

(a) Alhambra,—" the red house;" so called from the colour of the materials originally employed.

bold turrets, its gilded domes and minarets had now ceased to reflect the rays of the departed sun, but the deep purple of the sky rested like a glory upon the massy angles and buttresses of the lofty towers.

was frequently the sole possession of different contending monarchs during the civil wars of Granada. Its very desertion, after the conquest of the Moors by the Castilian monarchs, with the abandonment of the palace of Charles V. seemed to be dedicating it to ruin and decay—a mighty monument to the power and splendour of its founders.

Granada, the beloved city of this vast mountain-fortress, lay at its feet. Approached by steep winding avenues, through groves of fragrant beauty, decorated with temples, gardens, and fountains, the white, glittering edifices, the sparkling of the waters, and the golden light of spires and minarets, gave to the dark green foliage and the deep azure of its skies a splendour of relief almost dazzling to the eye. Through an antique Moorish tower of vast dimensions, opened the chief entrance leading to its grand portal, the Gate of Judgment, within which sat a public tribunal (a) to pronounce instant decision on the causes of the people. The arch of the grand vestibule extends half the height of the tower; on the key-stone is sculptured a gigantic hand, and in the same manner, on the inner side, a gigantic key : the former, it is believed, representing the emblem of doctrine, the latter that of faith, and borne as an armorial ensign on the banners of the Moslems in their early conquests, opposed to the Christian cross. A winding passage from the porch conducts the spectator to an open esplanade, the Plaza de los Algibes, where were situated the great reservoirs cut in the solid rock for supplies of the purest water. At this point, the magnificence of the prospect from the walls above, along the vale of the Darro, and through the Vega, is nowhere to be surpassed. Proceeding round a part of the imperial palace, the tourist next enters the interior of the palace by a plain, unornamented portal ; and it is then

(a) The Hall of the Two Sisters, and all the splendid suite of saloons and towers, as they will be found more particularly described in the appropriate portions of the work assigned to them.

In proportion as the last refulgent light of day sank in the horizon, the whole of the spacious structure—losing its brilliancy—seemed to dilate in solidity and extent.

the enchantment of eastern pomp, luxury, and refinement first bursts upon his astonished view. Here appears the Court of the Alberca, and at the upper end rises the Tower of Comares. Through an arch-way at the lower part he approaches the celebrated Court of Lions,—on one side of which lies the Hall of the Ambassadors.

The lavish splendour of the Alhambra gave rise to the popular belief that its great founder, Mohammed Aben Alahmar, must have dealt in magic. The first king of the noble line of Beni Nasar, he gained the throne by his reputation for wisdom and beneficence, in 1238. His former character as a governor seemed to actuate every movement of the monarch; with qualities at once brilliant and solid, he promoted many noble and useful institutions, and was beloved by his subjects as their guardian and their friend. He commenced the building of the grand fortress towards the middle of the thirteenth century, directed its progress in person, and was often seen conversing with the architect and the labourers. Though surviving to an extremely advanced age, he left his vast undertaking to be finished by his successor, Yusef Abul Hajig, who erected the beautiful Gate of Justice. Vieing with the example set by his illustrious predecessor, he evinced all the ardour of a great and good mind in promoting the happiness and prosperity of his people, and so strong was his attachment to learning and the arts, that at a period when the rest of Europe was lost in comparative barbarism, Granada presented a capital and a court surrounded with all the luxuries of taste and refinement, all that was elegant and emblematic in the genius of this active and extraordinary people. "Granada," says an Arabian writer, "was, in the days of Yusef, as a silver vase filled with emeralds and jacynths."

The above view includes the whole of the fortress, together with the Generalife. Immediately in the centre stands the Tower of the Homage, to the left of which rises the palace

" Holy Prophet!" ejaculated Aben Kassim, as he gathered his spangled kaftan * closer about him to resist the breeze which now blew keener from the snow-capped mountains,† wildly mourning through the groves;—" Holy Prophet!" he repeated, " thou wert not enshrined in splendour and luxuries like these, when the messenger of the supreme first taught thee

commenced by the emperor, Charles V. This is a very magnificent building, composed entirely of marbles found in the neighbouring mountains, and in any other situation it would be deemed beautiful. Here it is eclipsed by the splendour of the Moorish edifices by which it is surrounded.

Still farther to the left is the noble Tower of Comares, while the building on the rising ground behind is the Palace of the Generalife. Between that and the Tower of Comares, is the one of the Infantas, and the Water Tower. The hill rising in the back ground is called the Mountain of the Sun, high overhanging the whole, and with its summits wrapt in the clouds of the Sierra Nevada. That loftiest tower on the right is the Torre de la Velha, or as it is sometimes called the Tower of the Bell, which commands the whole view of the fortress, together with the extensive Vega, or plain of Granada. On the extreme right lies the Torre de Vermejas, between which and that of the Bell is situated the principal entrance to the Alhambra.

Descending the hill of the Albaycin, which is still partly surrounded by a long line of battlemented towers, between two of which is the entrance which forms one of the woodcuts,—namely that to the Albaycin,—and thence crossing a large square in front of the palace of the Captain-General, we ascended a winding and confined street, called the Calle de los Gomerez, from which point the artist took his view of the Vermilion Towers.

   * Decorated robe or mantle.
   † The Sierra Nevada, a chain of hills to the south of Granada, the summits of which are constantly covered with snow.

the ineffable mysteries of eternity ; when the glories of
a celestial paradise burst upon thy more than mortal
view.   Thy cave of refuge boasted no battle-towers, no
rampart walls of brass ; yet wert thou more inviolate
than steel-clad monarchs in that fort-girt sweep of
golden palaces.   He who veiled thee with the spider's
simple web, who bade the dove to build, and spread
her wings around his prophet's head,* whispered to
thee there more sweet and wondrous counsel than all
the wisdom of our learned ulemas,† the vain, weak-
eyed policy, the idler eloquence of our grand divans.
In the eyes of the most merciful and gracious thou
didst find favour and exaltation, for thy doctrine
breathed the faith of the compassionate and the
resigned.‡   Adversity opened to thee the stores of
experience § and truth, and Destiny guided thy steps
in the right path, till thou couldst behold all-joyful
Paradise prefigured in the " shade of the scymitars,"

* Incidents related by historians and followers of the prophet, in recounting Mohammed's escape from the pursuit of
his enemies, and referred to the immediate miraculous inter-
position of the Deity.
   † An order of lawyers next in rank to the cadhi.
   ‡ Of Islam, or resignation.
   § Witness the noble lines by the Sultan of Mousel, written
when deprived of his crown, and a prisoner :—

Hail ! chastening friend, adversity 'tis thine,
The mental ore to temper and refine,
To cast in virtue's mould the yielding heart,
And honour's polish to the mind impart.

Without thy wakening touch, thy plastic aid,
I'd lain the shapeless mass that nature made ;
But formed, great artist, by thy magic hand,
I gleam a sword to conquer and command.

beckoning thy young bright Faith's disciples to rush
into the groves of spears, to mark unquailed the
lightning of the battle clouds, and greet thy enemies
with a joy yet loftier than we welcome the pure
blessed season of thy earthly Bairam.* But where
is now the generous soul of thy early khaliphs, who
raised their golden thrones upon the necks of subjugated kings? where the thousand cities, and palaces,
and tribes, and nations? Fallen; fallen on the bitter
scorn and hatred of Islamite with Islamite, of brethren
and families, of ancient tribes with tribes! Once
were thy institutes of bravery and honour clad in
the royal robes of sovereignty, courteous and magnanimous; once were discipline and justice wedded
with the gravity of reason and sound discretion;——days
for ever fled! The season of alms, and prayers, and
pilgrimage, thy people flocked to the voice of thy
muezzins;† then were the faithful sheltered beneath
the sacred shield of their judge-kings, when they sat
in their gold and gem-embroidered kaftans at the gate,
and gave out even measure to the meanest son of Islam.
Where now is the impulse which bore thy Moslems,
with the Koran newly written on their hearts,——
graven on their flashing falchions,——beyond the utter-
most bounds of their native seas, built up kingdoms,
seignories, and states to its glory, and towered upon
the wings of conquest, till it out-soared even the

* The Mohammedan Easter.
† Appointed to give public notice of the five recurring
periods of prayer during the day.

chivalry of the mighty Charlemagne, and laid the loftiest crests of his favourite heroes in the dust?" *

Scarcely had the last words fallen from the lips of the old, impassioned Moslem, when the moon, a small silver crescent, was seen slowly surmounting the shadowy crests and broader minarets of the Alhambra. Aben Kassim felt like a mortal from whose eyes the veil of ages had fallen away; who was permitted to behold the secret fountain of his ancestral glory,—the mysterious shrine, in whose golden cells the banner of Mohammed had been treasured by the fates ere yet unfolded to the world. †

The Prophet had, beyond question, chosen well when he selected the half-orbed moon for the bright material emblem of his worshipped faith. For beautiful is the moon looking from heaven's azure depths over a city in all its living strength, its turmoil, and its greatness; beautiful is she when her beams fall thick and luminous over the field glittering with tents and spears. But still more lovely is she when pouring a chastened glory upon the ruins of empire slumbering in their time-hallowed desarts, she seems as if she were only watching the steps of the lonely traveller, or waiting to reveal some mystery to the ardent soul of a true worshipper.

> * " When Roland brave, and Olivier,
> And every Paladin and Peer,
> On Ronscesvalles died."

† A favourite tradition of the old Moslems, who abounded in gigantic imagery, and corresponding expressions, wherever their passions were concerned.

Mohammed knew well that his earthly followers would often need some visible celestial emblem to inspire them with the recollections of past glory, and never since the sword-planted tree of his faith took root, has that bright crown of his standard beamed through the veil of night, but it has awakened in some warrior of his tribes a more indomitable spirit; in some Imam's priest or pilgrim-poet, a deeper, more glowing enthusiasm as they bent at the sacred shrine, calling on Allah and his Prophet. Aben Kassim reverently raised his turban from his brow as he fixed his eyes on the clear calm heavens, till the planet had risen high above those palace towers, their shadowy courts, wooded avenues, groves, founts, and garden bowers,—the last and most beloved capital of the faithful. Then with the slow step of one whose thoughts ponder on deeds given to power, wisdom, strength,— not the feebleness of haste or low policy to fulfil,— he entered that magnificent area of the Alhambra, called the Court of the Lions. The splendid marble pavement, the capitals and pillars of the porticoes, the alabaster reservoirs, the water of their bright fount that threw its spray rejoicingly into the pure, still air,— all far and near received a new and mysterious touch of beauty from the silver light of the waning moon.

Aben Kassim paused for a moment in this proud, spirit-stirring scene; all was silent around him, but a quick ear might catch at intervals the mellow voices of the lutes, awakening the hours to love and song, amid the golden saloons and inner chambers, or the plaintive note of some bird from the myrtle gardens of the Linderaxa. It was none of these, however, that made the thoughtful Moslem pause; his step rested before one of those singular inscriptions emblazoned from early ages on the halls and temples, not less than on the swords, of the Prophet's children, teaching them how kingdoms were to be won, and how, when conquered, they were to be maintained. A sigh escaped him as he turned away from the admonitory wisdom of the past,—that sole despised heritage of our sires; and he proceeded with more hurried step and clouded brow to the palace residence of the king, into whose presence he alone, of all his aged council, ventured at any hour.

Muley Ibn Hassan was seated in one of those luxurious retreats of the Alhambra, prepared by the seductive genius—the elegant voluptuous flatteries of successive architects, painters, and poets of those brilliant times. Beauty in all its forms, under every species of capricious taste, rare fancy, and emblematic invention, was to be seen in the variegated labours of these delicious saloons. Through richly ornamented windows and flower-wreathed lattices, came the odorous air of gardens shut out from every eye but that of the prince and his favourite sultanas and friends. Glittering, half-concealed fountains of the purest water diffused a coolness which gave sweet anticipation of the approaching night, and could one human being have entered that enchanting seclusion, so lovely in its solitude, without the heavy sense in his heart of human sin and calamity, he might well have rejoiced to behold on earth so rich an earnest of something not of fleeting beauty, a type of man's recovered paradise with all its promises of delight.

But there was an expression on the features of the Moslem king which would have dissipated every gentle and loving thought,—all of peace, or heaven-inspiring solitude from the mind of the most unsuspicious of beings.

He was now long past the meridian of life, and his stately strong-knit frame had begun to bend and rock under the united force of time, enervating indulgence, the stormy passions of his breast. Still his countenance was more strongly ploughed by anxiety than by age. His swarthy brow bore traces of the most violent tempests that can shake the human soul. Not deficient in the light of intelligence, the mental characteristics of his face were themselves but interpreters of the pride —the terrible self-will which ruled all the thoughts and avenues of his being.

Aben Kassim then was the only one of his ministers who feared him not in his gloomy moods; and the stern monarch, as he greeted him with a few pithy words, seemed to admit that he knew him to be his only real friend, and that he had, therefore, a right to approach him when he pleased, and to speak what he thought. " Son of Ismael,"* said the noble scheikh, " methinks the hour is drawing nigh which must de-

* The peculiar veneration of the Moslems for the paternal authority, is in nothing shown more clearly than in this prevailing custom of individual address; nor could there be a higher compliment to the son, than thus to sink his own name in that of his father,—a fact which places Boabdil's usurpation in no very amiable light.

cide the fate of empire between thee and the descendant of thy vassal Goths. Fortune, my prince, like the heavenly emblem of our faith, shone on the Moslem arms till their glory had reached its flood—till wearing a paler aspect it began to wane with the revolution of days. Will it rise once more, fair as yon glorious crescent? will it ever more irradiate the world with its glorious beams? Or is it not in the book of destiny, oh prince, even from the beginning, that the fame of nations which hath risen like the sun in the east, shall set in the west amid a darker night; that they who have achieved deeds of splendour shall but feel the darkness of adversity fall more heavily upon their souls! Brave as thou art, didst thou do well, oh king, to hurl defiance at the Christian foe? Nay, chafe not; but having cast down the gauntlet to his teeth, draw the sword of the Prophet,—away with the scabbard, and let it woo the smiles of victory once again, as it were a new and hard-won bride. It is not war, nor the fortune of the open battle-field, which fills my prophetic spirit with alarm; I doubt not the onset of thy chivalry, the rush of spears, and the daunting clamour of our horsemen in the shock of steed with steed. It is not war; it is the deep designing policy, the cool and cautious treachery, the arts and intrigues of Arragon's king, the firm and fanatic spirit of his Castilian consort, which Aben Kassim most dreads. More darkly inauspicious than the chivalry of Christendom marshalled in frank array against our scymitars, with what weapons shall we resist his dastard arts? Vain to us is the aid of Afric's princes, and the fiery blood of her desart tribes, against the bribe which dissolves the ties of concord and saps the foundation of our empire, arming the hand of Moor against the peace of Moor."

" What think you, noble scheikh ? plots Ferdinand in secret to raise up enemies to our throne in the chiefs and children of the faithful ?"

" Yea ! in the tribes of your Zegris and Gomelez, in the palace, in the harem of Muley Hassan, oh king."

" And wouldst thou, therefore, pay him tribute, Aben Kassim? wouldst deprecate my policy—nay, my long craving—my burning thirst and passion, of war? retribution, long merited, in avengement of great Allah's and his holy Prophet's cause ? It is welcome to my soul !"

" Daringly great, but rash, unadvised, wert thou, oh king, when with taunts on his rejected claims thou didst spurn the royal envoy, and for vassal-pay present the glistening scymitar to the Christian court. But was it wise and well for a commander of the faithful— for a father of his tribes, and of horsemen—for a ruler of the people, and a judge of the city? was it prudent as it was honourable to the heart of the heroic chief of our chivalry?"

" Oh, Aben Kassim! and couldst *thou* have heard that vain-presuming knight remind thee of thy vassal lot, and call aloud for tribute before the assembled emirs and elders of the empire, seated amid thy symbols of sway, robed in thy royal kaftan on thy imperial divan, a throne won for thee by the sword of judgment wielded by thy Prophet? Had he sent to challenge us to open tourney, at the tilt of reeds, or to place the destiny of empire on lance with lance, more pleasing to me had been the sight of that malapert envoy in our lists. But his idle, vaunting embassy, told in so lofty a tone, made me tremble with rage to smite him spite of his sacred badge, even where he stood. And, methinks, he ought to thank thee, that he does not now look down from our battlements, in place of bearing our sharp-edged missive to the wily monarchs of Arragon and Castile. By Allah! it will rouse their chill, stagnate blood when they hear that all Granada's kings who once gave tribute-money to Castile are dead and gone—that our royal mint coins nothing now but blades of swords and heads of javelins. Yet it irks me that we let him wag his pert and impious tongue, when the flash of many a weapon told him that justice was near at hand, ready to sprinkle the mouths of our lion-founts with his impetuous blood."

" Nay, count not of him, my royal master, at an hour like this. Ye have struck the first blow—ye have perilled life and crown upon the die, be it for good or for evil result. Why a moment's delay? Haste, fall swift as death, an eagle from his mountain rock with the prey in view, on the scattered squadrons of the foe. Granada's last hope lies in the fiery combat; she can only foil her subtle enemy by rushing from field to field, reaping fresh harvests of the sword. Give him no breathing time to play his secret game, and stake the life of Moor against royal Moor. No more let the edge of Moslem steel smite the breasts of the Prophet's children !——seize on every resource——pour through all its wide-spread channels thy long-treasured gold, till it turn to steel-clad hosts. Yea, the magician of the war, strike the earth with thy golden rod, till there up-spring legions upon legions——bands of hardy mountain warriors cover all our plains. Let the old Moorish pennon, unfurled once more on the bright blue seas, bear Afric's fiercest tribes,——the swart sons of the desert——to confront the pride of European chivalry gathering round us from each Christian land in aid of our haughty foe. Let us, too, summon all of heroism and fiery zeal in the cause of our Prophet, to stand by us in the mighty struggle, to brace the hearts of the children of Allah, to conquer with renown, or still more greatly to perish. By our faith and our country, go forth with rapid heart-cleaving blows ! beat down the artful points and stratagems of thy enemy, as the sword of God,* wielded with the old resistless fire of his Khaled, consumed whole hosts of unbelievers !"

" It is now," replied the king, " I recognise the young companion of my victories——my staff——the light of my path; for thy looks are terrible as when, young in arms, we broke the strength of famed Pelayo's breed of mountain freemen, and bade their humbled monarch do obeisance to the dazzling glory of the crescent; terrible as when we opened a path through hostile squadrons on Cordova's plains, and brought

* The sword of God : a frequent figure in alluding to the exploits of Mohammed. His favourite, Khaled, was renowned for his brilliant success in the early battles of the khaliphs.

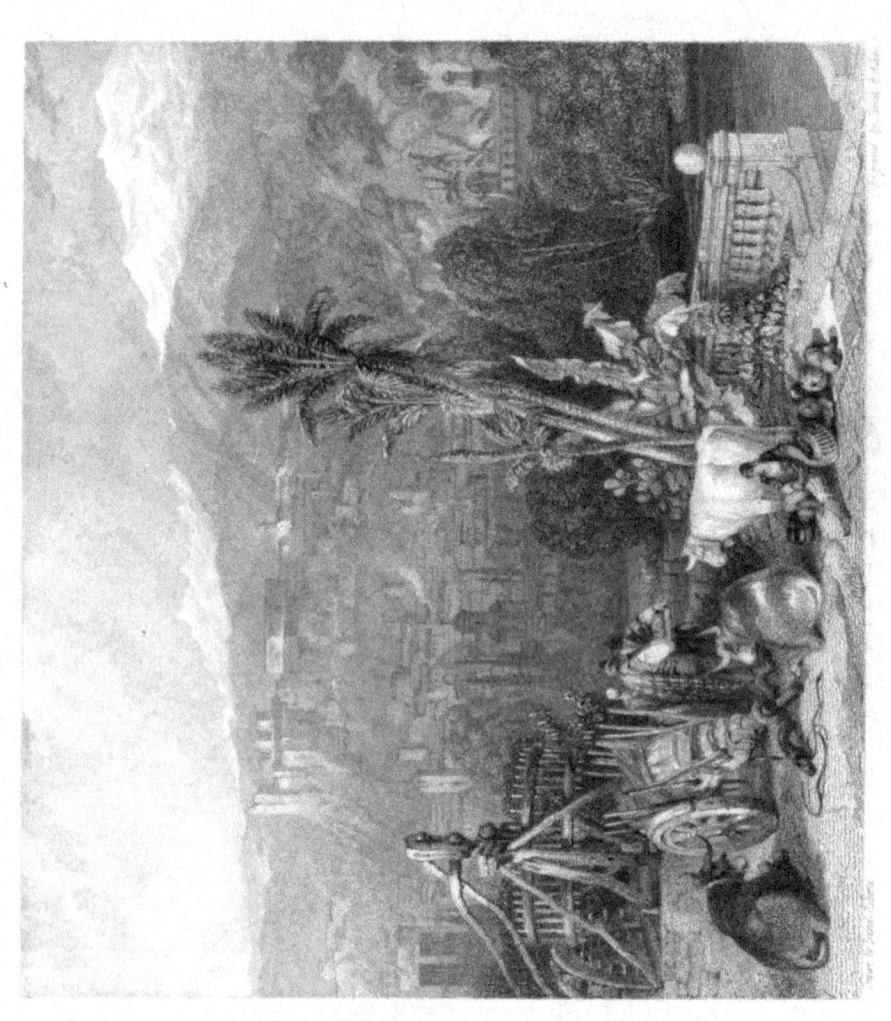

their chief a captive into our capital. Thy counsel, noble scheikh, comes from lips touched with the hallowed wisdom which inspired our Prophet. I see he is thy friend, and still be thou the friend of Muley Hassan, and let all be done as thy own brave heart would have it."

"Then Allah speed us! let us join the grand divan, and next, oh king, summon we to the sacred mosque our imauns and elders,—yea, the hajees,* every pious follower of their revered priests, even our faquirs and santons, to offer up their prayers for Granada! Thence let them proclaim through her cities, from end to end, the greatest of our holy wars; thence unfurl our Prophet's sacred banner, and hurl back the infidel from the soil of our beloved country!"

And was it not a glorious resolve, to hand down to their children and to their far successors the bright heritage of their heroic sires—those blissful seats so long illumined by the torches of genius, science,—by the lords of the sword and of the lyre—the glory of those heavens, the magnificence of nature arrayed in all the splendours and delights which mortal art and industry can picture to the eye and to the soul! Then who can wonder at the rapture with which the Moor looked upon the bright and beautiful city of his princes!† In the dewy twilight of morning, breathing

---

* Pilgrims;—hajee Baba, or pilgrim Baba.

† Wildly romantic, and strange as magnificent in its solitude, the aspect of Spain combines with the softer features and enchantments of the south, all the stern bleak air of grandeur so characteristic of the eastern desart. With its bulwarks

C

the soft spirit of its southern sea, mingled with the
pure breezy freshness of its snowy sierra; in the
radiance of the noonday sun, in the solemn shades of
evening, Granada burst upon his sight with a splendour

of dark sierras, its sweep of wide cheerless plains, alternating
with the most delightful and fertile regions, abounding in all
the exquisite beauties of its southern clime; it may be said
to resemble the architecture of its singular conquerors,—vast
and massy, dark and forbidding in its exterior, but suddenly
opening upon all the interior beauty, glory, and refined
luxurious taste, which pictured to their eastern imaginations
the paradise of the blest.   But the rugged, dreary hills, with
their ruinous towers and battlements, the broken aqueduct and
bridge, the wasted or diverted fountains, the lost, neglected
roads, the torrent-worn dells and ravines, the birds of prey
soaring from the snow-capped peaks above, the leafless site of
groves, gardens, and busy hamlets—haunts of the wild fowl
and the fox—the stern deep silence which wraps heath and
vale, and stream; what a wondrous contrast to the whole
scenery, under the impulse of the genius—the astonishing
activity, the colonial policy, and teeming fertility characteristic of the Moors!   It is this which gives to the loneliness of
its plains and valleys, the mouldering fragments of its moun-
tain-towns and castles beneath the deep blue skies, in a sunny
soil fertilized by its crystal springs and rivers, so peculiarly
mournful and almost unnatural an air.   Thus Granada, like
some mighty relic of vanished empire, every where presents
traces of her palmy days of splendour; the foot of the Moor
is still on her soil; the look, the accent, the very character and
manners of her regenerating Arab victor is visible in the
features of her children—in their habits and costume—in the
implements of husbandry as in the weapons of war.   Still
with their legend of the saint is mingled the romantic ballad
or love-song of the Moor, as the herdsman returns at even-
tide by the Darro side, the slow-journeying muleteers beguile
the hour, winding their way down the steep mountain-pass.
Within her chain of natural outworks, lofty sierras of marble
and granite with cloud-piercing peaks, glowing under a burning

unknown to any other city in the world. Loved with a species of idolatry, without parallel, perhaps, except in the glory of the Syrian Damascus, or the marble Tadmor in the palmy days of its famed queen,

sun, lay Granada, like some splendid beauty enveloped in rude attire, but whose dazzling charms and enchantments as you approach more near, rivet the eye and fill the soul of the beholder. In her city of palaces, filled with umbrageous courts and avenues,—a sylvan scene of garden, grove, and fountain-freshness wildly intermingled,—a labyrinth of exquisitely decorated nature in her wilderness of mingled sweets,—she bade the rocks pour forth their cool delicious springs through her thousand sparkling founts, her snow-clad hills, to supply her marble halls, her fretted domes, and sacred temples, their wild declivities to bloom with the cistus, the aloe, the fig-tree, the pomegranate, and the vine,—her vegas to teem with fruit and grain, and her garden-bowers with the myrtle and roses of Yemen, beneath their stately canopy of palm and cypress groves. From such a throne of beauty did the last queen of the Moorish capitals behold the approach of the storm, first cradled in the Asturian mountains by a handful of vanquished Goths, and now, having swept over her brilliant empire of the south, about to burst with exterminating fury upon the most beautiful and beloved of her mighty conquests. From her thousand frontier towns and fortresses, through all her thickly peopled plains and hamlets, came the sound of its ruin loud and yet louder upon the ear.

The view here given is taken from the banks of the Xenil. The trees in the foreground are the date palm; whilst that with the large broad leaves immediately below them is the plantain. The rude-looking but picturesque mill on the right is of Moorish origin. It is used for raising water for the purposes of irrigation. Midway in the distance appears part of the town, and immediately surmounting it rises the vast fortress of the Alhambra. One of the first objects that strikes the eye of the tourist on entering the town, is the old Moorish gateway, which conducts him to the entrance of the grand square of the Vivarambla.

far around her swelled the mountains which appear
to have been raised by nature for her lordly barrier,
their snow-bound crests emulating in whiteness the
crystal of the moon-beams——their deep dark woods
bending in bold contrast to the glistening clothing of
the summits, and the not less exquisite splendour of
the golden roofs of palaces and mosques that shone on
the plains below.   Wide spreading along the sunny
sides of the delicious site of this queen of cities, the
murmur of its golden river, the bloom of gardens and
orchards vied with the luxury of an eastern Eden.
Immediately on the skirts of those pleasure grounds
which appeared only lavishly adorned to skreen, in
their sylvan recesses, the most lovely of women from
the too ardent rays of the sun, extended yellow corn-
fields and purple vineyards far as the eye could reach
over fertile lands, richly peopled with busy hamlets,
strong thriving towns, with innumerable castles and
fortresses in the distance.

  In the midst of this spacious glowing scene of fertility, enriched with all the gems of art, lay Granada,
like some proud beauty calm and stately, seated secure
in her own spangled halls.   From the two hills which
she crowned with her numerous sumptuous edifices,
the Darro and the Xenil were seen mingling their
limpid waters, in which the peasants not unfrequently
gathered the purest grains of gold and silver.   The
most conspicuous objects in the direction of the Darro,
flowing through the valley of the two hills and dividing
the city, were the palace of the Alhambra and the
Vermilion Towers,——the former venerable in the eyes

of the Moor as the grand citadel of his country's glory; the latter, as one of those monuments which seem to defy the calculations of time, still glowing midst the surrounding ruins of a fallen empire. To the northward of the river rose the stern rude-looking towers of the Albaycin and of Alcazaba; while the broad intervening plain was covered with the light, airy, and variously adorned dwellings of the wealthy population. The city of Granada, thus beautiful in itself as in its situation, was probably founded by one of those colonies of Phœnicia, which the adventurous merchants of that country had established in several provinces of Europe. The Romans appear to have regarded it as a place well worthy of their attention,—calculated for a strong military station; and it was transmitted from them to the Goths. But it was reserved for the Saracens to invest it with all the strength and magnificence which it was naturally so well fitted to receive. Having in the early part of the eighth century fallen beneath the arms of the victorious Ommiades, it gradually assumed the character of a city, which had for its rulers the most polished and luxurious people in the world. It was not, however, till the close of the thirteenth century that the Moorish people conceived the magnificent idea of the Alhambra. Their coffers were then sufficiently well stored to enable the monarch to carry through his noble design. The plans adopted by Muley Mohammed Abdallah were further pursued by his successor; but the marble walls of the palace, the splendid shrines of the mosque rose not without stains of blood upon their glittering decorations. Moham-

med, the successor of Muley, was an usurper and a
murderer; the money itself, which defrayed the cost
of the sacred edifice, was wrung by oppression from
Christians and Jews.   For several years subsequently,
not a reign is described by the historians of the Moors
without the record of some deed of blood,—the work
of princely hands.

In 1340, Alphonso XI., taking advantage of the
divisions which existed in Granada, obtained a signal
victory over its sovereign, who perished by assassination, hated and despised for his misfortunes.   But the
calamities which followed were not sufficient to warn
the infatuated people of the declining grandeur of
their empire, and the king of Castile continued to
possess the complete ascendancy in the state.   When
Mohammed Alhamar, a dethroned monarch, fled to
him for help, Pedro, justly sirnamed the Cruel, accepted the gold and jewels which the unhappy prince
poured at his feet; but almost immediately afterwards,
seated on an ass, he paraded him, together with his
attendants, through the city, and stabbed him with
his own hand on the field of the Tablada.*   The king
whom the Castilian sovereign, after this barbarous
murder, established upon the throne, reigned in security, as did also his successor, Mohammed Abouhadjad,
whose mild character and virtuous moderation enabled
him not only to remain at peace with Castile, but to

* At the moment he was stabbed, he addressed his assassin
in these words, which became the subject of more than one
ballad : " Oh, Peter ! Peter ! what an exploit for a knight and
a king ! "

improve his territory with new and splendid additions to all its principal cities. It was but for a brief space, however, that the gleam of returning glory continued to shine on the Moors of Granada. The succeeding prince involved himself in bitter strife with the fierce monarch of Morocco ; and, like the hero of antiquity, perished in the envenomed folds of a poisoned mantle sent him by an artful enemy. A similar fate attended his successor who, in the agonies of death, ordered the immediate execution of his brother, whom he hated with so intense a hate that his last thoughts were employed in securing his destruction. The bearer of the death-warrant found Juzef, the intended victim, engaged in a game of chess. " Grant me time to finish the game," was the request of the prince, and with difficulty he obtained the desired permission. The brief interval which sufficed to conclude the game, was enough also to change the colour of his destiny. His brother had expired in the interim, and the loud shouts of the populace proclaimed him lawful successor to the throne. The humanity which formed a conspicuous trait in the character of this prince, contributed greatly to the improvement of the state. He took no vengeance on his enemies, recollected not the cruelty with which he had been treated by the partisans of his brother, but bestowed on the children of that monarch the strongest marks of affection.

The succeeding reigns exhibit few incidents that mark not strongly the rapid decay of that high and magnanimous spirit, which for a long time distinguished the Moors of Granada. At length, clouds, darker and more tempestuous than had yet been seen, lowered upon the horizon. Ismael, who obtained possession of the crown in 1453, found himself threatened by the strength of Castile, as by that of an enemy who had gradually grown up into the possession of a power that could no longer be resisted.

But all that prudence or valour could achieve was effected by this prince. He employed his people in recultivating the lands which had been laid waste by the enemy;——forests were cleared away to make room for the plough, and the villages that lay smouldering in ashes again furnished homes for the terrified and desolate peasantry. His efforts, however, could effect little while the wrath of the Castilian remained unappeased; a peace purchased at the expense of an annual tribute of six hundred Christian captives, or as many Moors when the Christians were exhausted, besides twelve thousand ducats, could alone protect the city of Granada from the horrors of renewed invasion.

Unfortunately for the Moors, as we have shown, his son and successor, Muley Mohammed Ibn Hassan, pursued not the prudent line of conduct by which his crown had been preserved from the hands of the enemy. Placing a false trust in his valour and resources, he ventured to dispute the claim of the Castilian monarch to the tribute agreed upon by his father; the tocsin of war again resounded through the streets of Granada, and sent its fearful echoes from the snowy sierra to the now chivalrous and splendid court of Ferdinand and Isabella.

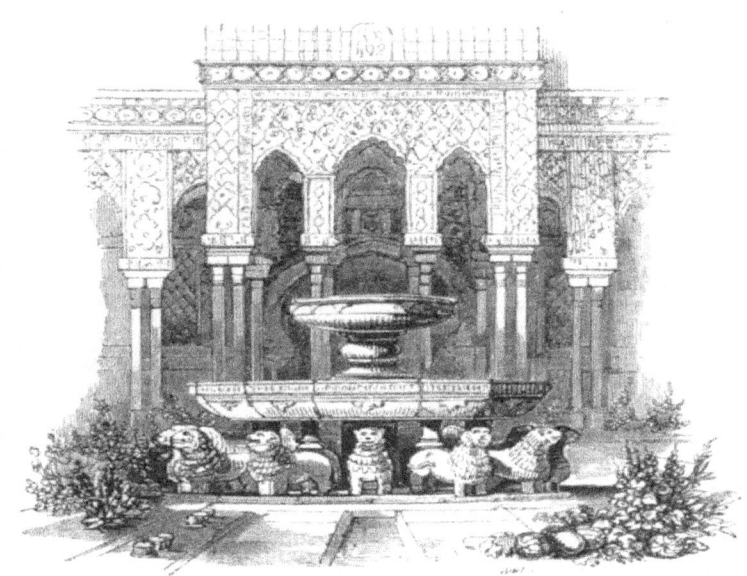

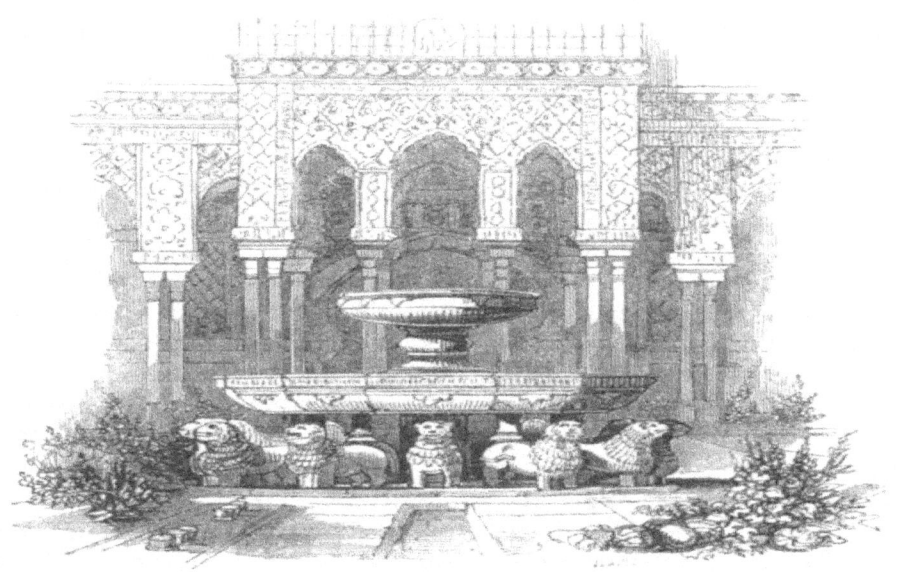

CHAPTER II.

Ventecico murmurador.

All the stars are glowing
　In the gorgeous sky,
In the stream scarce flowing,
　Mimic lustres lie ;
Blow gentle, gentle breeze,
　But bring no cloud to hide
Their dear resplendencies,
　Nor chase from Zara's side
Dreams bright and pure as these.

LOCKHART.

A PRINCE of the Abencerrages, in the yet chivalrous epoch of the Moorish sway, combining the brilliant qualities of his ancestral line with magnanimity and courtesy above those of his generous tribe, was reclining at the feet of the loveliest of Andalusia's maidens, famed alike for the softness and brilliancy of their charms.* She it was had first inspired him with the emprise of love and honour, borne in his heart and proudly emblazoned upon his crest. It was one of those rich, deep-glowing evenings of an Andalusian summer when nature, in all her luxuriant splendour, fills earth, and air, and sky, with a radiant beauty unknown to other lands. Every object seemed embued with a glory, an elasticity of existence, irresistibly inspiring, and enchanting to the eye. Each flower, and shrub, and tree, shone with their own peculiarly ripe and dazzling hues. The myrtle, the citron, the camellia, and the rose, over-arched by stately palm and cypress, and fed from the pure, sparkling waters and breezy incense of the hills, shed an ineffable sweetness through the clear, mild heaven, reflecting its deep purple light upon tower and stream ; while the nightingale from her favourite tree filled the garden-bowers with a thrill of passionate delight, in perfect unison with the hour and the scene. But was it the only music which fell on the charmed ear in these delicious retreats of love?† was there not yet sweeter melody which, breathed from

* " Their very walk would make your bosom swell ;
I can't describe it, tho' so much it strikes ;
Nor liken it—I never saw the like—
An Arab horse, a stately stag, a barb
New broke ; a cameleopard, a gazelle—
No, none of these will do."—BYRON.

† The Generalife ; the name of which imports, the Mansion of Pleasure.

the soul to the soul, lent a charm to the spot such as, in the vivid language of their clime, made those lovers feel as if paradise were indeed in that part of heaven which shone so radiantly fair above their heads?

Amid those bright and balmy bowers,—intermingled in lavish glory of bloom, and flower, and fruit,— and high o'er-canopied by fragrant murmuring groves, they sat, pure and lovely as the flashing waters of the marble fount which rose bubbling at their feet, ever catching some fresh beauty from each other's looks, like those scenes on which they gazed from the moon's chastened beams; there they sat, entranced in the first delicious consciousness of full, reciprocated passion;—and the passion of such a clime! You would have thought they were some bright realization in mortal form of that ideal-beautiful and heroic in the elysium of the faithful, as it is so fondly pictured in the fascinating strains of the fervent poets of their land.

" Great is Allah! and how good!" at length spoke the young, plumed chief, while his large dark eye still hung upon the enchanting features of his adored; " he alone, my sweetest Zelinda, who holdeth the secrets of hearts and the destinies of empires in his hands, could give to his faithful the rapture of moments like these."

" Tell me, are they so very dear to you?" breathed the melody of a voice which thrilled every vein of the noble Moor.

" By your fair self, I swear, a thousand times more dear amid these fierce tumults of reviving war,—dear as the sylvan couch where nestle his loves to yon warbler of the night,——as the spring to the parched lips of the desart-pilgrim, as the voice of its mate to the wild roe of the forest."

" Would Ibn Hammed, then, so often fly from his Zelinda's side to share the stern dark joy of the battle? or is it the will of Allah,——is it so written——that we must submit?" and her eyes met his with that deeply fond and confiding expression which told how easy it were to die *with* him ; that it was the idea of separation, not of death, which made her voice falter,——her bosom heave with sighs.

" Light of thy father's eyes,——my star of beauty midst a sea of storms,——brightest daughter of thy princely line,——sole sultana of my soul,——even thy sighs and tears are precious as the fragrant and dewy sweetness of the rose to her own enamoured bird ; for when near you I am happy above all the children of Allah, favoured more than other sons of the Abencerrages, thus to hear thee speak, drink glory from thy smiles, and read the truth of our promised paradise in those heavenly eyes."

" Ah ! flatterer !" murmured Zelinda ; " it was thus you taught me to love: ere my noble father placed my hands within yours, you already swayed my heart. If you so love to feign, I would you should become a minstrel, and doff those dazzling arms to sit ever near me, and do nought but sing me pretty lays and pastorals of our country's loves."

" Nay, THY love, Zelinda, sheds a glory on my path, and makes these delicious scenes, so captivating in their veiled splendour to those who love the night, a

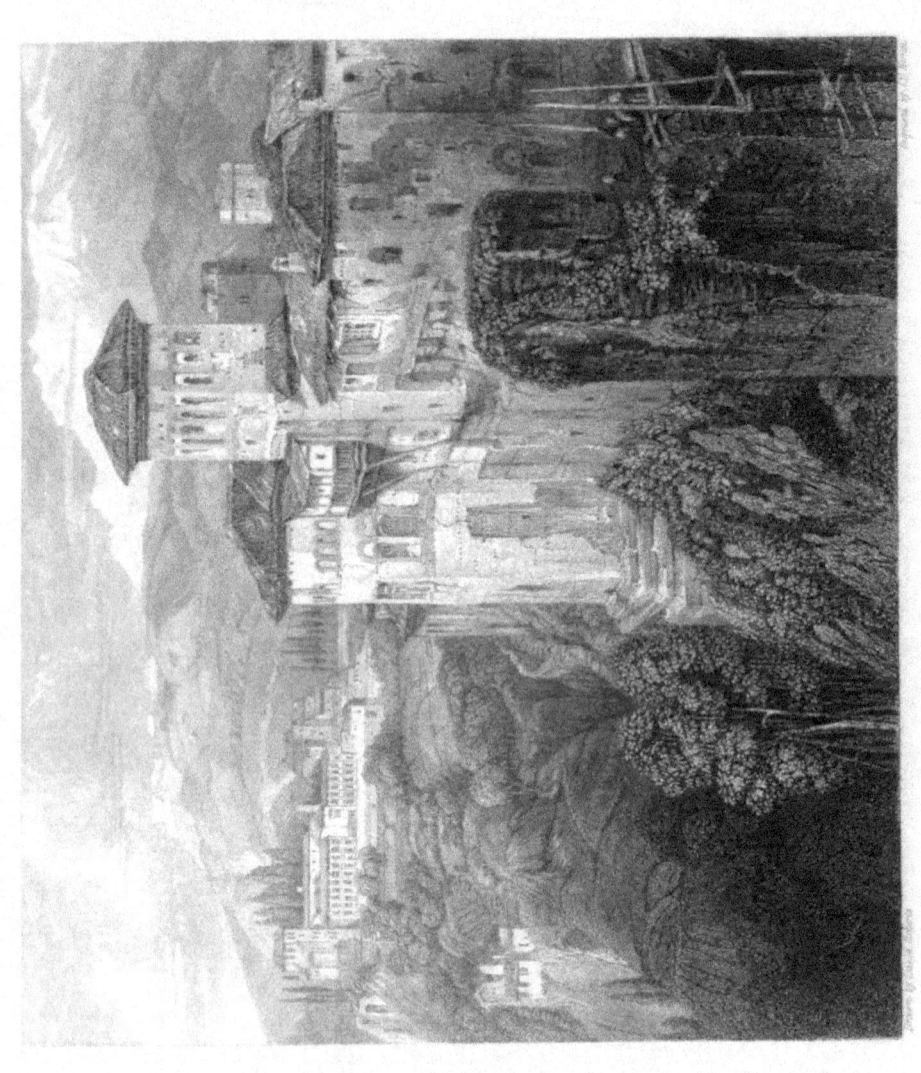

thousand times more refreshing to my soul. Well did
their royal conquerors to call them the retreats of love; *
for that are they, by our Prophet, without the gaudy
mantle of their sylvan palaces, with all their trickeries

* By a small postern, midway in the descent of the hill,
were the Moorish monarchs wont to proceed to their spring
residence in the delicious retreats of the Generalife. Luxu-
riously, most enchantingly adapted for the palace gardens of
royalty, it combined all that was exquisite in locality and
choice; being delightfully cool and fragrant, situated a little
east of the Alhambra, where the towers rise loftiest to the
eye, on a pleasant hill confronting that of the grand fortress.
The prospect it commanded over the vale of the Darro and
the surrounding scenery was picturesque in the extreme; the
golden spires of mosque, and minaret, and tower appearing
through the deep green woods and gardens, and reflected in the
waters of the Vega rivers, like stars studding the dark blue
vault of night. Hence, too, were beheld the old Moorish bridge
and tower on which were erected a noble line of galleries
forming a communication between the Alhambra and the
Albaycin. Amidst mosques and steeples the crystal stream
was seen winding its way into the heart of that beloved city.
The hanging woods and gardens of the Generalife, contrasted
with the fine verdant slopes crowned with the turrets of the
Alhambra, the banks of the Sierra del Sol, and on the north
the Albaycin, with innumerable gardens and orchards, and
subterranean dwellings,—altogether presented a wilderness of
beauties, a scene of fairy objects to the eye unequalled, perhaps,
in any other spot. Lavish nature, fostered by the luxurious
refinements, the captivations of ingenious art ; the distribution
of the entire edifice and surrounding gardens, tastefully adapted
to the aspect of the ground, all threw a species of enchantment
round the scene, such as is felt only on opening into the interior of the Alhambra. But its great charm consisted less in
external splendour and grandeur of design than in the uniform
study of elegant decoration and research, exquisite adaptation
to the tastes and manners of its possessors, the most refined
luxury and enjoyment mingled with the permanently useful,

of cunning art, in an hour like this.   Though they rise
so fair and brilliant from their rich flower-bespangled
hills, though kings revel in their delights and teach
their marble halls and spacious corridors to ring with
the wassal strains of pleasure, more dear to me are the

the seasonable, and even comfortable, so marked a feature in
the architecture of the Moors.   The symmetry of the portico,
bearing that frequent inscription, " There is no Conqueror but
God," has long been the admiration of the beholder.   Its
columns of white marble, the elaborate work above the arches,
the richness of the mosaic, and the brilliant diversity of the
colours produce a striking effect.   The intricate wood-work,
and stucco ornaments of the interior are of similar design,
adequately splendid with those of the Alhambra.   One of
the ceilings is considered the master-piece of Arabian art.
   With its canal and fountains, its gardens boasted perennial freshness and beauty, the glow but of a season in a less
favoured spot ; the purity of its air, its extreme salubrity, a
stranger to the usual sources of decay, while it expanded the
soul and gave elasticity to the frame, gave also deeper lustre to
its woods, richer fragrance to its flowers, and a warmer vegetation, which drew a finer spirit into its bright mellow fruits
of the magnificent east.   The gardens were laid out in the
Chinese style ; the dark cypress in the back-ground, with the
palm in their shady recesses, spread their stately branches above
the citron, the myrtle, the fig; and again, the aloe, the tamarisk,
the pomegranate, were surrounded by the roses of Tunis, the
jasmine, the mimosa, and sweet-blowing lilies of Yemen. Many
an aged cypress still spreads its venerable arms over the spot
once sought by the princely Moors in seasons of relaxation or
of pleasure, and you hear the murmurs of the same river which,
flowing through these delicious retreats, preserved that invariable freshness and fertility so remarkable in the aspect of the
soil under the sway of its former masters.   To this, their accu-
rate scientific knowledge, and in particular that of irrigation,
conduced in no small degree.   Rows of embowering trees were
planted on its banks so luxuriant as to form a sylvan arch

sweet, glad songs of our early pilgrim-poets, who drank inspiration at their Prophet's shrine ; and the wisdom of our ancient scheikhs who loved truth and justice, and made the precepts of the great Koran the guide of their faith and life."

from side to side, and in the centre of the gardens rose a lofty summer-house, constructed of canes, about thirty feet in height, and in the circular form of a dome. The high-arched fragrant bowers of the Generalife, overhanging the river, and reflected in its waters and those of its bright alabaster fountains, produce almost a magic effect upon the eye ; the perspective conveying an idea of the vast and indefinite, very favourable to the impression of such a scene. On the several sides appear clumps of the glowing laurel and other evergreens, to which the Moors were most attached, forming a skreen or guard for the magnificent flowers and plants,—the blooming product of an Arabian clime. Large beds of roses, fenced off with lines of ilex, shed their rich ineffable sweetness through the summer air, borne through bower, and balcony, and the trellised chambers of the high-born beauties with the delicious night-breeze, in pleasing union with the soft notes of the lute or the guitar.

With a southern aspect, and sheltered on every other side, the view from the end of the gardens is truly magnificent ; the golden waters of the Darro, with the blooming vega stretching into the distance,—the massy Albaycin with part of Granada at your feet, and beyond all, the vast chain of dim and dusky mountains encircling that once beloved region of chivalry and romance.

The view of the palace, as it here appears, is from the splendid Hall of the Ambassadors ; the edifice immediately to the left is part of the Alhambra, and the white tower, just seen peering over it, is named the Tower of the Infantas. The ruins of a fortification seen on the heights above are called the Seat of the Moor, from the circumstance of the last king of Granada having from that spot gazed sorrowfully down upon the splendid capital from which he had been banished by his people. Towering over the whole is seen the grand mountain-chain of the Sierra Nevada.

"Ah, my Ibn Hammed, would we indeed lived in those better, simpler days! With the grandeur of our country, with the splendour of her arts and learning, and all the wonders of her hidden science, her fortunes seem to desert her,—a fragment of her glorious and beautiful empire alone remains."

"Because her princes, my Zelinda, court honour less than power and luxury, and the sway over each other; dead to all true fame in arms. The sun of our glory, which shone on the thousand triumphs of our Mohammeds and our Tarikhs hath for ever set. With all its intricate beauties, the elegancies and splendours of our Alhambra—these soft delights of fragrant fountains, perfumed baths, cool groves with sylvan arcades, and airy palaces, with all Granada's wonders of wedded art and nature, how feeble are the joys they can inspire to those I feel in listening to the chronicles of our old exploits, and striving to transfuse the same daring, resistless spirit into the breasts of my Abencerrages! Their fame to me is dear; for it is the heritage of our fathers,—the bright torch, pure as the fire of the sacred lamp,—and it is re-lumined at that of our love. Sigh not that our country and our love are linked in one precious tie, before which all other charms, all the magnificence of state, the idle pomp of power look poor in the eyes of thy Ibn Hammed."

"And in mine too," whispered his betrothed: "when thou art absent, what to me are these fairy haunts, the loveliness of heaven and earth, and these enchanting views from our fragrant myrtle bowers! I

wander amidst their flowery sweets; list to the glad
music of the rich bloomy groves, the murmuring
fountains, and the soft low breathings of the summer
winds amid the reeds; I hear them and I sigh—I
tremble for my Ibn Hammed."

"You tremble for *me*, my Zelinda! you sigh for
me ! Let me hear you speak; speak thus for ever,
and I will dread no rival."

"Let others, my Ibn Hammed, envy the beauty of
our clime; the splendour of our halls and palaces.
Granada in all the pomp and triumph of her genius,
to which nature herself is but as a handmaid; Granada famed through all the east, beloved of the
mightiest khaliphs of ancient Cairo and Bagdad, who
vainly sought to vie with her in glory and in grandeur; all, all earth can give would I joyously resign
to preserve the love of my Ibn Hammed. Yet did
he really love as he is beloved, would he so eagerly
leave his Zelinda, to plunge into the terrors of the
gleaming battle field ? The ruin of Granada is written;
but if it be not Allah's will that we perish, I would
that we might even now flee to the desarts. Here we
are exposed to perils worse than death."

"And fearest thou, my love, for me in the strife
of honour ?"

"I fear for thee and for myself. I glory in thy
fame; for woe is me! I see that our loves may not be
happy upon earth. Snares are laid for our feet; the
air I breathe, though so bright and pure, oppresses my
soul, for it is poisoned with the presence of Abu
Abdallah. Amiable, generous as he appears to others,

and beloved by the people, his long unhappy passion that would snatch me from thy arms makes him our bitter foe. Great and benignant as thou art, the shield of thy country and thy king, yet wilt thou fall a victim to the deadly feuds of royal Moor with Moor, to the fiery and cruel Muley, or to his weak, licentious son. Dark and terrible as hath been the past; more fatal moments, I dread to think, are at hand. They cast their black shadows before; see you them not in the threatening union of the Castilian throne with Arragon and Navarre, in our monarch's defiance of the Christian princes, and in the ceaseless feuds between our families and tribes? The kingdom of the Moors trembles as with an earthquake, breathing fresh vigour into the Christian hosts."

Terrified and trembling, Zelinda ceased to speak, and drawing her closer to him, her lover supported her head upon his breast. "Why weeps my love? Is this spoken like the noble-hearted, high-souled daughter of my heroic friend? Was it my Zelinda who could listen to the tumult of the conflict unappalled; and shower her sunny smiles upon my Abencerrages, as we flew through Elvira's gates to the field of fame? Doth the name of the queenly Isabel thus blanch thy cheek? or the mean, perfidious arts of her consort of Arragon? Nay, daughter of a noble sire, summon back, bright as the radiant beauty of thy eyes, the brightness of thy spirit's joy!"

"I fear the Christian, Ibn Hammed; yet more do I dread the royal Moor."

"The Moor! ah! said'st thou? there is a dark

meaning in thy words. Hath Abu Abdallah,* of the close thoughts, mild eye, and open brow,—too well loved by Granada, too amiable in woman's eyes, dared again to insult thee with words of love?"

" Did I say aught of Abu Abdallah, it were to ask thee not to cross his path."

" What, if he should step between me and all I hold dearest upon earth? to dream of the peerless princess of my love; the adopted daughter of his royal sire; the betrothed of an Abencerrage!"

" Heed him not, my Ibn Hammed; again and again I reject his hated vows. In that thou may'st read the magic of thy love; for thee, I gladly scorn a sultana's throne."

" Nay, nothing can make thee dearer in my eyes; but, by Allah, it gives renewed bitterness, tenfold justice to my hatred and my scorn of the dark plotter against our peace. Gentle, generous, and just as he can show himself to others, shall he persecute thee thus with his obstinate, unrequited passion? Let him openly appear, and decide our loves in the field."

" Sooner shall you behold me die at your feet!" was the reply of the terrified girl, as she clung to him ere he hurried away.

" Fiery and cruel is Muley Hassan," he continued; " but he loves his country, he spurns at tribute to her foe, and the blood of the Abencerrages will freely flow to support his throne."

" Fearful omens, my Hammed, point to yet darker

* Better known by the name of Boabdil; and sirnamed El Zagoybi, the Unhappy.

days ; and it is therefore I tremble as I gaze upon the bravest of the brave, and am growing feeble-hearted now," and the beautiful Zelinda drooped her head upon his bosom, yielding to a burst of passionate grief she could no longer restrain.

As the young chief, with soft whispers and gentle caresses sought to dispel her fears, wild sounds came borne upon the night-winds, of mingled fury and lamentation. Gathering fresh strength as they rose into general tumult, which fell portentously upon the ear, he clasped the weeping beauty in his arms, and bearing her to the nearmost saloons, consigned her to the care of her maidens, and rushed eagerly to learn the source of so fierce an outcry at the dead hour of night. As he hurried down the shady avenues of the Alhambra, he saw approaching a vast concourse of the people, directing their rage towards the palace of Muley Hassan, and filling the air with deep universal lament.

" Alhama ! woe is me, Alhama !* Accursed be Muley Hassan ! How long shall he betray the faithful into the hands of the Christian spoiler !" With the same cry swelling far and wide, on they poured like a torrent, directed by the deep refulgent light of its Vermilion Towers,† till they reached the very walls of the vast

---

* The spirited version, by Lord Byron, of the old Moorish ballad will here occur to the reader :—

> The Moorish king rides up and down
> Through Granada's royal town :
> From Elvira's gates to those,
> Of Vivarambla on he goes.
>   Woe is me, Alhama !

† Of the Torres Vermejas, or Vermilion Towers, the most picturesque and striking among the conspicuous objects which

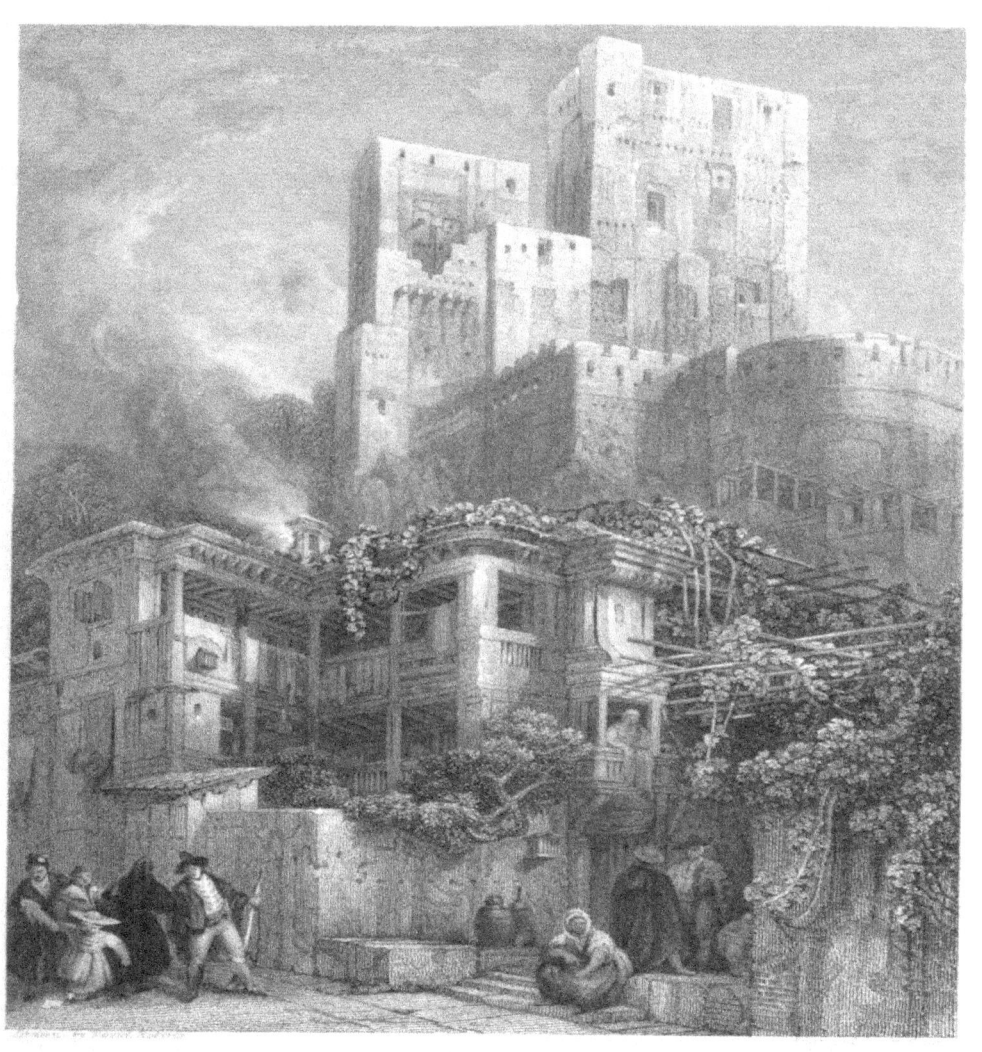

THE VERMILION TOWER.

fortress, where, renewing their execrations, they were in vain opposed by the Moorish sentinels and guards. But soon every tower and citadel along the whole sweep of its massy ramparts seemed alive with gleaming steel and swarthy visages; while fraught with darker terrors was heard the same shrill, piercing voice which, on the fall of Zaharāh, predicted the approaching doom. It was that of the aged faquir, to which the superstitious populace responded with shouts of vengeance which rang through the midnight air, and piercing the precincts of the Alhambra, bore the signal of insurrection through court, and hall, and corridor to the ear of the royal Moor. " Woe; woe to Granada ! " cried

arrest the eye of the tourist on entering the spacious Vega, no authentic account has survived as to date or origin. They rise boldly from their rocky height, rivalling the proudest of the Alhambra; and it is generally admitted that they are of greater antiquity than any by which they are surrounded. It is the popular belief that they were erected by the Romans ; but some writers assert, with more show of probability, by some wandering colony of the Phœnicians. This it has also been observed, in many instances, is the popular impression of the Spaniards themselves upon the spot, but upon what authority it would be idle to conjecture. It is, however, known as the regal home of successive races of warrior-chiefs through the eventful history of the Phœnicians, Romans, Goths, Moors, and Christians. Its present inmates, although of a more peaceful and less honourable calling, are, perhaps, more usefully employed than their predecessors. The place is inhabited by a colony of potters, and the proud Vermilion Towers, instead of reflecting the steel cap and morrion of the mail-clad warriors, are appropriated to baking the produce of their quiet labours in the sun, which is here almost sufficiently powerful to allow of dispensing with the heat of an oven for the same purpose.—*For the View, see the Frontispiece.*

the fanatic; " Alhama is no more. Are her children
captives ? Not one hath escaped the sword ; the ruins
of Zaharāh have fallen upon our heads ! Would that I
had spoken a lie. Do I lie, when I cry woe to Granada,
to the last of her Moorish kings?"—" Allah! Allah!
holy Prophet! hear him not !" re-echoed the tumul-
tuous people ; while the young chief, eager to stem the
tide of popular delusion, hurried down to the tents of
his Abencerrages. One shrill blast of his clarion drew
the brave around him ; and soon, marshalled in stern
array, they wound their silent course from the Vivarambla to occupy the gate of Elvira, leading into the
plain. " Here, my friends and brothers, you will be
first in the onset! await my return ;" and swift as the
wind he was borne by his fiery barb to the palace of
Muley Hassan, eager that he should retrieve the loss
of Alhama at the head of all his tribes.

Nor was the arrival of the Abencerrage unwelcome
to the king ; for the tumult had reached its height.
Such was the excitement of the infatuated Moors, impelled by the Zegris and other tribes, that they called
on Muley to pay tribute to the Castilian monarchs,
or to yield up the crown.

It was at this moment the Abencerrage showed himself on the ramparts, where he found Muley Hassan,
who had in vain attempted to allay the ferment, surrounded by his counsellors and the most distinguished
among the tribes.

The eloquent Aben Kassim, popular by his talents and
his virtues no less than his fidelity, and whose muni-
ficence had brought throngs of students and artists of

other lands to acquire knowledge in the learned institutions of the Moors, stood opposing his enchanting and divine art to the blind infatuated fury of the crowd. Nor could he give a nobler test of his friendship for a bold but misguided monarch, who, becoming the slave of his own passion, enthralled by the charms of a Christian captive, had brought his country to the very brink of ruin. But Aben Kassim, like the Abencerrages and the noblest Moorish tribes, struggled for honour and for country, beholding in its monarch only the symbol of its power ; nor was his appeal to the passions of the fickle people of Granada without its expected results. He addressed them with the noble confidence, the secret scorn of lofty intellect, born to command. He swayed the muttering surges of their reckless varying minds with the practised power of some skilful mariner ; he drew elements of the most opposite qualities,—concord, reason, and courage, from the rabble rout of violence, fanaticism, and dastard selfishness,— those national failings of the lower orders of the Moslems. It seemed after he had spoken as if oil had been poured upon the troubled sea of life around him.

" There is no conqueror but God," he concluded, " and Mohammed, his Prophet, was his sword. Are ye not his children ? the children of the faithful, victorious in a thousand battles ? Why tremble ye then at what is destined to come? is it not the will of Allah? doth he not gird ye with the same weapons which conquered the world ? His sword is unsheathed again ; and will ye bow your necks to the foot of the Christian ? Nay ; even then the hour of judgment, the day of

grace is gone by; and here," turning to the chiefs,
" here is the tribute you owe to Ferdinand and his
queen.   The breasts of Moslem heroes are henceforth
the only bulwarks of Granada and her happy homes.
If ye tremble, crouch beneath the shield of your glorious tribes, the sons of Mohammed and of Tarikh, not
at the feet of the infidels who will trample you into
dust.   If you will live, live renowned as your ancestors;
learn how to die for the country which they bequeathed
you. Go, prepare for battle; to conquer or to perish!"
Here the aged orator turned to the chief of the Abencerrages, who, waving his jewelled scymitar, flashing
through the darkness of the night, swore " to lead his
brethren to Alhama, if the king refused to put himself
at the head of Andalusia's chivalry, and to tear down
from the watch-towers of the devoted city the symbols
of the Christian sway."

At these words the wavering, unruly multitude, sent
up a shout of exultation. " God is great, and Mohammed is his Prophet! Down with Macer; away
with the lying prophet! Glory to the Abencerrages!
Allah, for Alhama; open wide the gates!"

With these cries the infatuated people of Granada,
ever fiery or depressed, and variable as the passions of
their conflicting rulers, hurried away to their homes,
resolute to second the ardour of their chiefs; and once
more the heart of that troubled city lay hushed in deep,
but brief repose.

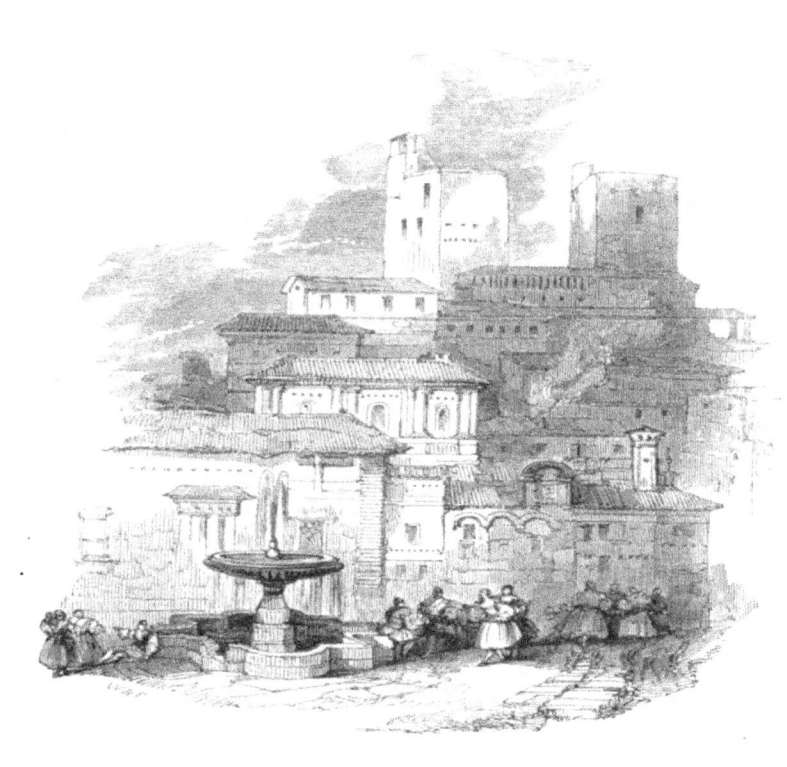

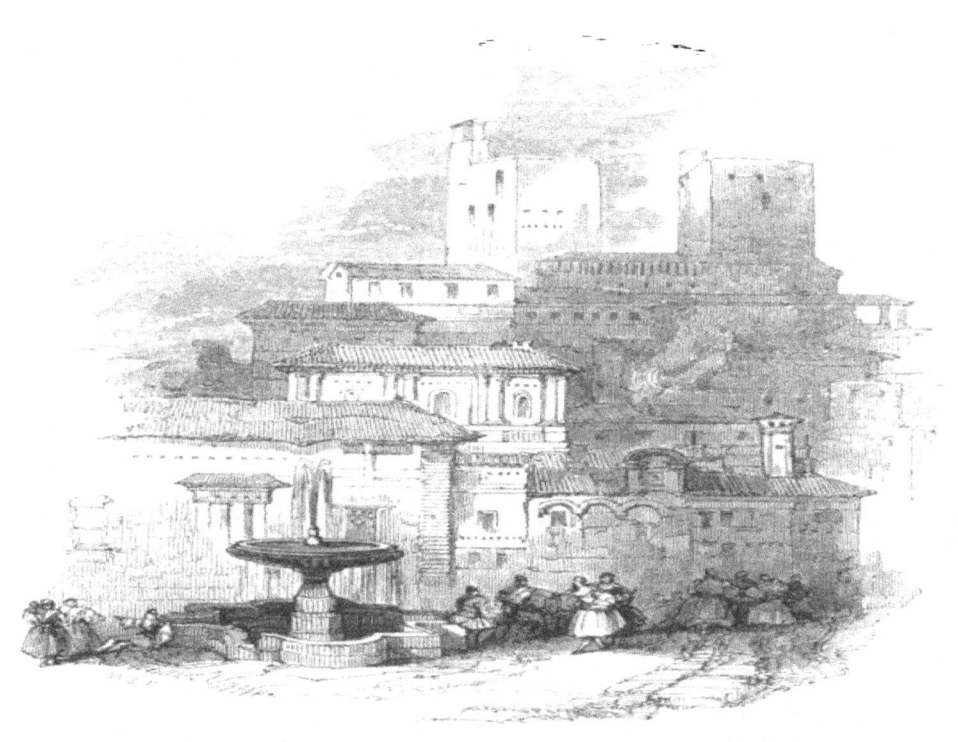

CHAPTER III.

They passed the Elvira gate with banners all displayed,
They passed in mickle state, a noble cavalcade,
What proud and pawing horses, what comely cavaliers,
What bravery of targets, what glittering of spears !
THE VOW OF THE MOOR.

IN the bitterness of his spirit for the calamitous fall of Alhama, the Moslem monarch smote his breast ; trampled his jewelled turban in the dust. His first impulse was to take vengeance on its governor, who had been absent when it was surprised. He was then quietly returning from the neighbourhood of Ante-

querra, whither he had gone to be present at some
festival.   The nobles and messengers despatched to
bring his head, are said to have met him on the way,
and the following part of the old Moorish ballad
commemorates the event :——

Out spake Granada's noble, " Alcayde, thou must die,
The royal Moor thy head will fix th' Albambra's gates on high,
With thy white beard and hoary hair beneath thy turban green ;
For thou hast lost the fairest gem of all his crown, I ween."

Then as he eyed the signet sad, the old alcayde said,
" Most worthy lords nought have I done to lose this aged head,
I went but to my sister's, the wedding feast to share
In Antequerre ; (I would the fiends had them who bade me there.)

Yet had I the Moor's gracious leave, writ by his royal hand,
For twice ten days, when fifteen was all I did demand,
Go tell the king, my master, Alhama works me woe !
A heavy cost it is to me, if I must pay it so.

Pray say, if he his city lost, my honour and my fame,
And on my soul, my daughter dear, Granada's flower her name,
Are lost to me ; for she's a thrall in Ponce de Leon's tent,
And to my proffered ransom, these are the words he sent :

' I count not of your golden crowns, her price you cannot bid,
For, Sir, she is a Christian maid, and of the Moor is rid,
Donna Maria de Alhama baptized is she now,'—
Alas, when only Fatima is her right name, I trow."

Thus grieving loud, the Moor he cast the dust upon his head ;
But nought it could avail, and soon, for all that he had said,
To the Alhambra's towers they bore the brave but sad old man,
And from its gates he grisly looked, a dreadful sight to scan.*

The rage and lamentations of his people had carried
Muley's indignation to the highest pitch, and none

* Romances Antiguos Españoles.

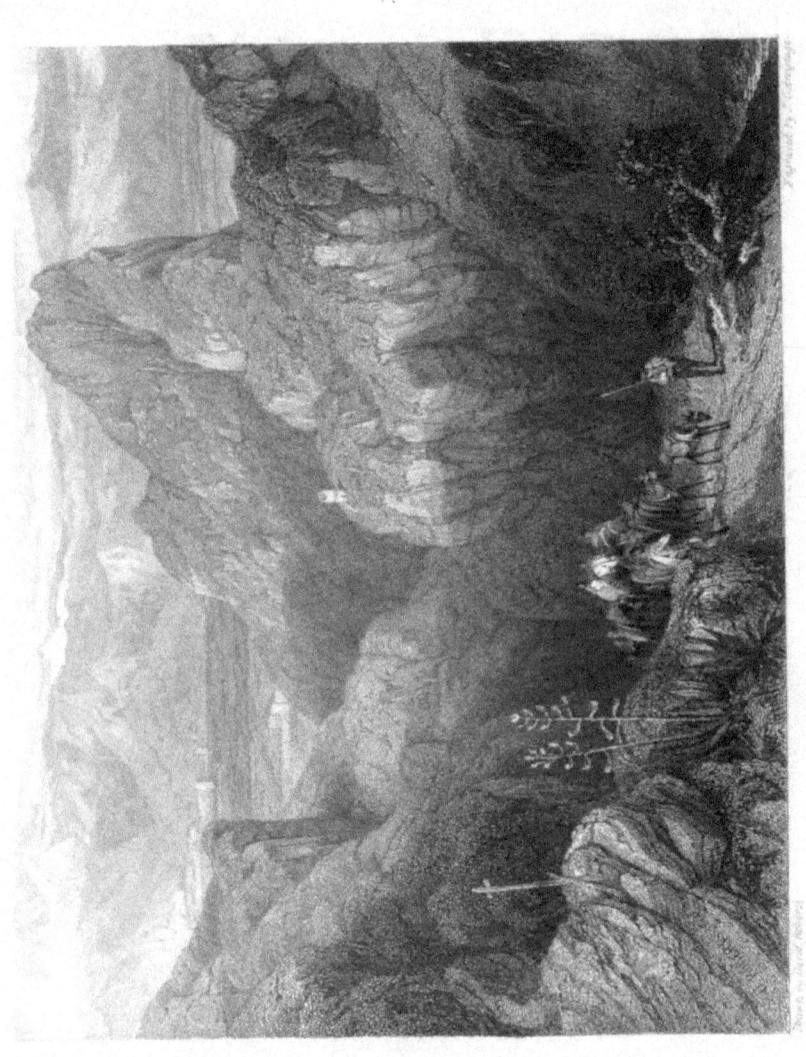

but his faithful Aben Kassim ventured to approach him. He was no stranger to these fearful moods, and aware how closely the passions of the great and the feeble, the hearts of princes and of slaves resemble each other, he was at no loss how to subdue those fierce quick impulses which govern both. The savage genius of Muley stood rebuked and abashed before the calm, deep wisdom, and the godlike faculty of arraying it in eloquent truth and beauty, which distinguished his old experienced counsellor and friend. He became calm; and when the wand of the mind's magician was again displayed, he burned with all the heroism of his race for revenge upon the foe.

Soon summoned around him, he beheld the chiefs and captains of his most chivalrous tribes, at the head of whom shone the high-souled Ibn Hammed, clothed in the dazzling armour of the ancestral princes of his blood.

The blush of dawn beamed on the pride of an oriental chivalry, refined and splendid as it was heroic,——on long serried ranks of gallant hearts and lofty miens, as they wound their dazzling path through the gates of Elvira, into the glorious scene of the blooming Vega, so long the idol of the old Moslems and of all their children.* Beautiful at once and

* This view of Granada was taken from the Mountain Pass, entering the plain early on the third day, during the traveller's progress from Cordova to the capital. No landscape perhaps which presents itself during his whole tour through Spain and Barbary, leaves a stronger impression on his mind, and no words could convey an idea of the sort of feeling it produces,——so peculiarly novel and absorbing. Having

terrible was the spectacle in the eyes of the assembled people, who burst into a wild shout of confiding exultation, in the strength and gallant bearing of so chivalrous a host.

In the front of these chiefs and brethren, all of princely lineage, rode Muley Hassan with his two sons, followed by their noble tribes, their gemmed and golden armour and burnished casques flashing in the morning sun. The standard of the empire, so rarely unfurled from the inmost sanctuary of the mosque, so deeply revered by every Moslem, displayed to their dazzled eyes the achievements of near a thousand years; and far shone its radiant crescent, the symbol

ascended to the summit of the hill, from which the view is given, the grand Sierra Nevada bursts at once upon his view; the peaks of the mountains were in part enveloped in clouds, whilst the dazzling snow with which it is eternally crowned, reflected as in a mirror the rays of the morning sun, while in the foreground, and nestled as it were in the lap of the vega at its base, rose the towers of imperial Granada. Then between it and the mountains, which lay at your feet stretched the noble plain and valley arrayed, even in the depth of our winter season, in all the bloom of spring. Far to the east wind the silver waters of the Xenil, whilst more near numerous towns and villages spread over that vast and fertile plain, giving additional splendour and animation to the scene. There among the most prominent stands Santa Fe, erected upon the site of the Christian camp, and from the same point, within a league, could be distinguished the beautiful estate presented to our great English captain, the exploits of whose gallant armies in that land of heroism and romance, may rank, in their way, with the proudest of the age of Gonzalos, or the old Campeador. Nearly in the centre of this romantic prospect, and in the very gorge of the pass stands one of those atalayas, or ancient watch-towers, which stretch in an unbroken line from

of those wondrous conquests which only stayed their
dread career in the heart of the mighty empire of
Charlemagne. Upon its green and golden field appeared emblazoned in the light of rubies and ame-
thysts, the crimson fruit which gave its name to the
beloved city of their kings.* Near it rode the high-
souled Muza Ben Gazan, chief of the Alabez, the
rival in honour, yet bosom friend of the Abencerrage,
followed by Ali Abu Fahar, Cid Yahia, with Hammed
El Zegri, Hassan of Gazan, leaders of the fierce Zegris,
the old Gomelez, and other princely clans.

High streamed their old Moorish pennons to the
broad, purple sky ; and gladdening to their thoughts

this spot to the city of Cordova. After descending the mountain, the tourist approaches Granada by the celebrated bridge
of Piños, long famed for many a desperate struggle between
the Moors and Christians. It is memorable, if only from the
devoted heroism of two Moorish brothers, who being reproached
by the people, on the fall of the fortresses they commanded,
asked permission to defend the pass of Piños into the plain.
At the head of a remnant of their veteran garrisons, they met
the onset of the whole Spanish chivalry, and long held possession of the bridge, like the Roman Cocles, performing incredible acts of valour. Disputing it inch by inch, till the stream
ran red with blood, every Moor died upon the foot of ground
he had occupied to defend, till the two brothers scorning more
to live amidst an ungrateful people, fell gloriously covered with
wounds. On learning their heroic and protracted defence,
with the great slaughter of the Spaniards, the admiration and
regret of the Moors exceeded even their reproaches ; and
eagerly extolling their generous daring, they erected to their
memory a column in the vicinity of the bridge, afterwards
distinguished by the name of the Two Brothers.

* Granada, said to be so called from the shape of the pomegranate, when cut into halves.

was the sound of their rattling mail, the flash of the scymitar, and the deep, low thunder of their rushing steeds.   For right bravely did the fiery barb, the war-clad Arab, and the brilliant swift-footed Andaluz, bear their favourite heroes over the resounding sun-brown plains, as if eager to meet the shock of their Christian foemen, the mountain-sons of the Goth.

But the evening of the second day witnessed another sight; when ere the sun's last beams ceased to illumine the peaks of the snowy sierra with a flood of golden fire, deepening the gorgeous hues of dome and spire, of mosque and minaret, her far-off watch-towers proclaimed to Granada the return of that brilliant host.   No songs of triumph, no trains of captive foes marked its course, as with slow-retreating van and battling rear, still presenting a flashing front to the invader, the blood-stained banner, the scanty horse, the soiled and battered armour, told a tale of fierce but unavailing conflict.

From the loftiest tower of the Alhambra, Abu Abdallah beheld the sight; and eager to ingratiate himself with the fickle, clamorous multitude, he put himself at the head of the royal garrison, and summoning the remaining mercenaries and the foot, hurried into the plain.   Here mingling with the retreating squadrons, he gave breath to the hard-pressed Moors, and for a moment turned the tide of battle upon their pursuers.   The delight of the people, on witnessing from the walls and watch-towers the deeds of personal valour performed by the young prince, knew no bounds; and never had the popular qualities of their favourite, his gentle courtesy and suavity of demeanour, now set in prouder relief by this brilliant action, won more rapturous plaudits from the voice of the Moslem horsemen, and the city of their kings.

The Christians having retired, the Moorish monarch re-entered his capital. Upon approaching Alhama, signals from the nearmost watch-towers had warned him of the advance of a powerful force led by Guzman Duke of Medina Sidonia, followed, at no great distance, by Ferdinand in person. But pressing the attack, Muley detached the flower of his tribes under the chief of the Abencerrages to surprise and fall upon the Spaniards in succession. The celebrated Ponce de Leon, Lord of Cadiz, had meanwhile thrown himself with a small veteran force into the citadel. And a mightier armament which baffled all the Moslem's designs, was at hand; the chivalrous d'Aguilar, the Marquis of Villena, with other lords of the frontier towns, uniting their feudal strength, bore down upon Muley Hassan, whose remaining squadrons after a desperate conflict found themselves constrained to retire under the walls of the capital.

" But where is the heroic Ibn Hammed? where the proud Abencerrages, the dauntless Alabez?" was the repeated inquiry upon the lips of the people. " By Allah! the compassionate and merciful; the blow of a friend is more severe than the sword of the stranger. Have their friends proved but spies? or hath injustice, like a cloud, hidden the light of faith from the king's eyes? But he who trusts in any but God, cannot succeed; and a wise enemy is more to be prized than a foolish

friend !'' were among the bitter sarcastic cries of the
fickle Moors, on the presumed desertion of the Abencerrages by their royal leader.   Any fate was preferable
to the keen reproaches, the wild lamentations of his
people ; and with the fiery genius of the unyielding
soldier, Muley Hassan seized the moment of returning
fortune to marshal anew his veteran squadrons.   Commanding the priests and faquirs to proclaim the Algihed,
or Holy War, he invoked the people, the whole surviving chivalry of Granada, to follow him to avenge
Alhama,—to the rescue of the faithful, or to perish with
them in the field.   The summons was responded to,
and seldom had Granada beheld a more puissant array;
horsemen and foot, all eager to vindicate the cause of
their prophet ;——their title to the last and most beloved
seat of their kings.

Slow and sullenly, the brave legions of retainers
headed by the frontier nobles, the most renowned cavaliers of the age, retreated before the overwhelming
might of the Moslems, falling back upon the royal
army advancing to the relief of Alhama.   But from the
surrounding heights the din of battle now fell heavily
on the ear, and Christian knight and fiery Saracen
burning to reach the scene, disputed the ground foot
by foot, till they came within sight of a yet deadlier
contest, with which they soon mingled, like the meeting
of two chafed and mighty torrents rushing from their
mountain sluices upon the vales below.   As they came
in contact with the battle already raging, burst forth
with louder and harsher breath the pealing music of
that stormy war ; for there, beneath the walls of their

fallen city, the Moors joined the conflict between the pride of all Granada and that dauntless Iberian chivalry, worthy the sons of Pelayo and the great Campeador.*

Though enclosed between the city and the foe, the Abencerrages and their adherents, in deep serried ranks of brothers, fought back to back with the combined spirit of a single hero,—beset on all sides, yet holding at bay the terrific charges of the Castilian horse. Maddened to loftiest deeds of daring by the example of their chivalrous chief, they at once met the furious onset of Ponce de Leon from the citadel, and that of the frontier squadrons led by the famed Marquis Villena, with the whole flower of the Spanish camp.† With renewed shock upon shock, they opened a path for their followers, engaging with the Moorish chieftains hand to hand. Every where beating back the most powerful of his opponents, Ibn Hammed, supported by Prince Almanzor and the Alabez, his friends Muza Ben Gazan, Ali Fahar, the Cid Yahia, struggled with heroic despair to cut his way through his fierce assailants, who vainly called on him to surrender.

At this juncture, the union of the Christians must have decided the fate of the Moorish horse; but fiercely

* Ruy Diaz de Bivar, the famous Cid, of whom so much has been chronicled and sung; witness our Poet-laureate, Mr. Lockhart, Mrs. Hemans, &c. &c.

† Such as Diego di Cordova, Alonzo d'Aguilar, Mendoza Zendilla, the Master of Alcantara, at the head of their frontier force and strong mountain-bands.

E

attacked by Muley Hassan, they fell back upon the force of Ponce de Leon, who now sought to regain the fortress. It was then a design suggested itself to the prince of the Abencerrages, worthy his lofty fame and commanding station ; his eagle glance at once caught the new position of the battle, and burning to add to his laurels the glory of recovering Alhama, he wheeled round his squadron, and advancing the standard of the Prophet with the war-cry of Alhama, rushed on Ponce de Leon, and entered along with him the gates of the disputed city. But ere they could be closed, the Spanish force pressing upon his rear as eagerly as he pursued the garrison, followed, and finally shut out the Moorish king as he was bearing down upon the place. He heard the clashing sound of the massy portals; he beheld the flower of his tribes which he had come to rescue, once more within the fierce and deadly grasp of their inexorable foe. But at the cry of Alhama, not a Moor in that vast host who strained not every nerve to reach its steep, precipitous walls ; and, unprovided as they were with their heavy engines, they rushed to the assault headed by their escaladors, uttering terrific shouts of vengeance which seemed to rend the heavens. Re-echoed from every mountain-height and cloud-capped citadel upon the cliffs, they were repeated along the gorges of the hills to the very watch-towers upon the pinnacles of the rocks. Nor was the spectacle less fearfully sublime, when that whole brilliant array rushed like a single escalador under the eye of their warrior monarch, prepared with heart and hand either to conquer or to perish. It was then the tempest of

the battle began to rage in its darkest terrors; when
the passions of the soul let loose, goaded by bitterest
religious hatred and thoughts of home and country,
panted to indulge that instinctive appetite for blood,
which, once excited, gives tenfold horrors to such a
scene. As fast as the storming Moors gained the walls,
they were hurled down by their terrific foe, forming
ramparts for successive bodies of their countrymen
rushing on to the assault. But the Christians, animated
by the presence of their illustrious leaders, hurried
to the ramparts in prodigious throngs, while others
were engaged in deadly conflict with the Abencerrages
in the streets. Ibn Hammed, under the impression
that he was followed by the whole of the Moslem host,
had traversed part of the city, displaying with shouts of
victory the standard of the holy Prophet; till, being
vigorously attacked, and receiving no aid from without,
he at once descried the fatal cause, and turning upon
his adversaries, attempted to regain the gates. Not a
Moorish turban was to be seen upon the ramparts; the
terrific shouts, the clash of opposing arms, the heavy
crush and fall of armour told him how fearful was the
hurling of the Moslems from the walls, how fierce the
reiterated assaults of their warlike king!

The noble Abencerrage, beset on all sides, had still
recourse to one desperate expedient to retrieve the
fortune of the battle, or to perish for his country.
Finding it impracticable to open a passage for the
Moorish army through the gates, he directed his last
determined efforts to reach the ramparts of the city,
at once to fall upon the rear of the brave garrison, and

to open a path for the assailants.   The ferocity of the
conflict to accomplish this daring exploit, incited by
every motive of country and of life, surpassed all
hitherto beheld in the chivalrous career of the Moorish
wars.   The princely tribes, for they were mostly of
high lineage, were opposed by the pride of Spanish
chivalry, fired by ages of national animosity.   Both,
nevertheless, evinced the courtesies, the generosity,
and that high soaring gallantry towards each other,
which marked the heroism of their times.   As noble
Moor after Moor fell on every side, the brave Alonzo
d'Aguilar besought their chief to spare his gallant
followers, and yield the sword and banner of the
Moslems.   But the thickly serried rank, presenting a
closer and closer front, still disdaining surrender, and
placing their sacred banner in the centre, replied only
by gathering heaps of slain.   Their desperate energy
at length opened for them a path ; they dashed boldly
on the ramparts, selling their lives dearly as they
encountered the garrison upon the walls.

But few, and broken, their heroic chief invited his
surviving brethren to follow him, and sprung with the
sacred banner over the lofty battlements, amidst cries
of mingled triumph and terror. *   For at the sight of
the hero and his gallant band with the golden symbols

* Though the event described in the text, may, at first
sight, appear incredible, it is not without a parallel in history.   During the treacherous massacre of Shahin Bey and
the other Mamalukes, by Mohammed Ali, in the citadel of
Cairo, in 1812, one of those redoubtable cavaliers, having
cut his way through the ranks of the Dehlis, spurred his
horse over the wall, and, notwithstanding the great height

of the empire, disputing the very ramparts of Alhama,
a sudden, fearful pause seized upon the rival hosts as if
they had beheld some vision, or the impregnable fortress
miraculously carried by the behest of the all-conquering
God.   But when they saw the dauntless Abencerrage
urge his fiery barb, at one tremendous leap, over the battlements with the Prophet's ensign broadly spreading
to the sky, there broke from the Moslem host a shout of
horror, as if they had beheld the fall of their beloved
Granada, or their great predicted day of doom.   Their
cry was re-echoed by the enemy, as they contemplated
the strangely daring exploit, which at once deprived
them of the bright trophy of victory, and the most
heroic of captives who had yet fallen beneath their
arms.   But the broad-streaming pennon dilating with
the wind, its beloved emblem streaming like some
aerial glory, bore its champion all unscathed and harm-
less into the midst of the awe-struck Moors.   And
again with hotter fury was the deadly assault renewed ;
again did he advance the celestial banner, and plant
his foot against the walls.   But he was met with an
energy and hostility as unsubdued as his own.   Muley
Hassan saw that he was enriching the field of the

of the bastion, escaped unhurt.   Of the four hundred and
seventy Mamalukes who entered the castle, this was the
only individual who eluded the vengeance of the Pasha.
" When I visited the citadel," says Mr. St. John, " the part
of the wall over which he is said to have sprang, was pointed
out to me : the height seemed sufficient to render scepticism
excusable ; but, as very improbable things are many times
found to be true, this almost miraculous escape, said to have
been witnessed by several persons still living, may, without
any extraordinary stretch of credulity, obtain our belief."

foe with the life-blood of his veteran tribes; that
Alhama's walls presented bulwarks, invincible as steel
to mortal heroism, and dark and sullenly he abandoned the assault, pitching his camp before the
leaguered city.

Cutting off all supplies, and pressing the siege with
unremitting vigour, Muley at length reduced the brave
garrison to the extreme of suffering, and Alhama was on
the eve of falling to the Moors, when tidings of dismal
import were borne to the monarch's ear.   Ferdinand,
at the head of an immense armament, was again
approaching to relieve the gallant victors of Alhama;
the newly blended banners of Arragon and Castile
were seen from the lofty watch-towers as they moved
down the mountain-pass into the plains; while in Granada his son, Abu Abdallah, was plotting to deprive
him of his crown.   Summoning the chiefs to instant
council, it was determined to make one more desperate
effort to surprise the place.   While the king made a
feigned attack on one side, a storming party advanced
in the dead of night, despatched the sentinels and
guards, and made their way into the streets.   But the
Spaniards were still on the alert, the walls bristled
with steel, every fresh shock was attended with the
same result; while more and more turbaned heads
flung from the ramparts, proclaimed that not a single
Moor who entered the fatal city had escaped.

Maddened with disappointment, the king drew off
his forces, and returned to Granada to preserve his
tottering throne.   But from that day Muley Hassan
was observed to have become a changed man; the

soul—the grandeur of enterprise which incited him to spurn at tribute, was damped; the unconquerable pride of Moslem heroism stood rebuked before his failing fortunes, and on learning the treachery of his son, he seemed to feel that he was no longer a king. His faithful Aben Kassim was more grieved than surprised to behold in the fiery and terrible Muley Hassan, well-proved in many a battle-field, only the wild and moody fatalist brooding over predicted evils,—the wreck of a princely mind. It tasked all his kindly skill, his brilliant eloquence, to sustain his master's courage under the first rude shock of his misfortunes,—a triumphant foe without, treason in his palace, and fast spreading sedition among his people. To the violence of his passions succeeded disappointment, regret, remorse; for he felt that he was the sole author of his own calamities, that he had driven a noble and virtuous queen from his throne and bed; forfeited honour and empire in the embraces of a too enchanting slave. * He was now only roused to acts of vigour by the earnest, impressive appeals of his venerable counsellor. In pursuance of his advice, Muley issued orders for the secret arrest of his son and the sultana, his mother.† Seized and hurried from their apart-

* Zorayda,—so termed for her surpassing beauty ; that is, "star of the morning." By her he had several sons, for whose sake, at the instigation of their too fascinating mother, it is supposed that he persecuted, and even put to death several of his own legitimate children. Such a motive is assigned, by many writers, for the rebellion of his son Boabdil, incited by the sultana Aixa.

† The sultana Aixa, sprung of a high Moorish family and

ments during the night, they were consigned to the
Tower of Comares,† one of the most conspicuous and
strongly fortified in the whole fortress-range of the
grand Alhambra.

But even in acts of policy and vigour, there appeared to be a fatality in the occurrences of this

termed by the Moors of Granada, over whom she exercised
considerable influence, " la Horra, or the Chaste," from her
pure and virtuous life.

† The lofty Tower of Comares, famed in Moorish history
for many a romantic incident, many a strange and dark event
or wild legendary tale, abounds in associations that cannot fail
to impress the mind. In its precincts were embraced the
Golden Saloon, or Hall of the Ambassadors, where the future
welfare, the destinies of a mighty people often hung upon the
pride, the insulted dignity, or caprice of a single despotic master.
There too were passed the prison hours of the unfortunate
princes—the sultanas who had ceased to please—immured in its
donjon keep, or its grated gallery, as they are to be seen at the
present moment. Here too, as we have noticed, was confined
the noble sultana, Aixa la Horra, whose devoted tenderness to
her son, and all her noble efforts to inspire him with a great
spirit, were so ill requited. In the extent and splendour of its
great hall—its rich and varied decorations sparkling with all
those starry colours in strong relief, and those combinations of
skilful art which threw a species of enchantment round the
scene, and in its saloons and courts, it displayed all the genius of
eastern magnificence. It abounded also in those national inscriptions from the Koran, or founded on some remarkable historical
fact or observation of their kings, which held the duties of prince
and people continually up to view. From the battlements
of the tower and its terraced roof, prospects spread far
around, nowhere surpassed in point of variety, novelty, and
grandeur. The dark rocky mountains in the distance, glittering more near with the snowy peaks of the sierra—the bright
green valley—the luxuriant plain—the whole scene lit up
by the radiance of the golden crescent reflected from mosque

strange eventful period, in singular unison with the belief of the people, with the predictions of old Arabian astrologers and learned men, at the birth of Abu Abdallah. There was something undefined and mysterious, approaching to the supernatural, asserted to have been vividly impressed on the popular

and cupola,—a magic scene of sylvan courts, groves, fountains, with the flashing waters of the crystal Darro, now hid, now revealed to the eye, exhibited a scene that might well excite the almost idolatrous attachment of its possessors. On one side, the Alhambra with its shady courts and gardens met the eye; there lay the Court of the Alberca, encircled with flowers, and beyond it the Court of Lions, its beautiful fountains, and light airy arcades; while embosomed in the midst of all appeared the myrtle garden of the Linderaxa, with its rosy bowers and shrubberies. The boundaries of the grand fortress presented a line of battlements, bristling with strong square towers, extending round the entire brow of the hill. On the northern side, the summits of the massy tower beetled high above the woods, which crowned the declivity of the lofty hill. Lower down, the deep narrow glen, widening as it opened from the mountains, led into the vale of the Darro; where, beneath its sylvan arches, the river wound its way among the terraced gardens and pleasure grounds which adorned its banks. The white pavilions glancing at intervals through clustering shrubs and plantations of olive, the melon, and the vine, showed the suburban retreats of the Moors, who carried to luxuriant refinement the study of domestic economy and cultivation of the soil. In another direction were seen the lofty towers—the spacious rich arcades of the Generalife, or summer palace, its hanging gardens, its cypress groves and myrtle bowers, bright with the perennial freshness—the glowing hues imbibed from the pure, fragrant spirit of the southern breeze. On the height above might be seen the spot where the last of the Moorish kings sat in trouble and dismay, when driven by his people from that beloved city on which he gazed, and wept to resign. From beneath could be heard the murmur of waters

mind, ushering in the final downfall—-the eclipse of
centuries of undiminished glory, which cast its broad
gathering shadows before, as it approached the appointed hour.

The severity of such a measure, therefore, was only
another step in the march of destiny; so far from
arresting its speed, it darkened the fearful perils which
overhung the beloved city of the Moors.   It gave a

conveyed by the aqueduct of the Moorish mills, situated in
the gorge of the ravine, or glen, that divides the palace of the
Alhambra from that of the Generalife.   The spacious lines of
trees beyond, mark the alameda, or great walk, extending far
along the Darro, with its long line of battlemented towers,
where the pride and beauty of Granada sought the enjoyments
of social converse in the refreshing airs of evening, when love
awoke the song of the nightingale, and the veiled beauties of
the Alhambra listened with heaving bosom and flashing eye to
the softer music of impassioned words and sighs. Overhanging
this walk rose the noble quarter of the city called the Albaycin.
Again, if you looked out upon the west, rose the distant hills
beyond the Vega, the scene of many a border warfare between
the Moslem chivalry and the Christian lords of the frontier.
Towns, towers, and cities, spreading over their declivities, were
shielded by their strong holds and castles on the summits,
commanding the mountain passes which lay between them and
their Christian foe.   The pinnacles of watch-towers apparently
springing out of the solid rocks, and displaying the green and
golden ensign of the crescent beetled above the loftiest cliffs,
but vainly sounded the alarm when that new, terrific arm of
war, the heavy artillery of the Christian, laid the mightiest
of their eagle fortresses a heap of ruins. It was then the hosts
of Ferdinand poured down from Alcala la Real, through the
famous pass of Lope, into the blooming Vega, trampling its
glories and its beauties with the unsparing foot of war.   There,
at the fatal bridge of Pinos, fell many a young heroic martyr
for his country,—beloved Granada, and its happy homes;
there was the Castilian chivalry mown down like the grass

foretaste of that grand catastrophe, of which the dreaded anticipation seemed to lie like a shroud on the spirit of the people, giving new impulse to those superstitious terrors which impelled the Moors to the very acts calculated to hasten their long-predicted ruin. Though aware of the startling prophecy, that " It is written in the heavens that this young prince shall sit upon Granada's throne, in whose reign shall be fulfilled the

under the scythe. Turn to the south, and the eye rested on a glowing tract of luxuriant harvests of the most precious fruits and grain, the rural villa, with its blooming grove and gay parterre reflected in the crystal waters of the winding Xenil, diverted into innumerable refreshing rills, which gave that brilliant depth of colour to every production of the clime. In the distance, to the south rose a chain of bleak, wild hills, crowned by the snowy sierra, like a white fleecy streak of clouds fringing the horizon of yon deep purple skies, reflected upon the hill of the sun. Often would it arrest the eye of the old Moorish navigator, or the home-bound mariner, when, in the pride of Moslem power, its royal navies swept the coasts of the dark blue sea which bathes that land of beauty and renown. In the same direction, situated near the city of Santa Fe, on the site of the old Christian camp, is the estate of the noble English duke of Ciudad Rodrigo already alluded to ; and again between the city of the faithful and the capital, is seen the bridge of Pinos, on the Xenil. From this point also, the spectator has a near view of the Tocador, or Toilet of the Queen ; and, passing the Darro by that bridge below the hills, seen in the foreground, Abu Abdallah made his escape from the vengeance of his father, Muley Hassan. The tower in the distance is called the Torre del Homage, where it is probable that the Moors observed the old custom of ascending the towers and houses in seasons of festivals, to pray with their faces to the east. The tourist, on retracing his steps, ascends the hill of the Albaycin, and arriving on the esplanade in front of the church of St. Nicholas, thence obtains the most favourable view of the fortress of the Alhambra.

predestined downfall of the empire," they were now eager to make him their king. They were as deeply incensed against his royal father, who, alarmed by these very predictions, and incited by the intrigues of his favourite mistress, would have sacrificed his unruly son at the shrine of policy under the cover of abject superstition. " It shall be seen," he cried, " whether the sword of the law or that lying horoscope be the stronger. Let it close the lips of the vain Abu Abdallah, as it has silenced some of his presumptuous brethren."

At the same time, Muley dreaded the people, who from respect to the sultana-mother, her strong affection for her surviving son, and her own wrongs, only required a spark to kindle their animosity into a flame. Apprised by her emissaries of the king's designs,— designs which he had not ventured to confide to his faithful counsellor,—the sultana, true in this fearful emergency to that virtuous courage and promptness of spirit which had ever distinguished her, resolved not to lose another day. Assisted only by her women, she concerted with her friends without, instant means for her son's rescue. At the dead hour of night an Arabian steed, ready equipped, attended by a single cavalier and his retainer, might be seen through the glimpses of the moon, on the banks of the Darro nearest the Alhambra, whose golden spires, and stately domes and minarets were imaged in its crystal stream. Summoning her slaves and maidens, the anxious mother took from each their veils and tunics, bound them firmly together, and then lowering her last and

favourite son from the lofty Tower of the Comares, may
be said to have held the destiny of all Granada in her
trembling hands. Hurrying down the winding and
wooded declivities, Abu Abdallah soon approached
the margin of the river, vaulted on his gallant charger,
and never drew bit till he knocked with his scymitar at
the gates of Guadix, amidst the lofty Alpuxarras. His
escape was the signal for an open appeal to arms ; the
various orders of the people declared themselves, and
prepared to decide the disputed sway. The far-famed
Zegris, the Gomerez, with others of the inferior tribes,
and the chief portion of the populace, were loud in
favour of young Abdallah. The nobler families, with
the Abencerrages, the Alabez, indeed all the principal
emirs, scheikhs, and ulemas,* supported the rights of
the reigning monarch.

After a severe contest, on returning one day from his
royal residence of Alexares, Muley found the gates of
the city closed against him. On all sides were heard
the proclamations in favour of his son. The old pre-
diction instantly recurred to his mind ; he no longer
sought to resist the existing impression become so
general among the people. " God is great !" he ejaculated ; " why contend against what is recorded in
the book of destiny ? I see it was no false prophecy
that young Abdallah should sit upon the throne. That
which was to follow, may Allah and his holy Prophet
in their mercy avert !" With these words the humbled
monarch turned his horse's head, and withdrew to the

---

* Anglicé,—the princes, learned men, and lawyers.

city of Baza.   Finding himself well received, he soon resumed the natural sternness and ferocity of his disposition.   Forgetting the recent lessons of adversity, his acquiescence in the course of destiny, and his respect for the most tried and faithful of his counsellors; alive only to the indignity offered to him by his people, he was seized with a paroxysm of passion, or rather madness, and burned for revenge against his own subjects. Selecting only five hundred of his most staunch and desperate adherents, he succeeded in arriving by night under the walls of the Alhambra.   In dead silence they scaled the battlements, and putting to the sword all they met, soon produced a scene of horror through its lordly courts and halls, almost without example in the civil wars of the Moors.   After thus wreaking his fury on his nobler foes, he descended into the streets and houses, where he attacked the people with the same insatiable thirst of blood.   When the dawn of day revealed the nature of so terrific an attack, and the trivial force with which it had been conducted, the citizens rose in a mass, and with indignation compelled the sanguinary monarch to relinquish his hopes of reigning upon the ruins of his country.

Muley Hassan withdrew to Malaga, while the startled and incensed Moors of Granada, joined by the greater number of the influential tribes, and the existing authorities, offered their allegiance to Abu Abdallah. From this period the progress and character of the war, and of the dark, domestic incidents connected with the fearful drama we are attempting to exhibit, assumed a new and still more terrific aspect.

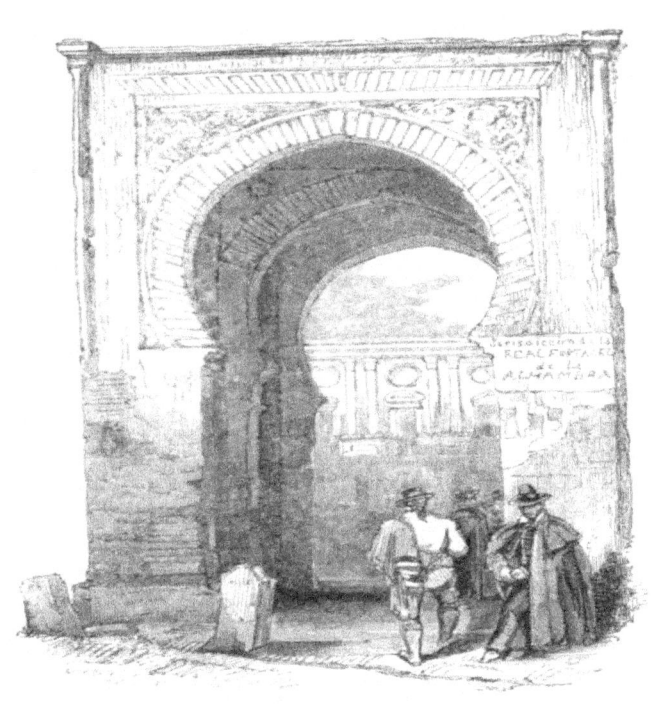

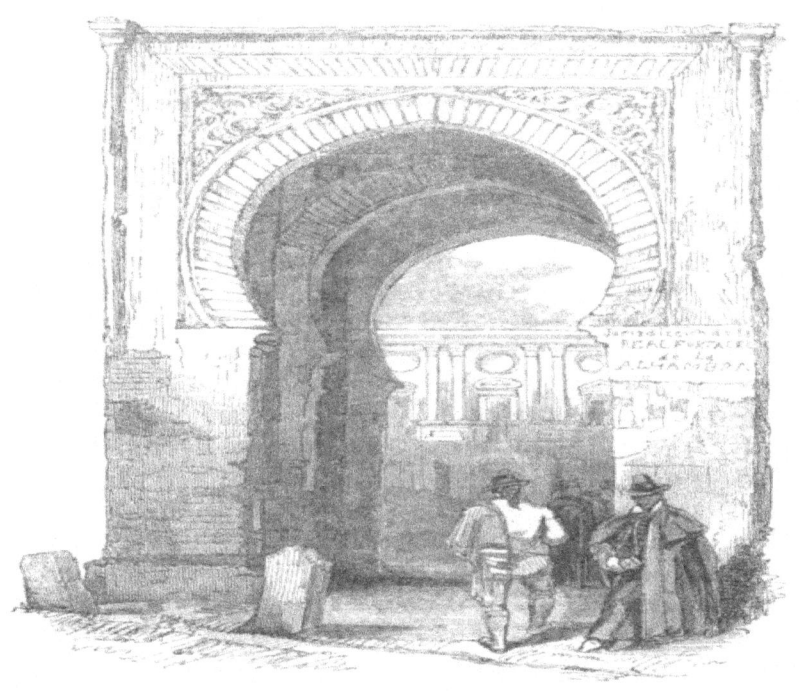

CHAPTER IV.

Not always wealth, not always force
A splendid destiny commands;
The lordly vulture gnaws the corse
That rots upon yon barren sands.
THE IMAM BEN IDRIS.

IT was not until after a succession of renewed conflicts between the father and the son, till Granada had
shed her richest blood under the scourge of hostile
factions, that these unnatural rivals paused in their
sanguinary career. Although acknowledged as king

by the popular voice, Abu Abdallah had wrested only a portion of the Moorish dominions from the sway of their aged and implacable sovereign. The important towns of Guadix, Baza, Malaga, with a number of frontier fortresses and castles, still continued to preserve their ancient fealty.

The alcayde, Aben Omixa, indeed succeeded in regaining for the new king possession of the Alhambra; and Abdallah soon began to display those qualities calculated to strengthen the superstitious terrors of the Moors, with regard to the dreaded season foretold by the eastern astrologers. Combining a remarkable degree of levity, weakness, and licentiousness with a latent fire and ferocity on the spur of action, he was at once the creature of his own impulses and of his worst advisers. Passionately devoted to public games and festivals, absorbed by the charms of some reigning favourite, sunk in luxuriant and indolent repose within the precincts of his splendid harem, he forgot the duties of the monarch and the hardy spirit of his sires. Amidst the enchanting scenery of the Generalife, struck with the transcendant loveliness of the betrothed bride of the noble Abencerrage, he had conceived for her the most violent passion: but as the adopted daughter of the king, brought up with the princesses of the court, and a child of the famed Ali Atar, the amorous prince felt it politic to restrain his ardour within the bounds of reason. Aware that she had long plighted her love to the chief of the Abencerrages, whom he hated not less as a rival than for his glory in arms, his intense passion had been chastened by respect

and even awe; but all better and nobler feelings lost
sight of in the intoxication of power, he could now
throw off the mask and appear in his real colours. To
secure the success of his criminal projects, he attempted
to consolidate his power by the removal of the former
authorities, and promoting the most devoted and abject
of his own partisans in their place. The emirs, the
venerable elders and scheikhs, the most learned poets,
artists, and philosophers,—all distinguished for their
rare science or their useful discoveries which conferred
lasting obligations upon Europe, were either neglected
or insulted by the new Moorish court. The most
renowned among the ministers and counsellors, not ex-
cepting the enlightened Aben Kassim, were not spared;
and to his deep-seated grief at witnessing the decline
of the empire, the outrageous actions of his royal
master, who had forgotten the respect due to his opinions, was now added the indignity of being struck
from the rolls of the grand divan. Several of the
chiefs, grown grey in the service of a line of monarchs,
were either expelled or doomed to behold the beloved
tribes with whom they had won their hard-earned
laurels headed by young presuming favourites, who at
the head of the populace had espoused the interests of
the new monarch. A few indeed there were, whose
high fame and influence in the council and in the field
he did not yet venture to impugn. Among these ranked
the Prince of the Abencerrages, Ibrahim Ali Atar, commander of the great fortress of Loxa, Muza Ben Gazan,
El Zagal, the brother of the deposed king, and the

F

powerful tribes and adherents attached to them by the most indissoluble ties.

Abu Abdallah did every thing in his power to win them to his interests ; he reminded them of the cruelty and horrors inflicted upon Granada by Muley Hassan ; he bribed their officers, and attempted to disturb the old warlike discipline still respected by the heads of the nobler tribes. By such policy he sought to smooth the way for the destruction of the most heroic of his opponents among the boldest of their country's champions, who spurned the idea of purchasing peace by the sacrifice of honour and independence. Pursuing the infamous policy of humbling the power of the Abencerrages and the Alabez, he secretly fomented the rivalries between them, the Gomerez, and the Zegris. By raising up a host of mercenaries, the dregs of the Moorish populace, wholly lost to the hardy spirit of their race, he ignobly sought to extirpate his noble rivals from the soil, instead of binding them to him by a free, frank spirit of conciliation, which at such a crisis might have consolidated his usurped throne, and given a new aspect to the fortunes of the war. But Abu Abdallah was a striking exemplification of the great truth, that the weak and sensual become incapable of any real excellence. Involved in the meshes of wild, insatiable passions, a prey to that most grievous and destructive disease, the insanity of the selfish instinct springing from early and excessive indulgence, which invariably brings down calamity upon others whether raging in the palace or the peasant's hut, Abu Abdallah now trampled on the eternal laws of order, justice, and reason. Instead of directing his vigilance, soul and heart, to arrest the progress of the foe, he attempted to make himself beloved by a series of splendid spectacles, of public sports and festivals, spreading royal boons and largesses among a corrupt populace.

Once a king, he attempted by every art of which he was master, to ensnare the virtuous and beautiful daughter of Ali Atar. With this view he had remained in Granada while her heroic lover was reaping glory in the field. But his intrigues had been met with a heroism, a scorn, and a constancy on the part of Zelinda, equal to the fiery passion which impelled him to seek the possession of her charms and the destruction of his rival. Vainly did he renew his detested solicitations in every form calculated to excite the feelings, to captivate the imagination or the heart. The bitterest threats and indignation succeeded the seductive courtesies of the royal Moor ; nor would respect for her noble birth, her plighted faith, or dread of her princely lover have longer deterred him from the most audacious of crimes, but for the noble conduct of the Moorish princesses and the daughters of Aben Kassim, who threw round her the shield of their rank, veiling her from his view till the arrival of her noble lover. As vainly did he display the allurements of a sultana's diadem, the honours and splendours which surround the partner of Granada's throne, to tempt her to yield to his wishes ere Ibn Hammed's return ; they were treated with the virtuous detestation due to motives so ignobly avowed.

It was then the designing Abdallah found himself
constrained to dissimulate; and with that refined
duplicity characteristic of the worst of the Moors, he
determined to accomplish his object by more slow and
wary methods. But the princely Abencerrage, receiving
tidings of what had passed, would on the instant have
flown, transported with fury, to confront the royal
invader of his honour. Forcibly withheld from so
rash a step by Almanzor and his friends, he was at
length induced to listen to reason, and adopt some plan
at once more dignified and more effectual. The aged
and gallant father of his betrothed, with numerous
other friends and leading families, were speedily summoned to attend a solemn council of the chiefs.

It was here discussed, whether Muley Hassan, having
forfeited his crown and the confidence of his subjects
by his late atrocities, it was not imperative on the
Abencerrages, the Alabez, and other influential bodies
friendly to their tribes, to adopt a new line of policy.
With patriotic desire of blending hostile parties in one
great cause, the experienced Aben Kassim recommended
to the divan an unanimous transfer of their allegiance
and services to the popular king. It was to be accompanied with specific conditions, of which the leading
were, that he should prosecute the war with the utmost
vigour, that he should enter into no compact with the
Christians without the solemn deliberation of his chiefs
and elders, and that he should lead his army in person
to oppose the foe. That in consideration of the signal
exploits of Ibn Hammed, he should command in the
field the forces entering into these arrangements, while

Prince Almanzor should be the leader of the Moorish foot. That in honour of the splendid achievements of Ali Atar in the border warfare, jousts of the reed and the ring should be held in the square of the Viva Rambla, to celebrate the nuptials of his daughter with the chief of the Abencerrages.

At the head of this warlike deputation walked the aged hero, still renowned as the most skilful lance in Spain, followed by the young Abencerrage. Next to them was Aben Kassim with the scheikhs and elders of the old divan, attended, according to their birth and prowess, by the whole of Granada's noble families and tribes which adhered to Ibn Hammed's cause.

It was an impressive spectacle to behold so vast an assemblage of the wise, and the chivalrous of that once fertile and superb empire of the Andalusian Moors, as they wound slow and solemnly through the aisles and avenues of the sacred mosque, offering up prayers to Allah for the preservation of Granada the beautiful —the beloved; her faithful children, and her happy homes. And first, they deposited in its sanctuary the holy banner of their Prophet, the great founder, the purifier of their religion and their laws, the father of their high-born chivalry, and of the thousand victories decreed by God, the only conqueror, upon the necks of prostrate nations. To God alone, and to Mohammed, his chosen, his sword, and his lawgiver, was the praise and the glory of having rescued the ancient tribes of the eastern world from ages of superstition, ignorance, and the feudal scourge.

" The light of a redeeming intellect," continued the

eloquent and aged scheikh, " shone on the sword of
our holy faith ; and with the might of our khaliphs, the
great vicars of our Prophet's will, came the regenerating strength of loftier times ; the civilization, the
science, the industry, and the arts which have at last
taught the Goths and Vandals of European thraldom to
turn their weapons against their teachers. Yea, from us
have they received the Kiblah,* showing the direction
in which they should go to attain all that is good and
great. We have, perhaps, fulfilled the Prophet's great
mission in this land of delights ; the genius of our
schools, our policy, and our discoveries hath illumined
the mind of Allah's children, the children of our foes ;
and we have now, it may be, only to gird up our loins
for travel, to go hence, and to be heard of no more !"

Then unfolding the pages of the inspired Koran,—
" that which is worthy to be read,"—he offered up
prayers to the one God, the conqueror, the elevator of
the humble, the humbler of the proud, the boundless,
the omnipotent :—" Oh hearer of prayer, source of
knowledge and of glory ; help us thou witness for the
just," he ejaculated as he closed the sacred volume ;
and, falling upon his face before the sanctuary of the
Prophet, he was followed by each of that noble train who
prostrated themselves before the majesty of the one
great God, finally appealing to the most Merciful for the
salvation of their beloved country. " Allah ! Allah

* Meant to point the attention of the faithful to the direction in which they should turn their faces or their steps in
prayer, or on pilgrimage in honour of the Prophet's holy tomb
at Mecca.

Achbar! the greatest of the great, the father of our Prophet and of his faithful," continued the noble scheikh,
" who metest out the might of monarchs in the hollow
of thy hand, who divest into the depths of their council,
and bringest their vain-boasting to nought : thou con-
founder of enemies, gird up thy faithful for the battle;
display before them the glories of that eternal paradise,
the heritage of the brave and the just. Do thou wing
our javelins, wield the scymitar, and sharpen for us
the sword and the lance. Fire the soul and strengthen
the arm of thy faithful ; clothe the necks of our barbs
with the thunder of the battle, and strike terror into
the hearts of our foes with the clamour of thy horsemen through the grove of spears ! For thou alone
art the God of battles, and didst call from the cave of
thy persecuted Prophet, the sire of mighty dynasties,
the reformer of an idolatrous and abandoned world.
Be near thy few and faithful in the day of conflicting
hosts ; raise them above a vile and grovelling genera-
tion ; and let them reap a harvest of glory worthy of
their omnipotent, all-conquering Lord ! "

The aged orator of the wise and ancient scheikhs
then arose, and with an impulse newly given by prayer
animating every look and gesture, he passed the threshold of the sacred edifice, and as he resumed his
splendid robe and glittering armour, the clarions and
the timbrels, with loud inspiring note, burst into a
flood of martial song. No more attired in weeds of
peace and devotion,* they wound their solemn way up

* In accordance with an established custom of early times,

the long, wooded avenues of the Alhambra towards
the tower of the Gate of Judgment,* amid scenes of
surpassing beauty,——the odorous-breathing air, pure
from its snowy fountain of the sierra, the bright, calm
heavens above, filled only with the swelling notes of

the Moslems before going to prayer divested themselves of
their usual attire, and entered the mosque in plain and simple
raiment.

* Of the splendour and beauty of this entrance to the grand
fortress, no description can convey so clear an idea as a faithful
and picturesque delineation ; how much more the actual contemplation of the singular structure itself. The Gate of Law,
or Judgment, with its noble portico and massive tower, the
first to arrest the eye of the traveller as he enters the precincts
of the Alhambra, was erected as a tribunal for popular justice,
being similar in its design and object with the ancient custom
of the Jews, on whose institutions and sacred writings so much
of the Mohammedan polity and the Koran itself was founded.
Thus, from the Israelite king sitting in the GATE was borrowed the characteristic appellation of the Sublime *Porte*.   It
was formed of white marble, and over it the elaborate mosaic
tiling extended to nearly three feet and a half high, with the
inscription in Cufic characters so often repeated, " There is no
Conqueror but God."   It is beneath this inscription appears
sculptured on the arch the famous key, one of the great religious symbols of the Moslems.   It is " the Key of God ;"
which, according to the Koran, opens to believers the portals
of the world and of the true religion.   As a national emblem
it was borne like the holy cross by the Christians, at once the
sign and signet of their faith.   With the older Arabs it had its
miraculous powers, resembling those attributed to the Catholic
church ; that is, to make fast or to loosen, to open or to close
the gates of heaven.   From its being considered an emblem
of power, it was not only borne as an armorial ensign, but in
conjunction with the gigantic hand it was supposed to denote
union and concord.   The door of the gate is formed of palm-
wood, and the capitals of the columns are wrought in the

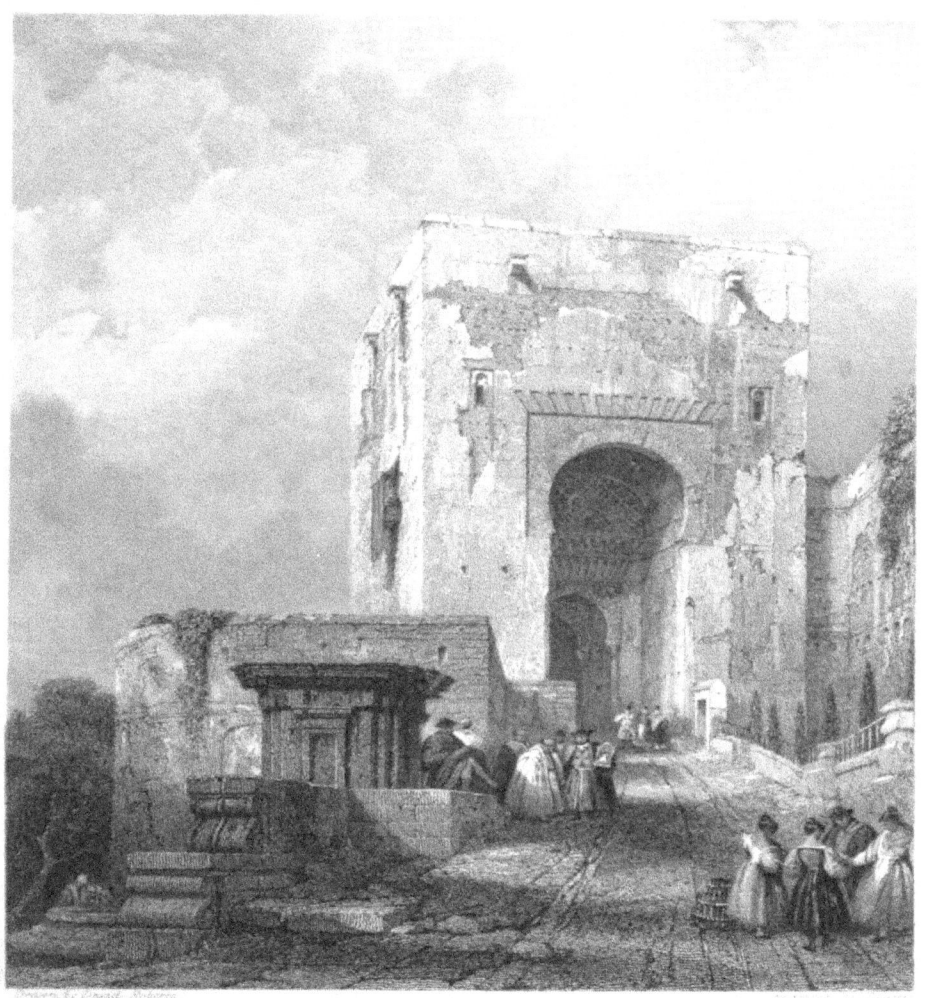

PUERTA DEL JUDICIO.

Entrance to the Court of Justice in the Alhambra.

martial hymns, reflecting in the founts and streams
the mimic splendour of mosque, and minaret, and
palace-tower.

Far as the eye could reach, the approaches to the
royal fortress, in itself a city of palaces, were filled

same delicate style as those so much admired in the Court
of Lions.

The porch, with its prevailing form of the crescent, has an
imposing effect upon the eye; it is on the key-stone of the
higher arch appears engraven that massy open hand, which
together with the key, as with all religious or national symbols, gave rise to a number of traditions current among the
Moors. We find frequent mention of the *omnipotent hand*
in the Koran, which conducts true believers into the right
way. It had, besides, various significations, being an epitome
of the law with its five fundamental precepts :—1st, Faith in
God, and in Mohammed as his Prophet ; 2d, Prayer, with all
its preparatory ceremonies and purifications ; 3d, the giving
of Alms ; 4th, Fasting, especially during the Ramadan ; 5th,
a Pilgrimage to the Kaaba, or sacred shrine of Mecca. In the
mystic hand, also, lay the power of enchantment, by giving to
it certain figures and changing them according to the courses
of the stars and planets. " According to this notion," says
M. Peyron, " when represented open, like this hand over the
Gate of Judgment, it had the power of weakening the strength
of the enemy." Both the gate and tower are framed of the
most solid masonry.

The large square pedestal to the left of the view here given,
forms part of a fountain, of which this is the back ; but it
is now choked up and in ruins. It was built by the emperor
Charles V. After passing through the barbican, you ascend
a narrow lane winding between walls, and come to an open
esplanade within the fortress, called the Plaza de los Algibes,
or Square of the Cisterns. Thence, leaving the magnificent
palace of Charles V. to the right, and passing through a low
portal, the stranger enters the Court of the Alberca, or great
Fish Pool, represented in the succeeding view.

with eager throngs, panting to gather tidings which
must reveal the colour of their future destiny.   As
the most aged and revered of the ancient council,
followed by the princes and elders of the tribes, paused
before the mysterious emblems which gave a sacredness to these portals in unison with the office to
which they were dedicated: the people,—inspired with
sentiments of awe and of reverence, stood in silent
contemplation of those sculptured emblems, the hand
and the gigantic key, which told stronger than any
language that it treasured the mysteries of that religion which had no God but God for its chief, and
Mohammed for his prophet.*

Within the sacred precincts of the gate sat the
venerable kadhis, prepared to dispense public justice
at the opening of the new reign, and at their head the
king himself, arrayed in his jewelled kaftan with the
golden diadem encircling his turbaned brows, eager to
ingratiate himself with the people by complying with
the ancient custom of the khaliphs.   He was about
to retire to receive the chiefs and elders with becoming
pomp in the Hall of the Ambassadors; but Aben
Kassim, seizing an occasion of enforcing their claims
with greater energy in the eyes of the assembled
people, suddenly presented himself before the monarch : " Justice ! justice ! " exclaimed the aged
counsellor; " in the united voice of Granada's chiefs
and elders, I ask for justice from the king who pre-

---

* The more exact meaning of the old tradition was, that
until the hand should grasp the key, the whole of that vast
and splendid edifice should remain entire.

sides in its gates. Oh, son of Allah, here shouldst
thou listen to the voice of wisdom and experience; or
prepare to forfeit empire to the infidel by the will of
the avenger of the injured, the great retributor for
deeds of injustice, oppression, crime. Listen, or
tremble at the vengeance prepared by Allah and his
holy Prophet, which will consume thee and thy people
as a mighty flame. But may the Father of the faithful,
the most merciful, Lord of all, direct thee in the right
way! Him worship, and ask assistance from him,
the King of the Day of Judgment, that he strike thee
not, as the unbeliever, with the sharp arrows of adversity; but that he lead thy foes astray. Behold thy
princes, warriors of families and tribes; behold thy
people, oh king, who knock with us at thy gate of
justice; and who in their monarch look for a father
of horsemen in the day. of battle. For here thou
beholdest the children of Mohammed, the brightest
of his faithful sons of the sword. Read aloud their
prayer, as becometh a king sitting in the gate, with the
words of discretion and gravity on his lips.''

There was a deep, solemn pause; during which Abu
Abdallah cast his eye over the protest of the chiefs
and elders, ere he trusted himself to give it a voice.
With all his assumed mildness and frankness of demeanour, dark, contending passions chased each other
over his features; his frame shook, his lip quivered,
and the sounds came harsh and broken, as he gave
utterance to the will of the chiefs and tribes. When
he ceased, no words of warm, or joyous assent infused
gladness into the hearts of the spectators. During the

portentous silence, his eye glanced from the protest to
the princely Abencerrage, who stood proud and indignant, confronting with fixed reproachful gaze, the
dark side-looks of the monarch, which had something
of sinister and terrible in their subdued glare.

"Speak, oh king!" burst forth Ibn Hammed in a
voice of thunder, as he advanced closer to the judgment-seat; "or is it that the light hath become dark
in thy eyes? Would it were so written, and pleasing to Allah, that I might dash the scales from thy
eyes, before the chiefs and people of the land. It is
before them an Abencerrage cries out for justice at her
gate, from him who sits, the vicar of our holy Prophet,
to dispense it pure from its fountain which runneth
by the throne of Allah, refreshing the paradise of the
just and good."

As he spoke, every nerve of the chief quivered with
emotion; the advanced step, the motion of his hand
seemed on the point of executing the bitter sentence
which spoke too eloquently in his large, dark eyes.
There was a solemn pause, during which the spectators, with alternate feelings of hope and dismay, bent
their eager looks, now upon the fiery chief, and now
upon the king.

"Is it thus ye speak, and thus ye look;" at length
replied Abdallah, with deep restrained ire visible in
every feature; "ye go to prayer clad in weeds of
meekness and of peace, but war and hatred enfold
your hearts. What! pray ye to Allah in his sacred
mosque, as ye now petition the son of his Prophet
upon his throne?"

" And are we not all children of Allah?" interposed the indignant prince; " hath he not said the good, the just, the noble-minded and compassionate are his children ? And who are the followers of the prophet, the fathers of horsemen in the day of spears ? Who the sons of his terrible and yet unsheathed sword ? Not the designing and the bad, the craven in heart and foul in spirit, who wrap them in their secret fears as with a garment to hide themselves from the day of wrath, when they shall be smitten from behind by a terrible and sharp foe. I claim, oh king, the daughter of Ali Atar as the betrothed of my soul,—mine by the will of her father, and of the father of Abu Abdallah, ere he ascended Granada's throne. Wilt thou accept our terms of amity, and victory over thy foes ? or prefer that half of thy tottering empire's princes and their tribes refuse to support thy throne ? Where *then* is thy justice, where thy throne ?"

At the same moment, the famed veteran Ali Atar, unbowed by half a century's brilliant campaigns, knelt before the judgment-seat and appealed loudly for his rights as a father and a soldier, determined to fulfil his honourable word pledged to a chief of the Abencerrages. As the king raised him from the ground, murmurs of applause ran through the assembled Moors, as if the royal hand were stretched forth in earnest of compliance with the terms proposed, auguring well for the success of that eventful mission. With the frank, placid features he knew how to assume, but with hatred at his heart, the king in harsh and broken speech announced his acceptance of the terms

required of him.   Then turning, with a peculiar expression, towards the chief of the Abencerrages, "I freely
bind myself to the fulfilment of these conditions, for
would ye mock Allah and his Prophet, by terming
them your petition,——your prayer?   I yield to one and
and all you ask of me, without help to deal with the
audacity of some as becomes the Prophet's vicegerent
on earth.   And for the fair daughter of Ali Atar——that
storm and terror of our frontier wars, as freely shall
that peerless beauty knit hands with the Abencerrage,
as the king accepts his amity, his promised victory
over the infidel foe.   Let him first redeem his pledge,
and Abu Abdallah will himself hold joust and ring
at his marriage festival; the noblest fame, the brightest
eyes that ever shone from the Viva Rambla shall rain
sweet influence on his exploits, as he brings us victory
a captive in his train.   Yea, let him bring us good
tidings from Ronda, and our frontier wars, and win his
lady by proof of battle with the infidels of Arragon and
Castile.   But it is easier to pledge words, than to
redeem them by deeds of proof."

"To thee, oh king, I have made no vow," was the
gallant Hammed's reply; "but be it so decreed, and
witness for me all, that I will conquer or forfeit
honour and love!"

"Recall your words!" interrupted Ali Atar; "ye
know not, prince, what ye promise!" while Aben Kassim fixed an eloquent and searching eye upon the royal
Moor.   "Ask not your bride on terms of victory,"
pursued the wary and experienced scheikh.

"Away!" cried the impatient monarch, "it was he

who proffered, not I! Sons of Allah! shall he speak
a lie; shall he babble of victory, and refuse to woo
her in the battle-field, ere he win his matchless
bride?"*

" Never!" retorted the chief with equal fierceness;
"she shall so be wooed and won, or for ever more lost.
Now I have made a vow," and he offered his hand to
the monarch; who, leaving his seat, embraced the too
ardent and imprudent prince,—policy which he well
knew would raise him in the estimation of the people.

In the generous impulse of the moment, Ibn
Hammed forgot the injuries of the lover, and received
the warlike mission with the brave, frank-bearing
characteristic of his distinguished tribe.

A tumult of applause from the spectators, caught up
by the assembled throngs without, gave glad assurance
to Granada of the reconciliation of her ablest chiefs
with the young monarch of her choice. Tidings of
the auspicious event went forth, and the troubled aspect

---

* Thus said before his lords the king to Reduan,
    " 'Tis easy to get words, deeds get we as we can;
    Rememberest thou the feast at which I heard thee saying,
    'Twere easy in one night to make me Lord of Jaen.

    " Well in my mind I hold the valiant vow was said;
    Fulfil it, boy, and gold shall shower upon thy head;
    But bid a long farewell, if now thou shrink from doing,
    To bower and bonnie bell; thy feasting and thy wooing."

    " I have forgot the oath, if such I e'er did plight,
    But needs there plighted troth to make a soldier fight?
    A thousand sabres bring; we'll see how we may thrive!"
    "One thousand!" quoth the king; "I trow thou shalt have five."
                                        VOW OF THE MOOR.

of a mighty city threatening anarchy and discord with
their train of woes, more terrible from the near approach of a proud relentless invader, became, for the
moment, one scene of exulting carnival, of anticipated
triumph.

But soon the harsh pealing notes of war summoned
to the exterminating contest; to decide the fate of
empire between two rival powers, the fame of whose
conquests had for centuries challenged the wonder of
the world.   Nor was the re-union of the Moslems
effected before the hour of need; the Christians under
the leaders of an age still breathing the spirit of the
heroic Cid, had borne the tempest of the war to the very
gates of their beloved city, scattering dismay through
their frontier towns and citadels.   The fairest plains,
the thickly populated hamlets of that delicious and
fertile region, with the blooming harvests, its thousand flocks and herds, its fruitful groves and gardens
clothing the banks of its crystal streams and golden
rivers, were involved in one indiscriminate ruin. From
the stronghold of Alhama, almost in the heart of the
kingdom, the enemy made fierce incursions into the
adjacent territories and castles, commanding the inlets
to Granada.   Jaen was already captured; the powerful and wealthy Malaga was on the eve of surrender, if
not relieved, and the fortress of Loxa was attacked
with the utmost fury by the frontier nobles, followed
by a stronger force under the cautious Ferdinand,
which burst like a thunderbolt upon the astonished
Moors.   It was to this point their combined efforts
were now directed to redeem the fortune of the war;

while at the same moment came tidings of victory from the plains of Malaga, inspiring them with hope. Their enthusiasm and old religious fervour, on learning its details, began to revive.

But eager to strike some memorable blow before the arrival of Ferdinand, the frontier nobles, led by Ponce de Leon, the Count of Cifuentes, and other lords, made inroads into the province, exterminating all before them with fire and sword. It was then Muley Hassan, the crownless monarch, still animated with deadly hatred of the Christian foe, called to his standard all of remaining chivalry or loyalty in the surrounding territory, and flew to the rescue of an afflicted people. At the head of his horsemen and bands of mountaineers, stern and wild as their native hills, he marched to the attack, aged and broken as he was. But time and grief, with every fiery passion, had wrought their fated work upon his enfeebled frame; and falling from his war-horse into the arms of his attendants, he was too exhausted to proceed. His eye fixed on the path he had been advancing, he pointed onwards, entreating to be again placed upon his faithful steed. But his brother, called El Zagal, the Valiant, and the famous Wali Ben Egaz now approaching, insisted on his resigning the conduct of the expedition, observing that he was no longer fit to encounter the perils of such a campaign.

The aged warrior, fiery to the last, answered them only by one indignant look, one effort to rise and vindicate his title to be their chief; but it was vain, and casting from him his useless arms, he trampled on

G

his jewelled turban, he tore his beard, and covering his face with his hands, turned away and wept.   From the spot where he sat, he could behold the new leaders separate his army into two divisions, at the head of which each placing himself, rapidly pursued his way. El Zagal taking the horse, bore down upon the Christians in the plain; while Redovan with the foot, javelin and cross-bow men, hastened to await them in the mountain defiles and passes.   The Moorish horse about mid-day overtook the Spaniards in the burning plain, heavily laden with booty, and desirous, for its sake, to continue their retreat.   But attacking with the utmost impetuosity, notwithstanding their superior numbers, El Zagal threw them into confusion; till after a brief struggle, the rout becoming general, the Christians betook themselves to the hills, where the terrible Redovan burst upon them from his ambuscades, and put them to the sword.   Numbers perished; the whole of the booty, banners, and captives became the prize of the victor.   The Count of Cifuentes surrendered his sword to Redovan, who found him valiantly defending himself against six Moorish horsemen, without a single soldier at his side.

Infusing redoubled ardour into the Moslems, this decided success was followed by more important consequences, as regarded the progress of the war.   The fame of El Zagal became the theme of every tongue; "For what," cried the fickle populace, "had Granada's favourite Abu Abdallah yet achieved to compete with an exploit like this!   Behold what it is to be a king;

to sleep without care is to have the best bed in the world. But woe to the people that have a ruler without desert! Look at El Zagal! an ambitious heart has heavy anxieties : see what he hath done! a courageous man is never poor! But Abu Abdallah is more useless than the old father he hath driven from the throne, who never turned his back upon a foe ; ah! his son's merits lie under his tongue!" And a large body of the caustic, bold speaking Moors, in the true spirit of their laws, declared that El Zagal alone was capable of saving the empire. So incensed was Abu Abdallah at his loss of popularity,—for not a few of these invidious comparisons met his ear, that hurrying on his preparations for the field, he burned to show Granada that its king was no craven, unworthy to lead its armies against the common foe. Learning that the town of Lucena was ill guarded, he there resolved to strike a first blow.

Loud blew the clarions that gave signal to Granada of their new monarch advancing at the head of the tribes, to seek the enemy in the open plain ; the gates of Elvira teemed with applauding throngs, half repentant and ashamed of their late popular strictures, as they beheld this sudden act of heroism in their no less fickle king. But the joy of the moment was damped ; a strange ominous silence followed the buzz of applause, when in passing through the gate the lance of the royal leader, coming in contact with the arch, snapped asunder* in the eyes of the astonished

* The Mohammedans have, in all ages, been remarkable for their faith in omens and auguries ; and Pashas have sometimes

and superstitious multitude.   As they started back
with an expression of dismay, the aged faquir, never at
a loss to seize an occasion for displaying his sinister
eloquence, and terrifying the abject and fanatical into
the fate he predicted, again gave vent to an ominous
howl, which broke the silence in no flattering language
to the monarch's ear.   Fearfully he recalled to mind
that it was at this exact spot, under the reign of Mohammed Alhamar, that the lance of the first knight
riding through the Elvira gave dismal token of the misfortunes so soon to ensue.   Enraged at the occurrence,
the king scowled darkly, as he passed, upon the prophet; and, drawing his scymitar with a smile of scorn,
he boldly dashed along at the head of his gallant
retinue.   But no farther symptoms of rejoicing filled
the air, as the silent ranks of horsemen passed in long
succession into the plains.   But where, in that brilliant array, shone the towering form of their brave
champion—the mirror of chivalrous exploit—the lion-
look which beamed like the rainbow of promised victory through the black clouds of the battle-dust in the
storm of war?   Why sparkled not the light of his

been removed from their governments for so slight a cause as
the falling of their horses, interpreted by superstition into a
portent of some grievous calamity.   In the late war in Syria,
the field-marshal of Anatolia was deprived of the chief command because he appeared to enter upon the campaign under
unfavourable auspices, and it was feared that the malignity of
his evil genius might involve the public interests of the state.
This feeling, however, is not peculiar to the Turks ; more civi-
lized nations are not free from it ; the only difference between
them and us, perhaps, is, that they acknowledge their weakness, and we conceal it.

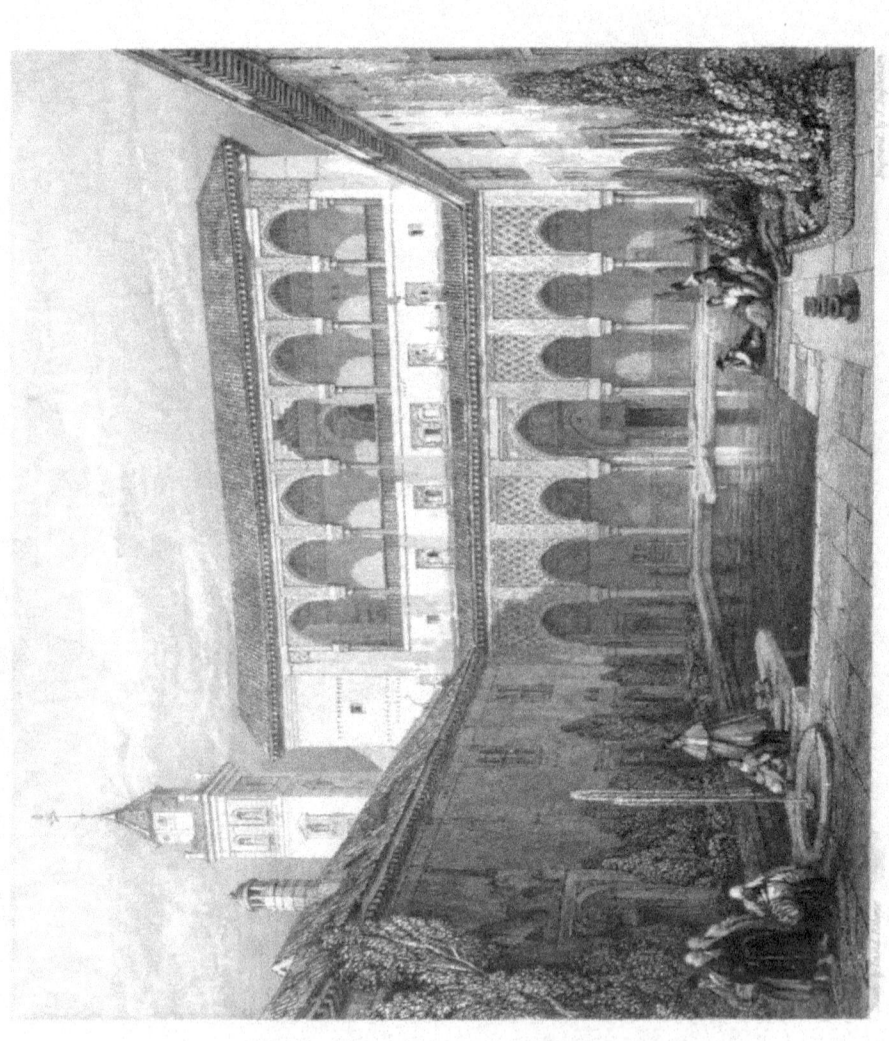

gleaming scymitar, the terrors of that brandished
lance——the harbinger of death to many a foe ! Ere he
flew to a deadlier field, the lover had sought to assuage
the deep absorbing passion of his soul in the light of
those bright eyes and sweeter smiles of the loveliest of
Granada's daughters, whose Andalusian fire is still
freshly visible in the glance of the dark eye and in the
elastic step, proclaiming their eastern descent. Swiftly
did he traverse the cool umbrageous courts, the marble halls and corridors which, through the famed
Alberca,* dreaded for its wild traditionary recollections, conducted him to the magnificent baths of the

* The Court of the Alberca, or great Fish Pool, situated
between that of the Lions and the Tower of Comares, with its
fountains sparkling through the clear balmy air, and glittering with myriads of gold fish, from which it is known to derive
its name. The apartments at the end of this quadrangle have
been much injured by an angle of the palace commenced
by the emperor, obtruding upon them. A great part of the
gallery and rooms attached to it were destroyed to make
way for it. The subject of the engraving is represented as looking
towards this end of the court ; but in order to give due effect
to that part of the building, the artist has, I think, judiciously
omitted the heavy abrupt angle which, by the side of this
beautiful court, looks little better than a dead wall. The
court is paved with white marble, and decorated at each end
with light Moorish peristyles. In the centre is an immense
basin, or fish-pond, which is one hundred and twenty feet in
length, by thirty in breadth. It is bordered by hedges of
roses, producing a beautiful effect with the bubbling waters,
the glowing fish, and the lofty Tower of Comares seen rising
at the upper end of the court. On passing from it, through
a Moorish archway, the astonished stranger next enters the
renowned Court of the Lions, forming one of the subjects in
the present series.

Alhambra. *   There the pure cool air, rich with the
incense-breathing herbs, antique vases of aromatic
treasures pouring their exquisite fragrance over bright
tessellated floors and fretted pavements, regaled every
sense with feelings of freshness and delight.   On all
sides the splendid decorations of Moorish art in its
last refinement captivated the imagination and the eye.

Entering the Court of the Lions, his eagle-glance
rested for a moment on its rich marble peristyles, its
noble walls and ceilings glowing with a thousand
brilliant hues,——those intricate mosaics,——fretworks
which baffle the minutest research.   They were farther
adorned by those frequent apothegms which every
where fill the recurring divisions of the palaces and
temples, as a record to the living of the old Arab
faith and customs.   And what more exemplary, what

* Of exquisitely oriental taste, these magnificent baths were
approached through a court filled with odoriferous flowers, at
the end of which rose a light and elegant hall, with a graceful
corridor above, resting on the delicate Moorish arch and
marble pillar. Alabaster fountains in the centre shed delicious
freshness, as you drew nearer their almost subterranean retreats.   On either side were recesses with small platforms,
in which the bathers reclined, enjoying the perfumed air and
the soft music from the corridor above their heads.   The
subdued light was admitted only through apertures in the
fretted ceiling.   Varying in taste and magnificence as appropriated to the monarch—the sultana—the beauties of the
harem,—they were the favourite resort of the Moors, no less
from a sentiment of religion than of luxury, even social and
conversational pleasures.   Almost in the vicinity were the
apartments of the Moorish princesses and ladies of the court,
the concert and music rooms, with the beautiful little myrtle
garden of the Linderaxa, skirting the splendid saloon of the
Two Sisters.

truer counsellors of wisdom than to be thus familiarly and daily reminded of the duties of patience, magnanimity, courtesy, hospitality, and prayer, as a refuge in the seasons of peril, of trouble, or of death. Though so often enjoined, Ibn Hammed dwelt on them, as if communing with his own heart. " There is no conqueror but God," he repeated, while his looks expressed high and holy feelings mingled with the gallant bearing of a leader of the war. As he turned away from the glowing colours and richly-pictured emblems around, he saw emblazoned in newer characters, " Obedience and honour to our Lord, Abu Abdallah;" and starting as if he had trodden on a serpent and with more hurried step, he passed along those marble colonnades into the silent hall of the fountain which bears the name of his noble tribe. Entering the tower of the Two Sisters, a splendid suite of saloons still more exquisitely and gracefully decorated, commanding most delicious prospects of the Vega through light-arched vistas opening into each other, he approached the wide illuminated window looking upon the magnificent country beyond, and reflecting the purple light in a stream of magic tints on every object. From the fountain of the Abencerrages could be seen the whole of this scene of splendour teeming with natural beauties wedded to all that was graceful and luxurious in art, rendering it delightfully adapted for a favourite residence of the princesses of the court.

Here, in these delicious retreats, so alluring to every sense, amidst sparkling founts, mimic groves, and odoriferous flowers, glided forms of surpassing mould and

beauty, whose dark, veiled eyes, whose graceful air and
fine elastic step threw a crowning charm around such
a spot.   At intervals, in the recesses and niches of the
saloons, were seen those rich-wrought golden censers
pouring fragrance over the glittering domes and walls,
the small incense-breathing urns and vases of the most
precious handicraft, elaborated with a thousand rare
and ingenious devices.   The chief slave having announced the prince's arrival in the interior saloon, the
splendid portals of the concert-room thrown open,
displayed rich groupes of the veiled beauties seated
on bright and costly ottomans; some listening to the
sweet-voiced music poured from the balconies above,
others directing the labours of their favourite slaves,
examining with critic eye the costly tissue of precious
stuffs, the rare embroidery, or stringing of pearls and
jewels of the finest water.

In the centre, along its bed of golden sands, ran an
open murmuring stream, which passing through a fair
alabaster fountain, again threw out its sparkling waters
in a thousand wild and graceful flights.   The entire
ground was of dazzling white and azure marble, the
product of those snow-clad hills seen towering in the
distance, pouring perpetual freshness through that
region of luxurious palaces, which embody the very
ideal of magnificence, utility, or pleasure,——embalm-
ing and purifying the air, which infuses a species
of ecstacy into the soul, and of elasticity into the
frame unfelt in any other spot.   And now the hero
and the lover panted to meet here the peerless lady
of his love, whose colours and device he wore, the

most fair of heaven's fair works in this enchanted ground.

Entranced for some moments by the spell of young, fresh-breathing beauty which met his view, the prince contemplated the sweet and glorious prospect before him. For there in soft and pleasant concord, with undisturbed hearts, ever-glowing eyes, and lips of a riper red from the clear perfumed spirit of their baths, mingled the high-born beauties of that favoured land, bright as its sunny soil, as lavishly gifted with the charms of nature as exquisitely embellished by the hand of taste, which stamped its impress on every object around. Here the young and enthusiastic repeated the tender lays of the old Arabian pilgrim-poets who strove for the great prize on the gate of the sacred temple, or breathed the tuneful effusion of later days. Others devoured with rapt eager ear the wild absorbing loves, the wondrous fates of the noble slave Antar, and his long-lost Ibla; and yet more drunk in the dreamy delights of those genii tales which charmed away the cruelty of those mighty eastern khaliphs, till they grew gentle in the light of woman's eye and the magic of her voice, as young hearts which first respond to the whispers of love. Some were themselves seen spangling the rich veils or velvets, wreathing the turbaned diadem or the tunic, emblazoning their robes with most precious stones, entwining flowery chaplets with the initials and devices of the one-loved heroic name.

As the thoughtful prince dwelt on the beautiful repose thus softening the dark, stern picture of Granada's fortunes, his prophetic spirit anticipated the hour when the hand of destiny should sweep like a hurricane over the scene, scattering the bright and beautiful in its rage.   Unconsciously he mused on the prophetic strains of his favourite poet, Alamary, and repeated, with a foreboding of events to come, the lament which he breathed over the desolated village, and home of his youth:——

> Yet 'midst those ruined heaps, that naked plain,
>   Can faithful memory former scenes restore,
> Recall the busy throng, the jocund train,
>   And picture all that charmed us there before.
>
> Ne'er shall my heart the fatal morn forget
>   That bore the fair ones from these seats so dear,——
> I see, I see, the crowding litters yet,
>   And yet the tent-poles rattle in my ear.
>
> I see the maids with timid steps descend,
>   The streamers wave in all their painted pride,
> The floating curtains every fold extend,
>   And vainly strive the charms within to hide.
>
> What graceful forms those envious folds enclose!
>   What melting glances through those curtains play!
> Sure Weira's antelopes, or Tudah's roes,
>   Through yonder veils their sportive young survey!
>
> The band moved on,——to trace their steps I strove,
>   I saw them urge the camel's hastening flight,
> Till the white vapour, like a rising grove,
>   Snatched them for ever from my aching sight.
>
> Nor since that morn have I Nawara seen,
>   The bands are burst that held us once so fast,
> Memory but tells me that such things have been,
>   And sad reflection adds that they are past. *

> * Specimens of Arabian poetry.

Amid these charming groupes, there appeared to reign a delightful ease and frankness, free from all invidious and tainted feelings, from petty rivalry or hate, arbitrary as was the conduct, and strict the regulations of their proud Moslem lords. Not a shadow of the fierce contention among fathers, sons, and brothers raging without, fell on the clear mirror of their unruffled hearts. But all were seen in glad social union, drawing richer draughts of pleasure from the peculiar restraints imposed, and nurturing feelings of contentment and resignation not unfavourable to woman's happiness,——so congenial indeed with some of her loveliest attributes, that full emancipation from them would prove the most perilous dower she could receive.

" Glows not that veiled light of living beauty," exclaimed the enthusiastic prince, " a symbol of the wondrous mysteries of our great reformer's faith,—— shrouded from mortal ken, yet breathing celestial grace and love, born of some higher, brighter sphere ? How refreshing to the spirit midst these dark unhallowed conflicts of the children of Allah, perishing by each other's swords, to behold an earthly vision of that holier and eternal beauty which arrays the fadeless meads and crystal waters, from whose fresh banks the amaranth flowers send up their purest incense to the throne of the supreme ! What blissful repose to the troubled breast, thus to partake the charm of love and amity still surviving in woman's gentler and better nature,——our heaven-directing Kiblah that points us

to its sacred shrine in this our sad and weary pilgrimage
through the desart of our mortal days !"

But vainly midst those lovely groupes the prince's
eye sought that of his adored Zelinda, till accosting
the daughter of Aben Kassim, reclined at the feet of
the royal sisters listening to the old traditions of the
Ramadan,* he was startled at the sudden confusion
which the slave's announcement of his presence seemed
to have excited. He observed the eyes of all directed
to the little garden of Linderaxa, and on the wings of
joy the lover flew to greet the fair object of his pursuit.

Sending his eager looks through the myrtle walks
and embowered recesses of this enchanting spot, they
rested on two objects which drove the joyous life-
blood from his cheek ; and pale and statue-like he
stood in the quick revulsion of his spirit, his eye
glistening with a fury strangely contrasting with the
fresh glow of delight. It was the princely Moor by
the side of her he loved ; her responsive smile, her
heightening colour ever as he breathed his whispered
words, apparently revealing a tale of treachery and
wrong. Rushing towards the sylvan canopy 'neath
which they sat, his hand instinctively grasped the
dagger. The shriek of the fair girl alone gave a moment to young Abdallah to unsheath his scymitar, ere

---

* The author perceives with pleasure the announcement of
a work by Mr. St. John, the able and enterprising traveller,
founded on these curious oral reliques of the Islam people,
and still repeated with enthusiasm in the season of their great
festival. It will furnish an interesting sequel to the valuable
narrative of his travels.

they were about to close in the death-strife of rival love. But the heroic daughter of Aben Kassim threw herself on the arm of the enraged lover, in the imminent act of his striking down the king's weapon; and the second clash of their gleaming steel must have met on the beauteous form of her whom they alike so passionately adored. Recoiling in horror at that sudden peril, there they stood with uplifted falchions, burning eye, and threatening gesture confronting each other, till the princess Zuleima appearing, explained the real cause of their meeting, and the groundlessness of the chief's suspicions. Giving breath to the transport of his rage, the lover in a moment became aware of the guilty excesses to which he had been thus suddenly impelled,—the perils, the ruin to which at such a juncture he had exposed Granada and her still faithful tribes. The youthful monarch, he was told, generously came to relinquish his claims to the daughter of Ali Atar, to communicate the delightful intelligence of his reconciliation with the chief and his noble tribe. Touched at once with sorrow and remorse, the frank-hearted lover acknowledged his error, his crime; and willing to expiate it, presented to the king his sword, dashing his turban from his brows, and bidding him fearlessly to execute his pleasure. But the terrors of Zelinda, the tears and intercessions of the princesses, with that sudden generous impulse to which he was no stranger, pleaded with the king:—" Charms like these," he exclaimed, as he returned to the prince his sword, " which outvie the full moon's rising splendour, or the glory of the morning stars in the depths of the summer heavens, more grateful than the waving palm branch, sweeter than Yemen's honey-dews, might well excite a lover to phrensy, at the idea of a royal rival in such a spot. But the noblest of my Abencerrages will himself blot out the memory of his fault, by redeeming his loyal pledge and the fortunes of his country at the head of his tribes. Follow me quickly at the head of our noblest Moslems to unfurl our holy banner in the open field,——thy glorious device of love and honour " in the colours of thy own brilliant maid !"

Transported by chivalrous feeling, the king for a moment triumphed over his master-passion, and with a feeling of remorse, often felt by the weak and licentious, he longed to regain the path of honour, and observe faith with the chiefs and people, even with his rival. But the regrets and resolves of the unprincipled, which have no sincere religion for their basis, are like the winds which blow whither they list ; yet the mere consciousness of meaning nobly, gave to the naturally mild and pleasing features of Abu Abdallah an expression of spirit and magnanimity they seldom wore, and a feeling of unalloyed pleasure to his heart. Unhappily, the seeds of one fatal passion only lay dormant, ready to spring up with noxious luxuriance : now, burning to reap his first laurels at the head of his princely tribes, clothed in refulgent armour, his jewelled steel-clad turban, his golden corselet, his shield glittering with gold and gems, he flew to lead his army, as we have seen, through Granada's gates into the open field. The chief had yet lingered in that garden of delights to bask in the sunlight of those eyes which directed his path of destiny, and which shone through their mist of tears as if to welcome the newly budding hopes of happier loves. The rich, heavenly smile, the fresh crimson glow again mantled on her cheek, as she hung enraptured on the words of her beloved chief.

"How could I suspect thee for a moment!" whispered the prince, "even though I beheld those looks, that soul-illumined face, all these resistless graces pouring their charm over the soul of Abu Abdallah. But a brighter sun hath pierced the clouded dawn of our loves; now dearer than before as inseparably intertwined with the wreaths of victory, or the sad ensanguined flowers which adorn a hero's urn."

"Speak not thus fearfully, my Ibn Hammed; wake me not from this brief, fleeting dream!"

"Nay, doubt it not, thou shalt yet preside my star-queen, the most famed and honoured of Granada's lists, the object of all eyes, the arbitress of honours, the inspiring theme of every master-poet, and of every hero's lance."

"Victor or vanquished, return my Ibn Hammed, light of thy Zelinda's eyes; return ever equally beloved." She was pressed to the bosom of the princely warrior with a rapture unfelt before; one last, long, enfolding embrace, in which their souls seemed to mingle, to breathe the language of unutterable love, an affection triumphing over separation and death. But sighs and tears soon told that Zelinda was alone; her hero-lover was bearing the sacred banner into the bloody fight; but as he left the spot, distant notes of music floated on his ear; the sweet, low murmur of

strains, like incense diffused through the balmy air,
leaving an echo in his memory as of some faint remembered vision of another sphere:——*

Tell me where is my young beaming light of life's dawn
    In that land of the sun, my own loved realm of flowers?
Dear home in the sweet lap of Yemen.——Ah, flown
    Are the fresh sparkling joys of those spring budding hours.

I wreathed thy bright roses, I sat in thy bowers,
    And all breathed of beauty ; the odorous air
Woo'd the song of the bulbul to charm nights like ours ;
    But where are thy flowers,——thy birds,——tell me where ?

Oh, vale of the Yemen ! I once had a fawn
    Like a young waving palm-branch, so gentle its grace,
So soft its dark eye ; and it loved me alone,——
    From my side it was torn in the wild hunter's chace.

Once mine too, the sweet smile of Leila, my young
    My fairy delight in the heart of our home ;
And glad was her spirit as wandering among
    Thy myrtles and palm-groves, she taught me to roam.

But she faded and left me, like all things I love,
    Home, country—sweet friends I hold dearest on earth ;
Till one nobler and brighter dream came, like the dove
    To heaven's Prophet : but Love too was doomed from its birth.

Round his brow beamed a glory that springs from the spirit,
    When the faithful of heroes their Prophet adore ;
He rushed to the fields of his sires, to inherit
    Their glory of ages,——but mine, ah, no more !

* Supposed to convey the Lament of Maisuna, wedded to
the khaliph she could not love, sighing for her early home
and the early ties from which she had been torn in her tender
years.

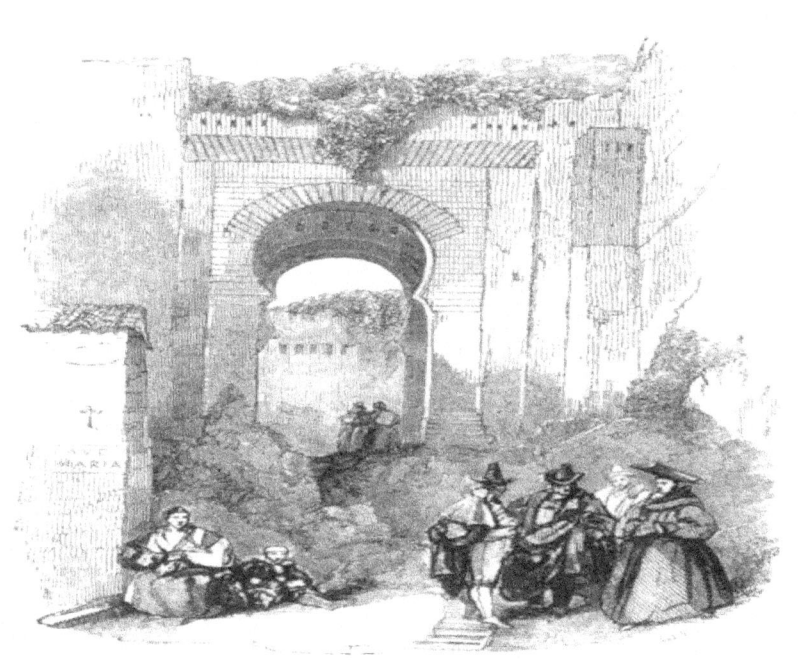

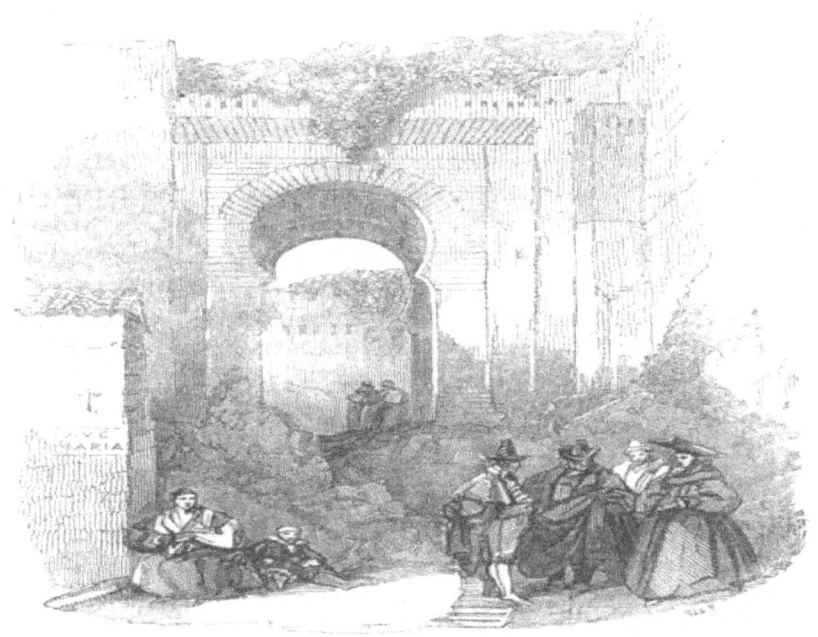

CHAPTER V.

Friends of my heart, who share my sighs,
Go seek the turf where Kassim lies,
And woo the dewy clouds of spring
To sweep it with prolific wing.

Within that cell, beneath that heap
Friendship, and Truth, and Honour sleep;
Beneficence that used to clasp
The world within her ample grasp.

HASSAN ALASSADY.

WHILE the Moslem chiefs at the head of their
mountain-warriors scoured the plains with the rapidity
of a whirlwind in pursuit of the foe, the aged monarch,
left desolate and stricken, like a tree blasted by the

H

storm, the red clouds of which had a moment before shed an ominous glory on its branches, sat brooding over his wayward fate. He had ceased to speak or to move, but his mind still retained its pristine glow and energy. His dark stern eye, still fixed upon the vanishing host, seemed to send after it a mingled stream of prayers and maledictions;——of prayers for its success against the common foe, of curses on the heads of those who had thus trampled on his fallen majesty, and left him to perish ignobly on the earth. Hours had already elapsed since he had been thus forsaken, when a single horseman appeared in the distance, and in a few minutes the noble scheikh, Aben Kassim, stood at the side of the spirit-stricken chief. There is a language which only the brave and the faithful learn in stern misfortune's school, which calls not for the aid of words. Their souls have power to commune in old age and death on things of strange and mighty import, as they sit and read each other's thoughts,——now dwelling upon the past, now upon the eternal future.

The expression of wrath and anxiety which had clouded the brow of the king, did not vanish as he turned his eyes on Aben Kassim. There is a period in the progress of death when he says, " that which I have written is written," and he seemed already vibrating his dart : a sudden ray of light mantled over that dark scornful look of the aged chief, and he bowed his head, as if willing to catch the last words of his friend. They were uttered in a voice low and deep : the breath of the dawn upon the desart,——soft, calm, and dewy, will give an image of those words. They brought to memory the thoughts of earlier times, and triumphs of the crescent in the tented field. They fed the time-worn, harassed spirit with themes that tended to reconcile it with fate and with itself, bribing even its offended pride into silence, its life's restless fever into peace. They touched it with a sorrow which had no alliance with the grief of the warrior or of the king, —with sorrow for those who had died in youth and loveliness ; and Muley Hassan listened patiently to the words of his companion, with the deep resignation on which the regenerating religion of the great Prophet was so mainly founded.

And when he proceeded to speak of the future, and, like a prophet, foretold the approaching calamities,— the ignominy of the Moorish people, sighs, heavy and quick, burst from the monarch's breast.[*] It looked as if his spirit were striving to escape that it might appear panoplied, not in a weak perishable body, but in darkness and power, to crush its adversaries, grieving it possessed no mortal engine to execute his terrific will.

[*] Cardonne, quoted by Gibbon, relates, that in the closet of the Khaliph Abdalrahman, the following singular confession was found after his decease :—" I have now reigned fifty years in victory or peace ; beloved by my subjects, dreaded by my enemies, and respected by my allies. Riches and honours, power and pleasure, have waited on my call, nor does any earthly blessing appear to have been wanting to my felicity. In this situation I have diligently numbered the days of pure and genuine happiness which have fallen to my lot : they amount to *fourteen* :—O man ! place not thy confidence in this present world !"—*Decline and Fall of the Roman Empire*, vol. x. p. 40 ; *Cardonne*, t. i. pp. 329, 330.

But Aben Kassim passed from these scenes of predicted misery, to others of a brighter hue; the words of faith fell from his lips, like golden dews from the full bosomed amaranth; and as he spoke, he stretched out his arm to support the feebleness of the aged prince. His head sank on his bosom; he lay subdued as a child, while the same low, calm voice, breathing the wisdom of love and reconcilement after life's long task, fell like some new revelation upon his ear.

The sultry hour of noon found the two aged men still seated in converse with each other. Aben Kassim then rose, and bringing water from a spring that flowed near the spot, he poured it upon the hot brow of the king, and moistened his parched lips. Muley Hassan looked up for a moment with an expression of love; and then again as his head sank on his bosom, the aged scheikh, with the fervour of the old pilgrim-poet, repeated in a deep sonorous voice these solemn strains,—the wild unpremeditated effusion of the moment :—

> Prophet! on thy golden throne,
>   In the depths of glory seated,
> When shall heaven and earth behold
>   Allah's firm decrees completed?
>
> Shall the circling ages still
>   Like an ocean onward roll?
> Still shall time and sorrow reign,
>   And thy children's fate control?
>
> See, the sword is red with gore:
>   See, the plains are strewed with dead;
> The dead! who are they? whose the blood
>   That dies the gleaming falchions red?

Prophet ! by the streams of life
   Leading thy celestial bands ;
Wherefore fall thy children thus ?
   Why drops thy standard from their hands ?

Hast thou not heard their voices raised
   For help in this their darksome hour ?
Or hast thou closed the starry gates
   To that bright throne where prayers have power ?

See, a king, a crowned king,
   He whose voice thy sons have led
On to a hundred battle fields,
   Where the proudest foes have fled ;—

Behold him now of glory reft,
   His sceptre broke, the earth his bier ;
A child of Allah fainting thus,—
   Prophet ! our cry wilt thou not hear ?

Thou wilt, oh sire ! I feel my soul
   With new and glorious visions fired :
Once more thy sons shall scour the plain,
   Like mine, their glowing hearts inspired.

But let those blissful gales that blow
   From Eden's bower now round us sweep,
Nor let thy crowned chieftain sink
   Unhonoured, thus in death to sleep !

Weak and powerless as a child, Muley Hassan suffered himself to be conveyed by his friend into his faithful city of Malaga, where the generous scheikh quitted him not, till restored to a frame of mind and strength equal to bear his lot.

Meanwhile, ere the Moors approached Lucena, the Christian army under Ferdinand had laid siege to the strong fortress of Loxa. But Ali Atar, at the head of three thousand veteran mountaineers, held his enemies

fiercely at bay, sallying forth with the utmost intre-
pidity, and even storming the intrenchments with
success.   After sustaining severe loss,* the Castilian
monarch was compelled to raise the siege, and the old
alcayde now charged the Christians with redoubled
vigour.   The subsequent victories of El Zagal, and
the no less heroic Redovan, infused fresh ardour into
the Moors.   All began to extol the valour of El Zagal,
and his royal nephew had found it behoved him
quickly to strike a decisive blow, if he wished to retain
possession of his crown.   Diego di Cordova, governor
of Lucena, having advice of his approach, despatched
scouts on every side to sue for succour ; but the
Moslems, headed by the king in person, were already
under its walls.

Summoned to surrender, under threat of putting
every Christian to the sword, the governor sought to
gain time by prolonging the brief period granted for
capitulation.   While engaged in conference, clouds of
dust, increasing in depth and blackness, gave signal
of approaching relief.

It was the Castilian army, and such was the terror
it inspired into the Moorish infantry, that under the
plea of protecting their baggage, they retreated across
the river without striking a blow.   But the horse, the
whole of the chiefs and tribes, with their characteristic
valour stood the onset of the Spanish veterans ; while
fiercely engaged, giving proofs of the most daring
heroism on both sides, victory was about to crown

---

* It was here fell Tellez Giron, grand master of Calatrava.

the chivalry of the Moors, excited by the brilliant
efforts of the princely Abencerrage and the presence of
their monarch. It was then the famous Alonzo
d'Aguilar, with his young brother, who subsequently
won the title of the Grand Captain, rushed into the
field at the head of a chosen body of retainers; while
the alcayde of the mountain-fort of Luque, * at the
head of a body of horse and foot, decided the fortune
of the day. Taking the victorious tribe of Ibn
Hammed in flank and rear, they turned the tide of
battle against him. The governor of Lucena, also
seizing the moment, sallied forth and completed the
overthrow of the Moslem cavalry. There fell, covered
with wounds, the old valiant alcayde of Loxa, defending the king; and the chief of the Abencerrages, after
all a skilful general or a brave soldier could achieve,—
twice beating back the fierce onset of d'Aguilar, fell,
overpowered by numbers, as the Prophet's sacred
banner was seen borne among the ranks of the enemy.
He was carried off the field by the broken remnant of
his tribe; and the Moorish king, now left alone,
attempted to fly. He had cleared the field of battle,
but being closely pursued, he threw himself among
the reeds and bushes skirting the banks of the river.
When dragged forth by the Christians who pursued
his track, he revealed his name and yielded up his
sword. He was forthwith conveyed to the royal camp,
where he was received with the consideration due to
his misfortunes and to his rank.

* See the Vignette.

Terrible was the shock of these tidings on the volatile people of Granada. Disaffection to their new monarch now spread fast on all sides; the old party of Muley Hassan began to raise their heads, and soon the unflinching old Moor himself, supported by his brother, El Zagal, by a strange vicissitude of fortune, took quiet possession of the Alhambra.

But the noble sultana, Aixa, was not idle. She despatched her swiftest adalid* with a missive, to treat with the Christian monarch for the ransom of her son; and at her solicitations he offered to do homage to Ferdinand, to hold his crown thenceforth as a perpetual vassal. He was to assist him also as a faithful ally, and to place hostages in his hands for the fulfilment of those conditions,——thus striking another blow at the declining fortunes of the Moors. Boabdil scrupled not to purchase his liberty at any price; and having been sumptuously entertained for a short time in the Christian camp, he was liberated by the wily Ferdinand. Calling him his friend and ally, he embraced him on his taking leave, and gave him an escort of cavalry to attend him in safety to the Moorish capital. By a lavish distribution of her treasures, the sultana, his mother, had already smoothed the way to his restoration, having secured possession of the gates of the Albaycin and the towers of the Alcazaba, so long the seat of the Almoravides since their expulsion from the hard-won dominion of the land. Proclaiming his return to Granada on the ensuing morning, the fickle

* A Moorish guide.

populace rushed in throngs up the avenues of the
Albaycin, and the city once more resounded with the
cry of King Abu Abdallah. By the usual arts he
soon regained his former power, and drew around
him all whom avarice and ambition find ever eager to
listen to the promises of restored kings.

Aware of what was passing, Muley Hassan had en-
trenched himself in the grand fortress of the Alhambra,
prepared to hazard one more struggle for the crown.
Denouncing the usurper's base alliance with the enemy,
the humiliations to which his weakness had subjected
him, and the invariable ill-fortune which pursued him,
he called on the noble tribes, the haughty wazirs of
Granada, to reject a chief so unworthy to command
the faithful, and to vindicate the honour of their
country. Summoning a divan, it was resolved to
expel him with every mark of ignominy from the city;
to attack him in the ancient fortress he now occupied,
ere he had time to consolidate his power.

Early on the morning of this eventful struggle between the Moslem sire and son, the heavy sounds of
the tambour, the shrill breath of the clarions, through
the winding avenues and shady courts of the Alhambra,
far re-echoed through the streets, gave fearful prelude
to a scene almost unparalleled in the annals of civil
strife and madness. With the Christian invader at
their gates, the infatuated people, unrestrained by the
remonstrances of the priests and elders, flew with
deadly hostility to steep their swords in kindred blood.
The whole capital assumed the aspect of a camp; the
more peaceful citizens with their families, amidst the

cries of women and children, closed their shops and houses, hurrying into the least exposed quarters, into the vaults and baths as a refuge from the gathering storm. Soon its distant, deep-muttered murmurs burst into those tempestuous shouts and tumult which marked the horrors of the Moslem wars in the fearful strife with sons and brothers for the supremacy of rival kings. Armed bands, rushing to their respective posts, were alone to be seen in the streets, and the shrieks of wives and mothers were drowned in the appalling din. Warrior tribes, whose long smouldering feuds and rivalries now blazed forth, fanned by the bitter wrath of king with king, marshalled their opposing ranks. On one side the Abencerrages, the Alabez, and the Vanegas supported the old hereditary monarch, whose late exploits and staunch-hearted hatred of the Christian foe had gone far to efface the impression of his former cruelties and excesses.

Among the adherents of his rival son, were the cruel and terrible Zegris, the old Gomerez, and the native African bands, led by the redoubted chief of the Berbers, followed by throngs of the Moorish foot and rabble, ever fierce and mutinous within their walls as they were panic-struck in the battle-field. As they drew nigh, each tribe commanded by its favourite chief singled out its hereditary rival, eager to redress some taunt or other insult to their honour, or to revenge some private wrong.

But ere they closed in stern array, the noble prince of the Abencerrages, still pale and ghastly with his wounds, threw himself between, as he entered the great square of the Viva Rambla, and sought to arrest the fury of his infatuated countrymen. But finding all his patriotic appeals in vain, he turned with indignant eye upon a chief of the Zegris, eagerly inciting his followers to civil wrath, and reproaching him in the noble language* of the hero-poet, Ibn Alabas, he called forth the acclamations of the other tribes and of all his kindred, even while they refused to be influenced by his love of country and his wisdom:—

> Why thus to passion give the rein?
>   Why seek your kindred tribes to wrong?
> Why strive to drag to light again
>   The fatal feud entombed so long?
>
> Think not, if fury ye display,
>   But equal fury we can deal;
> Hope not, if wrong'd, but we repay
>   Revenge for every wrong we feel.
>
> Why thus to passion give the rein?
>   Why seek the robe of peace to tear?
> Rash youths, desist, your course restrain,
>   Or dread the wrath ye blindly dare.
>
> Yet friendship we not ask from foes,
>   Nor favour hope from you to prove,
> We loved ye not, great Allah knows,
>   Nor blamed you that ye could not love.
>
> To each are different feelings given,
>   This slights, and that regards his brother;
> 'Tis ours to live -   -   -   -

* This animated poem, taken from the Hamasa, affords a curious instance of the animosity which prevailed among the Arabian tribes, and of the rancour with which they pursued each other when at variance. It was addressed to a kindred power at enmity with that to which the poet belonged.— *Specimens of Arabian Poetry.*

But the flashing steel of the terrible Hammed El Zegri, rushing in irrepressible hate upon his hereditary rival, gave signal for the furious onset.   Deadly and desperate was the encounter ; for though fewer in numbers, the adherents of the old king were opposed to a less gallant lineage of warriors.   Such was the terror of their once-repeated charge, that the Moorish foot, the dregs of the populace, pressing upon their flank, gave way in disorder, seeking shelter under their barricades and the close narrow streets of the Gomerez and the Zacatin.   But fierce and sanguinary was the struggle between the rival squadrons from the gates and courts of the Albaycin far along the banks of the Darro. Not a pause in the combat ! and yet more fiercely was it waged for possession of the old Moorish bridge,* round the entrance to the great square, and the vicinity

* Following the course of the Darro, and leaving the principal entrance to the Alhambra by the street of the Gomerez to the right, the tourist reaches the remains of an old Moorish bridge which crossed the river at this point, and connected the ancient mint, which lay on the opposite side, with the Alhambra. The battlements of the fortress immediately overhang the old houses which are built upon the foundation of the old bridge ; whilst in the distance is seen the summer palace of the Generalife, high overshadowed by its ancient cypress trees, said to have been planted by the fair hand of one of the sultanas. One of these is still pointed out by tradition, as being that beneath which the unfortunate sultana of Granada was accused of having formed assignations with the noble Abencerrage.   Still keeping along the bed of the Darro, the tourist comes to the Alameda, and crossing the stream ascends the ravine that divides the Alhambra from the Generalife by the pass of the Mulinos, immediately above which the judicious artist took his view of the Tower of Comares.

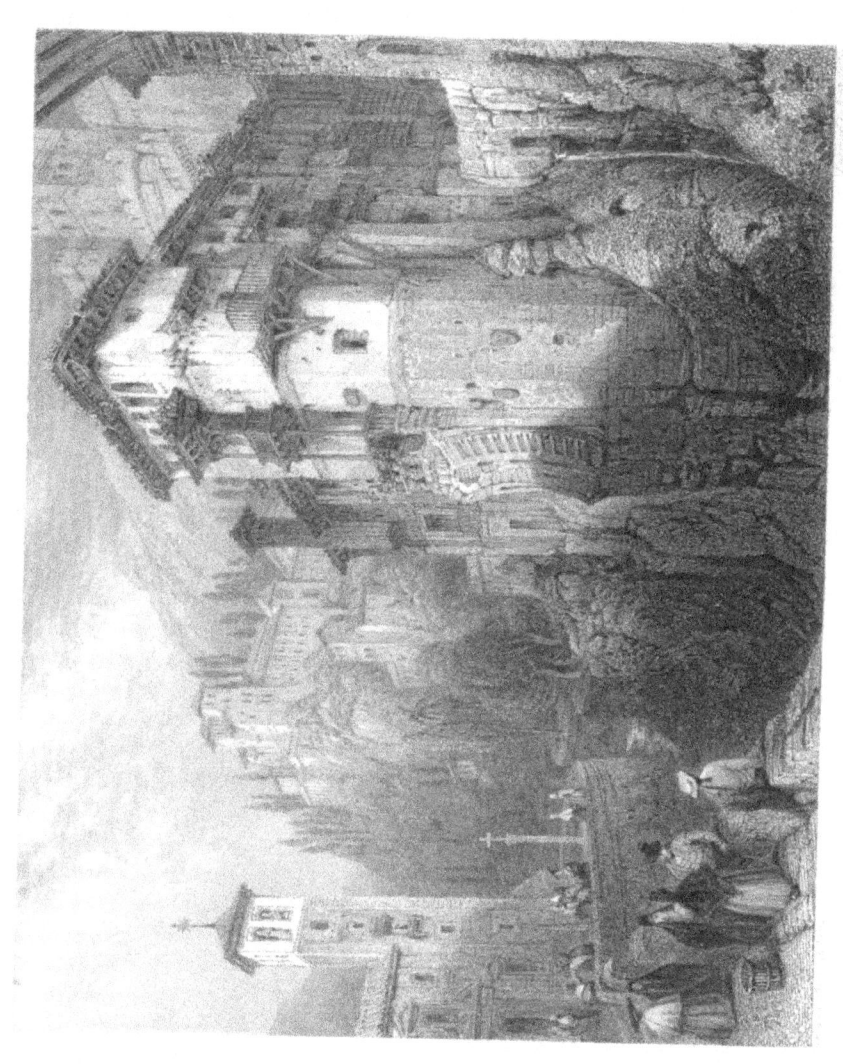

of the royal stannaries. Battling hand to hand and foot to foot, Hammed El Zegri, Lisaro, and other leaders, opposed themselves to the prince of the Abencerrages and the youthful Celim, exciting their adherents and the populace by their intrepid bearing. Fiercely beset, Hammed El Zegri stood the shock like some tower that repels the boisterous surge; his cleaving falchion descending on the head of the too daring Celim,* cleft sheer through buckler and turbaned helm, and smote its way down to the very chine. His bright locks bathed in blood, the fair device of his love all stained and trampled 'neath his charger's hoofs, fired the souls of the Abencerrages with the intense desire of avenging their youthful hero and the bereaved maiden of his love. Ibn Hammed fell with resistless vigour upon the slayer of his favourite brother; and a personal conflict ensued, which momentarily held suspended the minds and swords of the surrounding combatants. Eager to close, they at once cast aside their light-barbed javelins, by mutual impulse wielding their glittering scymitars, and dashing off in short curved career to give vigour to the first shock. The equal shock and the rebound, followed by a storm of swift repeated strokes aimed and

* Oh, lovely lies he on his bier, above the purple pall,
 The flower of all Granada's youth, the loveliest of them all.
 His dark dark eyes are closed, his rosy lip is pale,
 The crust of blood lies black and dim upon his burnished mail;
 And evermore the hoarse tambour breaks in upon their wailing,
 Its sound is like no earthly sound.——Alas! alas! for Celim!
 OLD MOORISH BALLAD.

foiled with the same skill, soon gave place to those
singular evolutions, the artful union of force and
fraud, in which man and steed alike bend every effort
to excel. Again they dart away;——they approach, meet,
and strike. The usual stratagems are exhausted; yet
both unwounded. Obedient to their least motions,
their noble barbs whirl round, plunge, or fly; and, as
if marking the deadliest blows of the foe, anticipate
their master's motions, and avoid, where they cannot
be resisted, the more imminent attacks. Their scymitars are shivered in the repeated and close shocks,
and their dreadful falchions now gleam on high.
With these they try their deadly skill anew; they
cease to urge their steeds in airy circles, and abandon
the previous manœuvres of the battle. As swordsmen,
for the last effort, they exhaust their various remaining
skill; red drops are seen trickling down the armour of
the Abencerrage, and the shield of El Zegri is cleft
and shattered. The generous prince threw aside his
own, and precipitated himself upon his foe. Their
swords now bathed in blood seem to scorn the skill
and science which they before obeyed; but it is only
a more rapid game of death, as they feel their strength
and breath dying away. Each sought to sheathe
the steel in his rival's bosom; it was one continued
assault. As their strength, their life-blood ebbed, all
their artful points became absorbed in rage. They
draw closer, till stirrup strikes with stirrup, that they
may inflict more deep, decisive wounds. They clasp
each other, and are dragged from their steeds——still
clinging together in the close embrace of hate. But

the sword of Ibn Hammed was about to pierce the other's heart, when some of the more treacherous Zegris rushed forward, and rescued their kinsman from his grasp. As the Abencerrages conveyed their hero from the bloody field, the conflict was renewed in all its horrors. His gallant tribe took bitter vengeance on the breach of faith which had robbed their chief of his hard-won triumph; but the horse of Muley Hassan, galled by the light-barbed lances and other missiles of the enemy, were compelled to retreat towards the Alhambra, taking advantage of the long wooded avenues and acclivities which commanded its approaches from the streets of the city. Here the combat raged with alternate fortune during the day, and the shades of evening fell on the unnatural strife which deprived Granada of her noblest and bravest defenders. Wearied, but still frowning defiance, each party withdrew sullenly to their respective strong holds, awaiting the returning dawn for a more decisive trial of their prowess. Spite of their deeds of desperate daring, the lofty enduring spirit of the Abencerrages had been met by a resistance equally formidable, and they held the same positions from which they had rushed into action. Their party had suffered severely from the irregular attacks of the African mercenaries, and the sort of Parthian warfare of the common herd.

On summoning a council of his chiefs and elders, Muley Hassan lamented the fearful havoc made in his bravest ranks, all the horrors of that strange unnatural conflict which had brought no result. As he spoke, his eyes rested on the benign but troubled fea-

tures of his venerable friend and counsellor, as if
appealing for his decision to guide him at this fearful
juncture of his fate.   But he turned away from his
look of calm reproach, as the virtuous Aben Kassim
spoke, the big tears starting into his eyes :—" Would,
oh king, that Allah had subdued thy heart to listen to
words of counsel ere the morning's sun had gone
down in a sea of blood.   But now I can only beseech
the most gracious and most merciful to endue our souls
with patience and resignation, for ' how straightened
and wretched would be our life, if our hope were not
so spacious and extensive.'*   Only by noble suffering
may we vanquish the days of trouble, and return into
the right path.   But if this bitterest of troubles, the
unhallowed strife of brother with brother, of fathers
and sons be ordained, we must submit, and cry woe
to the children of Allah, and the faithful of our holy
Prophet !   Rather let me raise the voice of a dying
and prophetic spirit in the name of the Supreme Ruler
of kings ;—the father of his prophets, I advocate
the cause of peace and union,—the last hope of the
Moors.   How willingly would I pour my last breath
in that sacred cause.   Never have I deceived thee, oh
king ; the companion of thy youth and of thy age, I
have lamented thy faults and errors with tears of

* Such was the exclamation of Mohammed Abu Alhahmar,
King of Granada, when he returned from the conquest of
Seville, in 1248.   He had been compelled, as tributary to the
throne of Castile, to bear arms against his own countrymen,
and when hailed by the title of " the conqueror," he, sighing,
made the memorable reply,   " There is no conqueror but God,"
which he subsequently adopted for his motto.

blood. I grieve to speak it, but the madness of the people, and thy own declining powers, alike call upon thee to resign the crown."

The exhortations of his favourite son, Cid Alnayar, were added to those of the noble scheikh, while the nobles and wazirs, who by their silence seemed to sanction the advice, gave a fresh pang to the soul of the aged monarch. "Is it not well, my father," spoke the young cid, "to seek a retreat from troubles and calamities like these? The fortunes of Granada, like a frail bark on a troubled sea, call for other hands to guide them through the dark, perilous flood."

The unhappy monarch replied not; he turned away in deep emotion, and hurrying to visit the different outposts of the Alhambra, he gave orders to sound the tocsin of war at the first break of dawn. It came, with the passions of rival tribes more keenly exasperated by the loss of friends and brethren, whom they were eager to avenge. As they were about to renew the dreadful conflict, the aged Aben Kassim, with outspread arms, his white beard streaming to the wind, threw himself between the clashing scymitars: "Arrest your fratricidal hands," he cried, "and turn your fury upon the common foe! What demon——what fell magician's arts thus impel ye to immolate your country to your crimes? Back, madmen! slaves of Eblis!——hateful and horrible as the ghouls themselves to the pure eyes of Allah and his holy Prophet! Is it your own impious daring, or is it at the bidding of your dark invader that ye sacrifice your wives, your children, and your happy homes? Infidels as

I

ye are, is it thus ye fulfil the Prophet's laws?   For
alms ye distribute daggers, curses for the daily seasons
of prayer,—and for hospitality and love the poison-
cup and the bowstring among each other!   Oh
unworthy the revealed, glorious truths of our great
reformer and master, who rescued ye from the de-
grading servitude, the abject superstitions of the
king of evil—Eblis and his horrid angels, ye refuse
to be directed by the Lord Supreme, and how shall
ye prosper?   Behold your weeping wives, your ravaged plains, your bleeding brethren!   But Allah
hath sealed your hearts and your hearing, a dimness
covers your sight; you see not that ye shall suffer
a grievous punishment.   Lo! his sacred volume!"
he cried, exhibiting the Koran, " in which there is
nothing doubtful; but admonish you as it will, you
cease to believe its mysteries—to observe the appointed times of prayer.   Believe ye in the last great
day, and call yourselves the children of Allah?   How
then have ye become the slaves of infidels, and paid
tribute to the Christian foe?   Like one who kindleth
a fire and then shuts his eyes, your light hath suddenly departed; deaf, drunk, and blind, you have
gone from the right path, and ye will not repent! Ye
tear each other like wolves; but when the foe, like a
stormy cloud fraught with darkness and thunder,
cometh nigh, ye put your fingers in your ears, because
of the noise of the battle and the dread of death.
Insensate people! God encompasseth the wicked,
his lightning wanteth but little to take away your
sight.   While you walked in his path, it was light; but

when the darkness of your deeds fell upon you, ye faltered and stood still. Look to it that ye fall not utterly in the blackness of a night, which shall wait in vain for the appearance of another dawn."

Startled at the sudden vision of the aged scheikh,—at the vehement eloquence with which he uttered his fearful denunciations, the assembled tribes paused as if struck by some more than mortal power, with abashed looks and drooping weapons gazing upon each other. Their fiery passions,—absorbed in wild and gloomy mood, gradually yielded to strange feelings of remorse and horror. They felt the truth of the picture thus brought, in such dark colours, before their eyes. They bent their looks upon the speaker, then upon each other; thoughts of hate and vengeance died away; other and better feelings began to prevail; and murmurs of regret and sorrow for shouts of fiery onset were heard, as they stood confronting each other, more like mourners over the grave of some beloved brother than the stern resentful visages of war.

The din of approaching battle had ceased; the shrill sounds of the clarion, the deep-repeated thunder of the tambour, and the hollow tramp of steed, were followed by a silence as mournful as it was eloquent, proclaiming the power exerted by the aged orator over the hearts of his fellow men. He hastened to improve the advantage he had gained: "I speak the truth, my countrymen and brethren—it may be harshly—because it is for your good. I speak as one about to depart from you; I salute you as a dying man. I go to ren-

der up my earthly trust and rejoin your celestial chief.
For our faith in Paradise is not a dream; there *are*
glorious mansions assigned to the faithful and the
just.   I mark the sting of shame that reddens on your
brows, oh sons of Mohammed, the heirs of his fame
and of his sword!   And well may you bow your heads
and droop those ensanguined arms, while you evince
your love for your religion and your country by a
dire unnatural contest, in which only the Christian
triumphs.   Had the torrents of blood shed yesterday
but flowed in the battles of our country, your Prophet's
banner would ere now pour the splendour of its golden
crescent upon the crystal waters of the Guadalquiver;
the thunder of your ambitious foe no longer be heard
at your gates.   But what hope ye from the vain, faithless usurper of a father's throne? what from the noble
Muley Hassan, bowed beneath the burden of years—
of a hundred brave campaigns?   Is there none among
you, boasting the lineage of kings, favoured by Allah
and by destiny, capable of coping with the peril of the
empire, and guiding you to fresh fields ?   Let him
come forth, advance the sacred standard, and wield
the Prophet's sword ! Who has not heard the exploits
of Abdallah the Brave, the terror of the Christian
frontiers—the soldier of happy fortune!   Glory to El
Zagal, the brother of your king !"
He ceased to speak; and a shout went up from the
assembled host, which rang through every court and
avenue of that troubled city.   The flash of a thousand
scymitars and the glistening of spears, showed the
spirit with which the appeal of the noble scheikh was

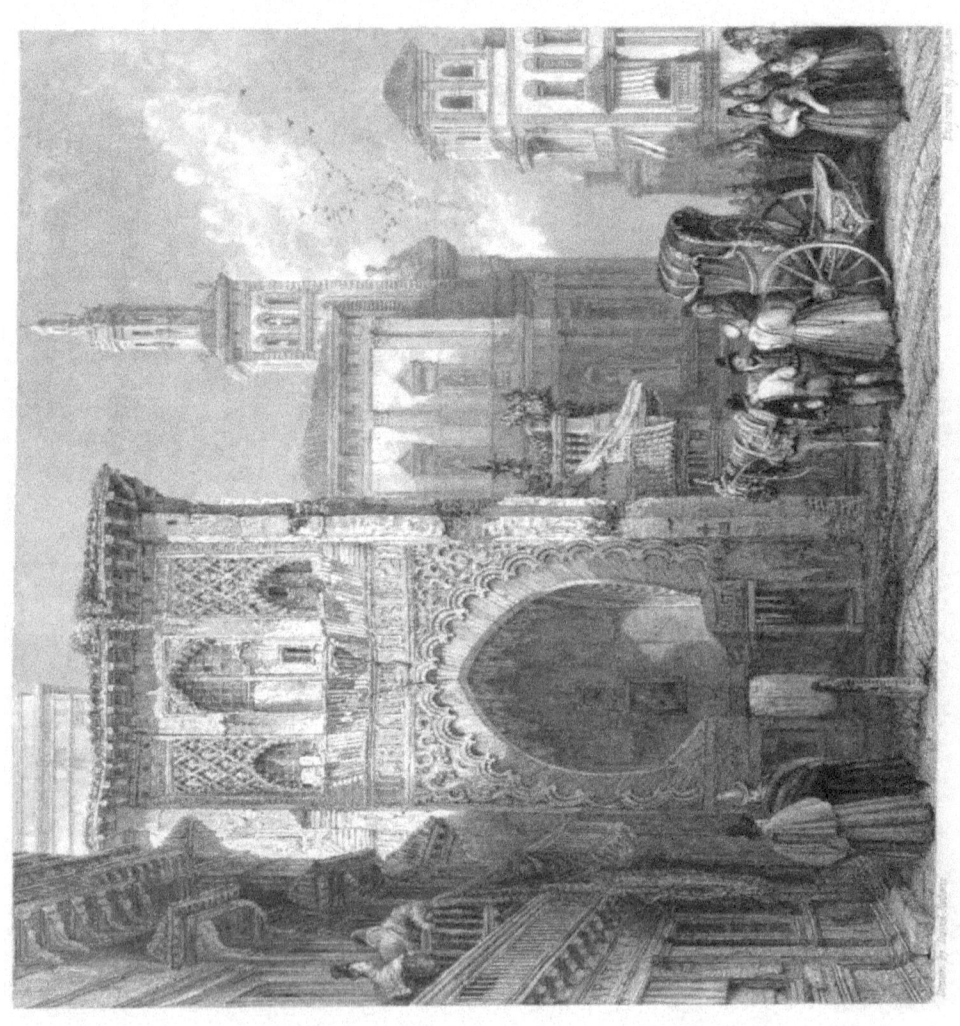

received : "Long live El Zagal! the brave alone shall rule us, and avenge us upon the foe !''

Moorish corredores were on the instant despatched from the Casa del Carbon, * on the fleetest Arabs, to the city of Malaga, where he was then in command, and to the different towns and fortresses of the kingdom, announcing to all the happy tidings, and inviting

* The Casa del Carbon, or House of Charcoal, as its name would import, is situated nearly in the centre of the city, between the old Zacatin and the ancient Moorish bridge, and, like them, close upon the banks of the Darro. Its more modern appropriation to the purpose of a warehouse for the sale of charcoal, has nothing in common with the objects of its founder, or its special occupation and uses in the bright chivalrous days of the Moslems. Admirably placed for its original destination by its vicinity to the river and the entrance to the plain, as well as to the great square of the Viva Rambla, the Casa del Carbon was the great post-house, or national stud, where the fleetest Arab, and other high-bred corredores, were kept ready caparisoned for bearing the missions of the state ; and no exhibition in the world, perhaps, of the kind, equalled that of the beauty, the admirable strength and speed of the animals forming this grand equestrian establishment, and the excellent methods, in addition to its extent and costly magnificence, upon which it was conducted.

The humane and generous Abu Alhamar carried it to its highest degree of perfection, greatly facilitating the purposes of its foundation by the skilful manner in which he effected improvements in the breed of the war-horse by new combinations, as well as preserving pure the blood of the barb, the Arab, and the fiery Andaluz, and obtaining the best palfreys and corredores for despatch of missions, and other useful admixtures of the breeds. For the following remarks on the modern stud of Mohammed Ali, I am indebted to Mr. St. John, the traveller, who, with his friend, Mr. Monro, seems to have paid particular attention to the subject. " There

him, in the name of the people, to accept the throne
of Granada. But long ere their return, the Moor himself
appeared in the city at the head of his veteran horsemen. With him came a train of captives, bearing the
heads of Christian soldiers suspended from their saddle-
bows. At a mountain-pass, on his way from the city of
Malaga, he had fallen in with a Spanish division from
Alhama, every soldier of which he had put to the
sword,——an event received with renewed acclamations,
as of happy augury, by the Moors. Accompanied by
the veteran Redovan Ben Egaz, he proceeded to take

were a great many horses," he observes, "in open places,
ranged round a yard, like bullock-sheds in England; several
of them were milk white. The grooms pretended they were
all Nejdis; but this was not true, as some few were from
Dongola. There were, however, many genuine Nejdis.
Amongst others, I remarked a small chestnut horse of the
true blood, as his points would testify. He had a fine snake
head, with an expanding and projecting nostril, but a remarkably small, pointed ear. His forehead was wide, with
an eye expressive of boldness, generosity, and alacrity. From
his muscular thighs and longish drooping pasterns, there is
no doubt he would be elastic, speedy, and lasting. The
groom said he was worth some hundred thousand parus; and
there were several other Nejdis partaking more or less
of the same formation. They carried no flesh, had very
rough coats, and reminded me much of the Hungarian cavalry
horse. The Nejdi, however, is higher than the Hungarian,
but looks small only from his fine proportions. The tallest
horse I have seen of the breed was fifteen hands, one
inch. In walking through the caravan encampments, about
to leave Cairo for Mecca, we were admiring a finely formed
horse, when his owner pointed out another which he valued
more highly. He was smaller and remarkably short and
thick in all his proportions. He had what the dog amateurs
call "a coarse stern," his tail being entirely out of place, and

possession of the Alhambra, where his brother, the aged Muley Hassan, welcomed him with apparent good-will, regretting less the loss of a throne now it could boast a warrior and defender.

But a deposed monarch like Muley, could ill brook appearing in a capital whose sceptre he had ceased to sway. He determined to retire to Allora, with his two sons, the Cid Yahie and the Cid Alnayar, the whole of his slaves and treasures being generously left him by his successor. Ere taking his departure, he went to bid a last adieu to his aged counsellor, by whose efforts to

his hind quarters cut off like those of a camel. The Arab spoke much of his great speed, and said he was a Nejdi of the famous Hassan breed. He was surprised at our preferring the other; they were both chestnut. The Dongola horse is black, with long white legs, and upright pasterns. He has a coarse, Cleveland head, and when out of condition, grows flat-sided and scanty in the loin. There is altogether a soft useless look about him. A certain French writer has stated, that these horses are highly prized by the young gentlemen of Alexandria, who mount these long-legged nags for an hour or two in the morning before they mount their long-legged stools; but as their judgment may possibly not have been matured on the Hambledon hills, it is not to be blindly adopted. It has been said, that these horses are very perfect in Dongola, but that they degenerate when exposed to a colder climate. The method in use among the Arabs, both of the cultivated country and the desart, for securing their horses, whether in the stable, the field, or the camp, seems highly injurious."

The Casa del Carbon is said to offer a favourable specimen of the style of architecture employed in the private Moorish edifices—plain and unstudied—even destitute of order or symmetry in the exterior, but spacious, splendid, and highly elaborate within. In this view, perhaps, it bears no slight resemblance to the mansions of the Jews, from whom the

spare the effusion of Moslem blood, he had been shorn
of his diadem and constrained to abandon the unhappy
contest.   It was a strange and trying meeting; for the
pride of the monarch refused to acknowledge how
deeply he felt injured——betrayed alike, as he considered,
by his relatives, his people, and his early friend. From
each and all he had received the sternest lessons of
adversity ; but though his dark spirit might break, it
would not bend, and while he did justice to the noble
motives of his early counsellor, he felt the indignity
——the dishonour heaped upon a royal head.   Aben
Kassim, while dealing the blow that went to the heart

Moslems would appear to have borrowed more than their religion—in many particulars assuredly—their polity and laws.
I may as well mention, that the clumsy-looking vehicle in
the centre of the picture, is called a " calésa," and plies in
the same manner as our cabriolets ; the drivers are called
caleséros, two of whom are introduced.   They invariably wear
the jacket, (which is of a peculiar cut, with patches of gaudy
coloured cloth—being arranged in stripes from the wrist to the
elbow), across the left shoulder, and on no occasion is it ever
worn, as it ought to be, namely,—to cover the back and arms ;
on the contrary, should they alter the position I mention, it is
to put it across the breast with the arms hanging down the
back, and, of course, the back left to provide for itself.   The
vehicle is of the clumsiest make imaginable, without springs and
gaudily painted, being decorated with some vile daub, generally
representing a picador, or bull-fighter, attacking that animal.
Nothing can be more miserable than the torture of sitting in
one of these machines, whilst trundling through these narrow
and ill-paved streets.   The caleséro himself either sits on
the foot-board, or runs alongside at the same pace with the
mule, and remounts or dismounts with the greatest agility.
The mule itself is in character with the vehicle, being
decorated with numerous bells, tassels, netting, &c. &c.

of a king, still loved and respected him; for to himself, at least, he had uniformly been a kind and generous master. There was something great and noble in the characters of both, notwithstanding the king's errors and excesses, which had produced a sympathy between them, strengthened by years.

If Muley Hassan, therefore, felt keenly the shaft of fate, which came barbed with fiercer anguish from his hand, its effect was yet more disastrous on him who aimed it. It required all his magnanimity and love of country to nerve himself for a task, which, loaded as he had been with honours by that master, made him appear an ingrate in his own eyes. Though he did not shrink from so trying a duty, from the moment his efforts were successful he reproached himself with ingratitude; and while he resigned himself to his destiny, he bowed his head in grief, and felt that his days were numbered. When he heard that the dethroned monarch had come to take his leave of him ere departing to his place of exile, the aged servant of the unhappy Moor covered his face and wept. It was in this situation that the minister and his master, who had experienced together so much of the grandeur, the power, and the vicissitudes of mortal life, met for the last time.

Muley Hassan stood for some moments contemplating the old man, as if doubtful whether to break upon the sacredness of a sorrow so deep, or to withdraw unobserved from the spot, for he had never witnessed aught but firmness and magnanimity in Aben Kassim. But a strange sympathy seemed to call him to his friend's side; the thoughts of his heart brought the picture of his own desolation before his eyes, when abandoned by all, he sat upon the ground and beheld the pride——the glory of his life, vanish from view. Harsh as was his nature, tears started to the old Moor's eyes; hastening towards him he took his hands, and seated himself at his side. Pressing them to his bosom, it spoke a language beyond words, appealing to the inmost heart of the sufferer. It came as the balmy breeze, or the honey dew-drops to the dying pilgrim of the desert, for he had thought the king was come to upbraid him. In the revulsion of his feelings, he returned that pressure of the hand, and raising his eyes to his master's face with an expression of gratitude which spoke to the heart of that stern warrior in a language he never before understood, he leaned his throbbing brows upon his breast. That look smote the hard rock; the waters of life issued forth, and he felt within his changed spirit that there is a joy greater than that of sitting upon a golden throne amidst all the magnificence and luxuries of a royal Alhambra.

As they sat thus absorbed, reading perfect reconciliation in each other's looks, the soul of the aged scheikh——ever grave and contemplative in its communion with the sublime mysteries of religion, and the no less mysterious secrets of this mortal life, so strangely linked with higher, invisible powers it beholds but dimly through the mirror of the mind's faith——began in a deeply mournful tone to give expression to its over-wrought feelings. It was to the spirit of faith he now addressed his solemn musings :——

Bright, heaven-born offspring of immortal mind,
  High o'er these spheres in cloud and tempest shrouded,
In the far Kaaba of yon Mecca shrined,
  Whose spirits watch its sacred fires unclouded :
The soul's lone pilgrim to your prophet-land,
  Where earth's fam'd teachers of thy language pure,
In robes of radiant truth and beauty stand
  By Allah's throne, on works which aye endure ;——
Divinest minds, I seek your holy band
  Of kindred love and soul-ennobling deeds,
Lavish of life to plant your godlike creeds,
And raise us from the dust by bright faith's hallowed hand.

Illustrious chiefs ! from whose resplendent line
  Of the world's sages, sprung that far, clear light
Of deathless song and wisdom all-divine,
  Scattering earth's dread idolatries, black as night !
Prophets—redeemers of a lost fallen race,
  Clothed in the strength of Heaven's enduring might,
Who made the rocks and caves your dwelling place,
  To teach the paths to Eden's mansions bright !
Oh, pure all-seeing Father of my faith,
  Whose is the power—the victory alone——
Yours is this fire which triumphs over death,——
  The soul's sweet peace which smiles o'er duties done.

Hear thou the prayer of thy faint, dying child,
  Ere yet he join the faithful and the just !
Allah, great Allah ! stem the torrent wild
  That whelms my country ! raise her from the dust !
Restore thine empire, thy loved shrines despoiled,
  Flash forth thy judgment-sword—thy Prophet's trust,
Ere yet their failing fame shall wax too dim,
  And sinks the glory of our ancient race !
Oh, breathe into their breasts the might of him,
  Who in his mountain cave thy will could trace
Through destin'd times,—thy law, thy sword, thy stream,
  Of heaven-born mercy, and thy work of grace !

Scarcely had the aged scheikh given utterance to

these sentiments, with the glow of fervid piety which animated him through life, when his head fell upon his breast. Still breathing words of consolation, of the most perfect confidence, the exiled monarch thanked him for his fidelity; and most of all for the last best gift of his noble eloquence, which, while serving his country, had created within him a new spirit, and brought him acquainted with himself. He felt restored all his earliest affections and aspirations, ere reason and humanity were shrouded beneath the blood-stained robe of royalty. What delicious feelings thrilled the bosom of his dying friend, as he listened to the king's words, and marked in every tone and feature that he was now the being he had so fondly wished him to become. He faltered out his gratitude, his joy; his lips moved in secret prayer, one pressure of the hand, one benign smile, and the spirit of Aben Kassim was no longer a dweller in its worn and broken tenement of clay.

The bereaved monarch hung over the lifeless form of his faithful counsellor, with all the bitter, remorseful feelings which his past errors and excesses were calculated to produce. No longer a king, the natural sentiments of the patriot and the man resumed their empire over his breast. He looked back with sorrow upon a life of clouds and storms, ere he sank in the still, gathering darkness of the valley of death. He thought of his bright youth-tide, when he listened to the voice of Aben Kassim; and now, in the spirit of his adverse lot, he again obeyed the generous impulses of his youth, such as he had felt ere corrupted

by the fatal boon of power. As he gazed upon the
calm, noble features of him he had lost, he involun-
tarily breathed forth the following touching eulogy,
from the lips of the sweet poet Shebal Addaulet:——

> Thy virtues famed through every land,
> Thy spotless life in age and youth,
> Proves thee a gem by nature's hand
> Formed out of purity and truth.
>
> Too long its beams of orient light
> Upon a thankless world were shed,
> Allah has now revenged the slight,
> And called it to its native bed.

The unhappy king then rejoining his family, set
out for the retreat assigned him * ; but even thence

* By some of the Spanish historians it is asserted, that
Muley Hassan perished by order of his brother, El Zagal,
who possessed himself of all his treasures, and seizing the
person of his favourite sultana, cast her with her two sons into
the Tower of the Comares ; the same in which the noble Aixa
and her son Abu Abdallah had been confined. It was thus
considered a sort of retributive event, after the persecutions
sustained by the virtuous Aixa at the fair captive's hands.
Such a crime, however, only anticipating a natural event
so near at hand, is hardly probable, because it was fruitless.
Besides, Muley had not opposed the elevation of his warlike
brother. The report was nevertheless industriously spread
among the deluded people; who, on hearing of the old king's
decease, began to extol him as the bravest of their chiefs—a
worthy scion of their ancient kings ; forgetting that it was by
his rash counsel the storm of war, in which so many had already
perished, had fallen upon their heads.
He was himself spared the grief of beholding the fearful fall
of the great fortresses of Moclin and Illora, emphatically
termed " the right eye, and the shield of Granada." Their
alcaydes were brothers ; nor did they yield the sacred trust
reposed in them, till they had no longer walls to defend, and

was he driven by the inexorable foe.   Taking refuge
at Salobreña, by direction of the reigning prince, he
had not continued there many days, before he followed
his beloved friend and counsellor to the tomb.

beheld tower and rampart blown into the air, leaving only a
heap of shapeless ruins.   Terrible was the storming of the
Christian, for it was before Moclin of old that the Master of
Santiago and his entire squadron had been surrounded and cut
to pieces.   The Castilian sovereigns at the head of their proud
prelates and an army led by Ponce de Leon, (a) took possession of these reliques of Moorish empire, and found enclosed
in subterranean dungeons numbers of Christian captives, who
had been taken in the ambushes and forays of the garrisons
in the mountains.   The brave governors, repairing to Granada, were received by the ungrateful and fickle multitude
with scoffs and insults, as if the surpassing valour which had
caused their lives to be respected by a chivalrous rival, after
such a defence, were matter of reproach.   Filled with sorrow
and indignation, the noble brothers sought the presence of
Abdallah, entreating that he would employ them in some desperate enterprise, in which there lay not even a forlorn hope.
The King pointed to the bridge of Pinos, by which Ferdinand
was about to inundate the plain of Granada with an overwhelming host.   Instantly they seized the hint, and with a
select and veteran force took possession of the bridge, awaiting
with desperate and unflinching purpose the attack of the
whole Christian army.   There they long held the fierce foe
at bay with a despairing fury, which made the spot memorable as the tomb of " the Two Moorish Brothers."

(a) For the splendour of his actions compared with the Cid Campeador.

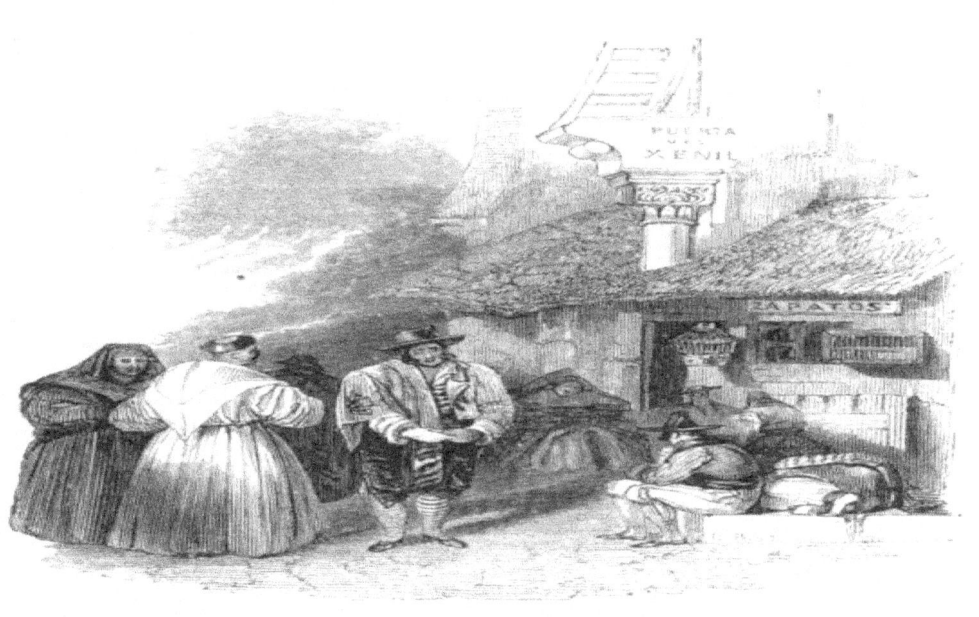

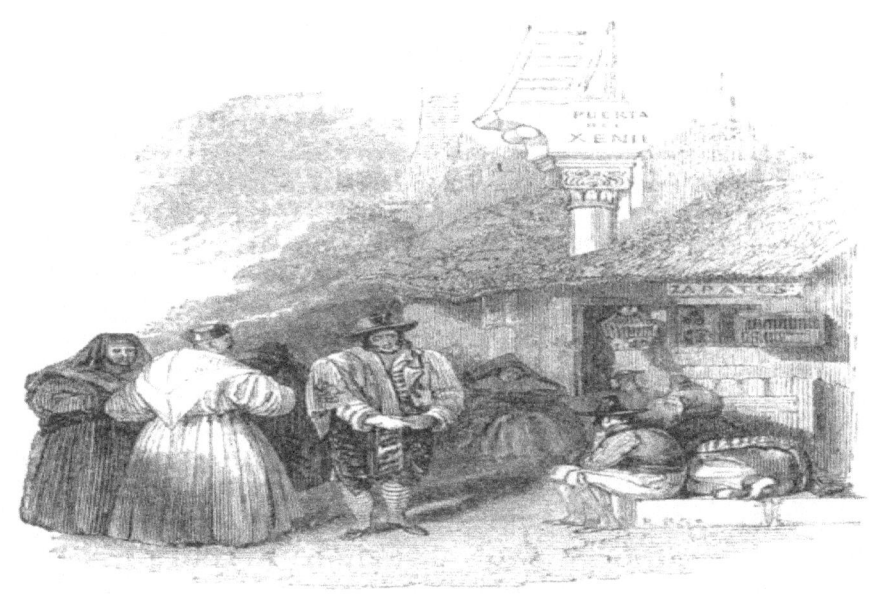

CHAPTER VI.

Those radiant cheeks are veiled in woe,
  A shower descends from every eye ;
And not a starting tear can flow,
  That wakes not an attending sigh.
        MOHAMMED BEN ABAD, SULTAN OF SEVILLE.

WHILST the foregoing changes gave a new, but not
less sombre aspect to the fortunes of the Moors, a
struggle yet more wild and terrible shook the bosom
of the unfortunate prince of the Abencerrages. Borne
on the shields of his friends from that memorable
encounter on the plains of Lucena ; he had the horror

of at once beholding the glory of his country eclipsed; and the desolation of his fondest hopes.

When, opening his eyes to returning consciousness, he saw the form of her he loved bending over him in the agony of her sorrow, the full extent of his misfortunes rushed darkly across his spirit. The dreaded penalty of his rash vow pierced, with the sharpness of the barbed shaft, to his inmost heart. He had lost her; and, in the impulse of his despair, would have torn the bandages from his wounds, alike inaccessible to the consolations of his friends, and the sad appeals and prayers of his beloved. For all other calamities he had been prepared, but to awake thus startlingly from his long-cherished dreams of victory and love, — after periling life and honour upon his fortune in the field, was a shock far heavier to his soul than the penalty of death itself. Exposed to the vengeance of the Moslem monarch,—to the last punishment of the laws on the chief who lost the sacred standard to the foe, he was bound to submit to the stern decree. His sole hope lay in the triumph of El Zagal, whose interests he had espoused since the ignominious treaty entered into by his nephew with the Spaniards. Nothing but the special grace and clemency of the ruling sovereign could rescue him from so harsh and revolting a fate, — falling by the hand of the headsman. Such was the terrific position in which the young prince found himself at the close of the disastrous expedition to Lucena, and the civil contests which ensued. Enclosed in the toils of fate, there was no escape if Abu

Abdallah continued to reign. For though he had long struggled with his passion, the royal Moor was now more deeply fascinated with the charms of the young chief's promised bride, and he still wielded the chief power of Granada.

As he refused also to listen to proposals to divide the empire, El Zagal was constrained to write to his brother-in-law, Zelim, governor of Guadix, and to his nephew, the Cid Yahia, at Almeria, to engage them in his interests. His rival, on the other hand, applied for aid to Ferdinand, which that perfidious monarch eagerly promised, grounding upon this alliance his great enterprise for the entire subjugation of the Moors. He forthwith despatched subsidies to Granada; but for every Spanish soldier who entered the slave-Moor's service, numbers deserted it to embrace the cause of El Zagal.

Ferdinand, meantime, assembling a large army at Alcalà la Real, laid siege to Allora, under the specious pretext of assisting his Moorish ally. A fortress of immense strength, erected upon the solid rock, it was a fearful enterprise to attempt to carry it by storm. The heavy artillery, therefore, then first brought into the field, was directed to open the attack by battering its walls. After an obstinate defence, the garrison was reduced to capitulate, and the fall of this frontier bulwark was followed by that of Cazara, Bonelù, and the submission of the surrounding people.

The Moors along the borders of Antequerra now flew to arms, and attacking the Spaniards with ex-

treme fury, carried their lines, driving them beyond
the walls of the captured fortresses, but again were
ultimately routed with great slaughter.   Elated with
victory, their fierce invaders poured down upon their
fertile plains and valleys, ravaging the country almost
to the gates of the capital.   Setefial, with a number
of smaller towns and villages, submitted, on their
approach, to avoid perishing by the sword.

From the watch-towers of Granada, the rival kings
beheld the progress of the enemy without attempting
to strike a blow.   El Zagal gnashed his teeth with
rage on his nephew's refusal to unite with him against
the common foe.   To the potentates of Barbary, and
the other African powers, his applications at this
trying juncture proved equally unavailing, owing to the
counter-measures pursued by Ferdinand and his allies.
The spirit, too, of the ancient khaliphs had become
extinct ; and, as if predestined to fall by the hands of
her own children, the last—the most beautiful of
their cities, in vain looked for succour from the land
of their early fame.

Like one who had nothing to dread from his Castilian
ally, Abu Abdallah viewed his progress as a triumph
over his rival ; but he was soon convinced that Ferdinand drew no line of distinction between the respective domains of the two Moorish kings.   He
made an attack for the third time on the strong fortress of Loxa ; and, having reduced it to the last
extremity, was about to carry it by storm, when El
Zagal,-—his fiery spirit scorning tamely to witness his
country's ruin, rushed forth at the head of an immense

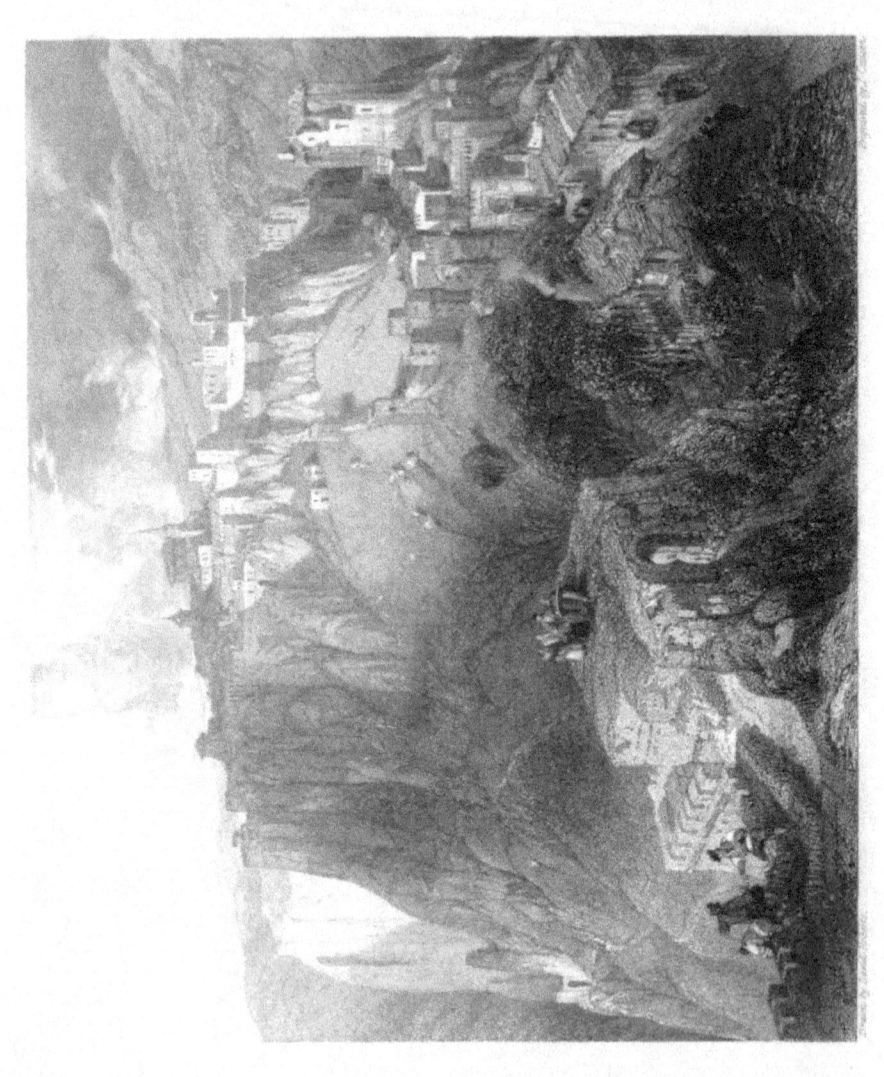

body of horse, attacked the besiegers in their intrenchments, and forced the Christian camp. The siege was raised, but no sooner was the old warrior engaged hand to hand with the enemy, than his treacherous rival made a furious assault upon the Alhambra, in the hope of becoming entire master of the capital. The governors of Almeria and Guadix then flew to the support of their absent master, and compelled his degenerate nephew once more to shut himself up within the walls of the Albaycin. Fresh dissensions, fomented by the arts of Ferdinand, soon enabled him to assume the offensive, and the strongholds of Cohin, Cartama, Marbella, and Ronda were summoned to surrender in the name of King Abdallah —the faithful ally of the Castilian crown. Cohin was taken by storm, every inhabitant put to the sword, and its walls were levelled with the ground. Struck with terror, the town of Cartama offered to capitulate at the moment the Spaniards were advancing to the attack. But Ronda,* a city of superior strength, presented a more formidable resistance. Growing as

* After leaving a small village, called Atajate, the road ascends till it gains the summit of lofty mountains, whence the traveller sees for the last time the rock of Gibraltar. On proceeding a little way, he beholds Ronda, an irregular town, encompassed almost entirely with a double enclosure of rocks. Its appearance is highly picturesque, but in other than warlike times, natural fortifications like these are more impressive than useful or convenient. In the bed of the deep and narrow valley runs a small river, called the Rio Verde, or Green River,—often celebrated for its beauty and freshness, as well as its warlike associations in the lays of the poet. The exquisite *Rio Verde* of our own sweet poetess, Mrs. Hemans, will

it were out of the rocks, and towering from its eagle heights,——the pride of mountain bulwarks, it was surrounded by double rows of flanking towers and bastions; its walls could boast a garrison of hardy, experienced veterans, well supplied with all the munitions of war.

An incident also, of a romantic kind, excited a noble and chivalrous feeling, which threw additional interest on the progress of the siege. Narvaez, governor of Antequerra, had despatched a party of horse

recur to the reader's mind, and a little farther, he will meet the no less romantic and pathetic strains so exquisitely adapted by the ingenious Bishop of Dromore.

A modern bridge of stone has been erected over the yawning chasm below, which from its prodigious elevation actually excites a feeling of terror in the beholder's mind. To the north-east, the environs of Ronda are well cultivated, and abound in fruits of various kinds; a thing of rather rare occurrence, as though a prolific country of figs, olives, and oranges, Spain seldom gives forth those exquisite fruits, which form the delicacy of our richer desserts,——owing most probably to want of care and skill, more than to any natural disadvantages. That such is the case, would appear from the state gardens of San Ildefonso, and of Aranjuez, which, by well directed cultivation, supply the royal table with the choicest of autumnal fruits. Paxarete, so celebrated for its wine, lies about four leagues from Ronda; it formerly belonged to M. Giron, one of the leading inhabitants,——subsequently better known under the name of the Marquis de los Amarillas. After passing Ronda, the tourist approaches the wretched looking town of Cañete, traversing a long, rugged, and dreary region, although occasionally broken by extensive corn-fields and plantations of olives. It is this wild and savage region also, which supplied the noblest animals for the arena of that favourite national sport, the bull-fight, the breed here being remarkable for their surpassing strength and ferocity.

to scour the neighbouring hills and plains; when in a lone mountain pass looking towards the vega and the snowy sierra, they suddenly came upon a Moorish knight magnificently armed and mounted,—so suddenly that he had as little time for defence as for flight. Evidently belonging to some family of rank, the young cavalier was conducted into the presence of the brave and vigilant Narvaez, who inquired on what expedition he was bound? The noble youth replied, in a voice broken by sighs, that he was the son of the alcayde of Ronda; but, as he spoke, the tears sprung into his eyes, and he could not proceed.

" You astonish me," said the brave governor; " the son of a valiant and distinguished chief,—for I know your father well,—and you shed tears like a woman! You must be aware that what has happened is one of the common occurrences of war."

" I lament not the loss of liberty," exclaimed the young man ; " but a misfortune a thousand times more grievous to bear." In more gentle tone, the governor entreated him to explain the cause of his affliction. " From my earliest years," replied the Moor, " I have been tenderly attached to the daughter of an alcayde residing near this spot. Sensible at last of my long, devoted affection, she returns my passion, and on this very evening she was to have become my wife. Ah, she is now looking for my arrival, and I am a prisoner here! You may imagine my feelings, for she will be distracted with fears for my safety; I cannot bear to think of her grief. It is for her I weep."

" You are a loyal lover, and I trow not the less brave
a knight," replied Narvaez, touched with pity. " If
you give me your word to return, you shall proceed
on your way, and fulfil your engagement with her."
The young chief was all gratitude, and ere the dawn
he reached the castle of his betrothed bride.   On
preparing to take his leave, perceiving his emotion,
she was soon informed of what had happened on his
way, and addressing her young consort with a noble
frankness;

" I knew you loved me before, but this is indeed a
fresh proof of your affection ! And from tenderness
to me, you were about to become a solitary prisoner:
but now I am your wife, do you believe I will be less
generous than yourself?   In captivity, as free, I will
equally partake your fortunes.   Here are precious
jewels in this casket; either they will suffice to pay
our ransom, or to support us in our prison hours."

Taking their departure from the castle, they arrived
on the same evening at the town of Antequerra, where
they were received by the governor with every mark
of honour.   Commending the young chief and the
devoted affection of his young bride, he not only gave
them their liberty, but sent them with a strong escort
and enriched with presents, to rejoin their father
and friends at Ronda.   The report of this adven-
ture spread through the kingdom of Granada, and
became the theme of many a romantic ballad; while
Narvaez, in hearing himself extolled by the voice of
his enemies, must have experienced one of the purest
of human pleasures.

The siege proceeded slowly ; the most heroic efforts were made to obtain possession of the bridge ; desperate sorties, directed simultaneously against the works, compelled Ferdinand to throw up intrenchments for five separate camps to protect his army. Behind these were erected batteries of heavy artillery, tremendous bombs and mortars loaded with all the combustibles calculated to scatter destruction, and pouring forth volumes of flame. Like a mighty watchfire, the blazing fortress was seen far and wide, one red towering pillar rising out of the pinnacle of the rocks. Horror and despair seized upon all hearts; women, children, and aged men made the air ring with their shrieks, while preparations for an assault, announced from the lofty atalaya, gave redoubled horror to the scene. All hope vanished, and Ronda fell,——bewailed almost like Alhama, and made the subject of many a melancholy lay.* No longer the

* Associated with the scenery of the Rio Verde, is the exquisite ballad so admirably adapted by the Bishop of Dromore, applying to the famous Alonzo d'Aguilar and his brave companions in the vicinity of these lonely banks, ever bright and blooming, watered by the fresh green-gemmed river :—

> Gentle river, gentle river,
>   Lo, thy streams are stain'd with gore,
> Many a brave and noble captain
>   Floats along thy willow'd shore.
>
> All beside thy limpid waters,
>   All beside thy sands so bright,
> Moorish chiefs and Christian warriors
>   Join'd in fierce and mortal fight.
>
> Lords, and dukes, and noble princes
>   On thy fatal banks were slain :
> Fatal banks that gave to slaughter
>   All the pride and flower of Spain.

impregnable city of the rock, the ensigns of Arragon and Castile were seen floating from its towers and battlements.   The Christian army next directed its efforts against the lesser towns and fortresses, which impeded its march towards the Moorish capital.

The most terrible of all the campaigns which Moor or Christian had ever yet witnessed,—soon the closing struggle was about to stamp its character upon ages to come.   But first, after such continued series of successes, Ferdinand gave an interval of repose to his veteran troops, preparing for his grand attempt of carrying the war into the heart of the capital itself.

Breathing also from their frantic feuds, which exhausted their best energies, the Moors saw the last of their exterior defences, the important towns of Moclin,

> There the hero, brave Alonso,
>   Full of wounds and glory died:
> There the fearless Urdiales
>   Fell a victim by his side!
>
> Lo! where yonder Don Saavedra
>   Through their squadrons slow retires;
> Proud Seville, his native city,
>   Proud Seville his worth admires.
>
> Close behind a renegado
>   Loudly shouts with taunting cry,
> " Yield thee, yield thee, Don Saavedra,
>   Dost thou from the battle fly?
>
> Well I know thee, haughty Christian,
>   Long I liv'd beneath thy roof;
> Oft I've in the lists of glory
>   Seen thee win the prize of proof.
>
> Well I know thy aged parents,
>   Well thy blooming bride I know;
> Seven years I was thy captive,
>   Seven years of pain and woe.
>
> May our Prophet grant my wishes,
>   Haughty chief, thou shalt be mine:
> Thou shalt drink that cup of sorrow
>   Which I drank, when I was thine."

Velez, Malaga, and Loxa, on the eve of sharing the
exterminating fate which had befallen their weaker
neighbours. Struck with terror, the elders of the
council within the divan, and the emirs, the scheikhs,
and faquirs in the presence of the people denounced
the conflicts of the rival monarchs,——conflicts rapidly
plunging the empire into remediless ruin. Bitter im-
precations fell upon the head of Abu Abdallah from
the lips of all but his immediate adherents; while the
more respectable classes repaired in a body to El
Zagal. Expressing their horror at witnessing these
continued scenes of bloodshed, they besought him to
put a stop to the desolating strife, and to adopt some
means of arresting the alarming progress of the foe.
El Zagal declared, that he was only deterred from

Like a lion turns the warrior,
   Back he sends an angry glare;
Whizzing came the Moorish javelin,
   Vainly whizzing through the air.

Back the hero, full of fury,
   Sends a deep and mortal wound;
Instant sunk the renegado,
   Mute and lifeless on the ground.

With a thousand Moors surrounded,
   Brave Saavedra stands at bay;
Wearied out, but never daunted,
   Cold at length the warrior lay.

Near him fighting, great Alonzo
   Stout resists the Paynim bands;
From his slaughter'd steed dismounted
   Firm intrench'd behind him stands.

Furious press the hostile squadron,
   Furious he repels their rage;
Loss of blood at length enfeebles,
   Who can war with thousands wage?

Where yon rock the plain o'ershadows
   Close beneath its foot retir'd,
Fainting sunk the bleeding hero,
   And without a groan expir'd!

taking the field by the treachery of his nephew, who attacked his authority the moment he left the capital. At the same time, marking the general wish to avenge the sufferings of their ravaged towns and hamlets, he assured them that he was ready to marshal a formidable force, and hurl back their fierce despoilers from the soil.

Rejoiced at their success, the deputation proclaimed the glad tidings through the city ; while the brave old warrior, summoning the chiefs who embraced his cause, proceeded to enter on a more decided campaign than had yet shed lustre upon his arms.   As he rode at the head of his veteran squadrons, turning to Muza Ben Gazan, he deplored the weakness and bad faith of the usurper, who had become the servile tool of the Christian king ; nor could he leave the capital without anticipating fresh disasters.   " But it is the will of Allah ! " he continued, " and it is more becoming to die in opposing the common enemy, than to divide with Abu Abdallah a blood-stained throne."   With these words, the royal warrior cast a last look on those gilded towers and massy battlements, the scene of his brief sway, and dashed through the gates of Elvira, eager once more to confront the foe.

His suspicions were not unfounded ; the moment the perfidious king felt himself freed from the presence of his rival, he gave full scope to his ambitious designs. He resolved to strike a blow at the power of the Abencerrages in the person of their illustrious chief ; and while he humbled the adherents of El Zagal, to accomplish his long-cherished design with regard to the betrothed bride of Ibn Hammed. Here he could display that promptitude and decision in which he appeared so deficient when engaged in a noble or patriotic cause : a trait which called forth that well-merited reproach of his heroic mother, when driven from a throne which he knew how to usurp, but not to defend. To one capable of throwing off all paternal authority, so revered by the laws and customs of the Moors, and of bartering his country for individual liberty and power, the criminal indulgence of passion and the infliction of private wrong could cost few scruples of conscience, nor did it prove a very difficult task.

Hastily summoning an assemblage of his adherents, —the creatures of his will, with the few emirs and elders who espoused his cause, in grand divan, surrounded by hired mercenaries and the dregs of the populace, he dictated to them the edict which placed the life of the princely lover in his hands. He next proceeded in solemn procession to open the trial of the unhappy chief in the tower of the Gate of Judgment, where he was summoned to appear in the name of " our sovereign lord, Abu Abdallah, and his faithful people." The satellites of his power were despatched to secure the person of the prince, whom they expected to find disabled by his wounds and no longer surrounded by his valiant tribe, who united with his friend, Muza Ben Gazan, had hurried to the field. But they found the gates and avenues to his palace in possession of a chosen band of horsemen all equipped for action ;— their leader, having abandoned the cause of the faithless Abu Abdallah, and become the supporter of El Zagal.

Few as they appeared, their unsheathed scymitars
and every lance in rest, showed they were on the spur
of some bold enterprise.   As the party of the king
paused at this unexpected sight, the sounds of a lute,
strangely contrasting with that stern panoply of war,
fell on the ear; and a voice of enchanting sweetness
threw a charm over the soul of the lover, preparing to
lead his gallant little band to rejoin their brethren in
the field.   He drew up for a moment as it fell, like
the soft night dews upon the burning brow of the
lonely traveller to some far shrine of his holy love,
and gazed up to that leafy canopy above his head
with a last fond look; for he had just torn himself
from the side of his beloved, eager to meet his
country's foe:——

> The dove, to ease an aching breast,
>   In piteous murmurs vents her cares ;
> Like me she sorrows, for opprest
>   Like me a load of grief she bears.
>
> Her plaints are heard in every wood,
>   While I would fain conceal my woes ;
> But vain 's my wish—the heart-sprung flood
>   The more I strive, the faster flows.
>
> Sure, gentle bird, my drooping heart
>   Divides the pangs of love with thine,
> And plaintive murmurings are thy part,
>   And silent woe and tears are mine.*

As with an eye of defiance he gave his barb the
rein, a chaoush, advancing from the hostile band
with the insignia of envoy on his arms, presented on

* Specimens of Arabian Poetry.

the point of a spear the summons of Abu Abdallah, while its captain called on him to surrender, and attend him into the presence of the court. Instead of returning a reply, the prince, casting it back in derision, commanded the guard to make way; and, uttering a loud shout, his followers rushed after him through his opponents, who quickly fled.

The gallant Abencerrages then hastened down the avenues leading to the vega; but being apprised by one of the fugitives of Ibn Hammed's escape, Abdallah hurried in pursuit with his savage mercenaries, having already secured the different passes into the plain. Brief, but terrible was the ensuing struggle; nor was it till the narrow streets round the bridge of the Darro were heaped with slain, and thrice the hired legions of Abdallah had been beaten back, that the heroic chief was taken captive.

Hurried into the Hall of Judgment to undergo the mockery of a trial, where only the kadhis and ulemas in the king's interest presided, the insulted prince refused to admit the competence of a tribunal in which El Zagal, whom he alone acknowledged, held no voice. He scorned to answer a single inquiry of his ferocious judges. But on the proclamation of the presiding emir, the kadhi proceeded to pronounce judgment of death " on the chief, who had failed to restore the standard of the Prophet to its sacred shrine." At the same time, in accordance with the old Mohammedan law, the condemned would be permitted to apply to the " fountain of grace and mercy on earth, our lord and sovereign, Abu Abdallah."

" Oh Abencerrage!" exclaimed the heartless king, advancing from the midst of his African guards, " behold, the warrant of thy doom. Thou art justly condemned; yet doth our sacred law, wielding its judgment-sword with a restraining grace, urge thee to seek the royal mercy. Speak! wilt thou renew the allegiance thou hast broken? wilt thou renounce Abdallah El Zagal? wilt thou yield the old chief's daughter, and live honoured by all his court,—the pride and bulwark of Abdallah's throne?"

" Never! lead me to death! and tyrant," he continued in a voice of thunder, which made every hearer start, " tremble! thou ingrate and unjust; for I warn thee that the wrath of Allah is gathering round thee, —will encompass all thy paths, and hurl thee from thy usurped and blood-stained eminence."

" It is well!" rejoined the king, with fury in his looks, " ingrate and traitor as thou art!" and turning towards his guards, " convey him to the lowest dungeons of our Seven Vaults; and there let him chew the bitter herb of his own culling, till his hour of doom! We must have recourse to softer materials upon which to build our towering hopes."

" Out with thy dagger, and finish thy dark plot!" exclaimed the noble chief; " that is the only mercy I deign to ask at thy hands," and he bared his bosom, yet freshly gored with honourable wounds. Abu Abdallah started back with pale and conscience-troubled look, while murmurs from the spectators and the ominous silence of his troops made the oppressor tremble for the permanence of his power.

" Lead him away ! " he whispered to their captain ;
and with confusion and dismay stamped upon his features even in that hour of triumph, the king turned
towards the emirs and elders, the kadhis yet seated in
their robes, and directing them to dismiss the court,
retired in the midst of his African guard to his royal
strong-hold of the Albaycin. With returning calmness
came his deep-seated hatred of the nobler tribes, by
whose patriotic efforts he had been foiled in possessing
himself of unlimited sway. Still more eager to gratify
a passion even more absorbing than his vain ambition,
he forgot all the nobler resolves which he had made,
and prepared to take advantage of the power which
fortune had thrown into his hands. But, as he approached the spot where he intended to hold parley
with that unhappy one, a pang of remorse shot through
his frame ;——distant notes of music floated on his ear,
——strains such as he felt could be breathed from one
voice alone ; but the feeling was soon stifled, like all
those nobler thoughts and energies which, unhappily
for his country, were obedient only to his caprice.

With the fatal mandate in his hand, he now entered
the palace-gardens of the Generalife, and having announced his arrival, was conducted by the chief slave
into the presence of her he sought. Scenes of unmiti-
gated wretchedness, of exulting treachery and wrong,
can never be described without a feeling of indignation
and of poignant pain. To convey the feeblest impression of the terrors which shook the bosom of one clinging to the existence of the beloved being, whose image
mingled with all that was dear and sacred to her, would

almost require to witness or to feel that nameless woe,
—a woe it is beyond imagination to pourtray.   When
she beheld the heartless Abdallah with the signal of
her lover's doom, and a look of exultation which made
her feel as if a serpent were coiling round her heart,
she knew that their fate was decided.   The icy chill of
despair seized on every faculty, on every feeling,—
crushing at a blow the whole energy of her spirit,
leaving her spell-bound under that enchantment of
fear which draws the fluttering bird within the infec-
tious folds of its dreaded enemy.   Her eye rivetted
with frenzied appeal upon that of the dark-souled king,
seemed to ask whether the last dread act had not even
now been perpetrated?   Long silent and absorbed in this
dread communion of thoughts,—" Lives he?" at length
faintly articulated the trembling girl, n ia tone which
fell like that of the accusing spirit on the ear of Abu
Abdallah;   and he too almost trembled, averting his
looks from that strange, appalling gaze, like the eye of
Heaven, searching the inmost recesses of his conscience.
And such indeed is the might of innocence, given to
awe the guilty, and blanch the boldest tyrant's cheek
with dread !

    " Ibn Hammed lives, lady," was the faltering reply,
as he sought to recover his composure and re-assert his
daring design : " he lives but in thy smiles, so long
as they shine on thy servant and thy slave."   Relieved
from the dire suspicions of his death, Zelinda almost
breathed forth her gratitude at the feet of Abdallah,
for the boon of a life which the high-souled Abencerrage had spurned.

Marking the power which this sudden excitement of her fears had given him, the king, enchanted at her disordered, yet all lovely charms, lost the last touch of pity, honour, and justice, in one deep, absorbing passion. Ere she could recall her presence of mind, or seek refuge even in the resolution of despair, he eagerly improved the advantage he had obtained, allowing no pause of anguish till he should terrify her into becoming his bride.

Gently raising her from the ground, and seating himself beside her, " He lives, fairest of women," he continued, " but his fast approaching doom has been decided by his country. Still his life is in thy hands, bright beauty of all eyes ; and he shall yet drink joy and ecstacy from thy smiles, for thou shalt see him honoured and favoured above all of Abdallah's court, if thou wilt consent to fill a sultana's throne. But a word from thy lips will consign him to the shades of death ; for if the beauteous princess of all my thoughts shall reject my proffers to share with me Granada's throne, to sway her subject realms and cities bright—Ibn Hammed dies. Nay, within the hour he dies the death of a public offender beneath the stroke of our headsman's steel ! Speak, wilt thou be mine?"

" Never ! away ! kill me ; kill us both a thousand and a thousand times!" shrieked the unhappy girl; at the same time conjuring him to have mercy, and throwing herself at his feet, and even clinging round his knees as he pretended to depart.

" Yield, then, to thy destiny,—to what is written for thee ; or I vow by Allah you shall behold him die!"

L

" Oh God! then he must die!" she exclaimed.
" Would I had the soul of Hammed, or Heaven's
lightning to strike thee dead!   Ah! go not yet—only
give me time—"

" Not a moment!" insisted the relentless monarch,
as he drew her towards a balcony which looked upon
one of the courts of the tower of the Seven Vaults.
" See where the sword of judgment hangs suspended
by THY hand over the head of yon noble chief; and
thou shalt see it fall!"   It was no vision, no hideous
dream from which she could awake; but one awful
sense of waking horrors which rushed upon the soul
of his unhappy victim.   And it was enough to freeze
the life-blood in her veins; it was her noble lover in
the grasp of his merciless enemies,—the gleaming scymitar brandished within a hair of that dear and sacred
head.   Then, for the first time, she yielded to the terrors
of her soul; speechless, breathless, as if dreading that
the next moment might come too late, she placed her
hand within that of Abu Abdallah, her eyes still bent
on that appalling sight with a fascination of horror too
intense for outward sign or expression.   From this one
pervading feeling, he gave her no respite, till, like
Niobe, "all tears," she resigned herself, a statue of living
woe, into the arms of him from whom, like that sensitive
flower which folds its leaves from the touch, she would
have shrunk even had her heart not been filled with a
love which threw its radiance round her youthful years.
But it fled! extinguished in the gathering shadows of
a night of woes, which must for ever shroud all of
good, and bright, and noble from her view; render

the purest passion itself a crime; and condemn her to
live a wretched martyr, to spare the life of one of whom
she must no longer even dream.

And the next hour beheld her the bride of Abdallah,
the sultana of Granada,——hailed by the deafening acclamations of the people. Borne, half unconscious, in all
the sumptuous array and stately magnificence of those
royal nuptials along the vaulted aisles, rich spreading
marble pavements, and decorated walls of the grand
mosque, how sad and strangely fell those joyous
plaudits of the fickle populace upon her ear.

The event of the king's marriage, followed by lavish
distribution of alms and largesses, the public festivals,
the projected tournaments and tilts at reeds, had a remarkable influence on his fortunes, and in consolidating
his throne. During a national crisis, in the midst of
an exterminating campaign, the Moors were as eagerly
engaged in their favourite exhibitions, their games and
bull-fights, as if they were celebrating a victory,——offering another trait in the character of a people, whose
whole history and exploits resemble rather the dreams
of some fairy tale than the soberer hues of historical
truth. Thus the least justifiable, perhaps, of their
monarch's actions had a more beneficial effect on the
mind of the people than the redeeming features of his
character, and the few really patriotic efforts he made
to save his country. And from the moment his royal
nephew had given a new sultana, the daughter of the
famed Ali Atar, to the throne of Granada, his warlike
uncle had an infinitely worse chance of sharing with
him its sovereignty than before.

Having ingratiated himself with his people while he gratified a passion which had long absorbed his whole heart and made him forget the dictates of honour, Abu Abdallah now panted to crown his ambition by some warlike exploit.   Fortune too, which had hitherto shone on the banners of his rival, deserted him in the very flush of victory, and destroyed that illusion which had made him the idol of the fickle Moors. He had experienced no check in his victorious career since his surprise of the unfortunate knights of Cala-trava ; and learning that Ferdinand had left Cordova and encamped at Alcalà la Real,* threatening the town of Moclin, he sallied forth, as we have seen, to give him battle.   The Castilian monarch, confident in his resources, was followed, at no great distance, by his

---

* Leaving the mountain-fort of Luque to the right, the tourist first enters upon that high chain of hills which forms the great frontier of Granada, and which is, indeed, an exten-sion of that grand range of natural bulwarks known as the famed Alpuxarras.   Intersected by streams which, at some periods of the year, are much swollen by the rains, the artist, in obtaining the view here given, had to encounter considerable risk and difficulty, the more so from the total want of bridges in any part.   Still he must have felt that the wild grandeur of the scenery by which he was surrounded, the highly romantic situation of the villages and towns, with their old Moorish castles, together with the historical associations connected with them, amply compensated him for his exertions, even at a season wholly uncongenial in a more northern latitude. Among these old castles, not the least striking and attrac-tive is Alcalà la Real.   The tourist's approach to it, when the setting sun rests upon its jutting angles, and tinges with golden light its ruined battlements, is still more striking and impressive from the relics of Roman grandeur which lie scattered around.   The only approach to the old Roman road,

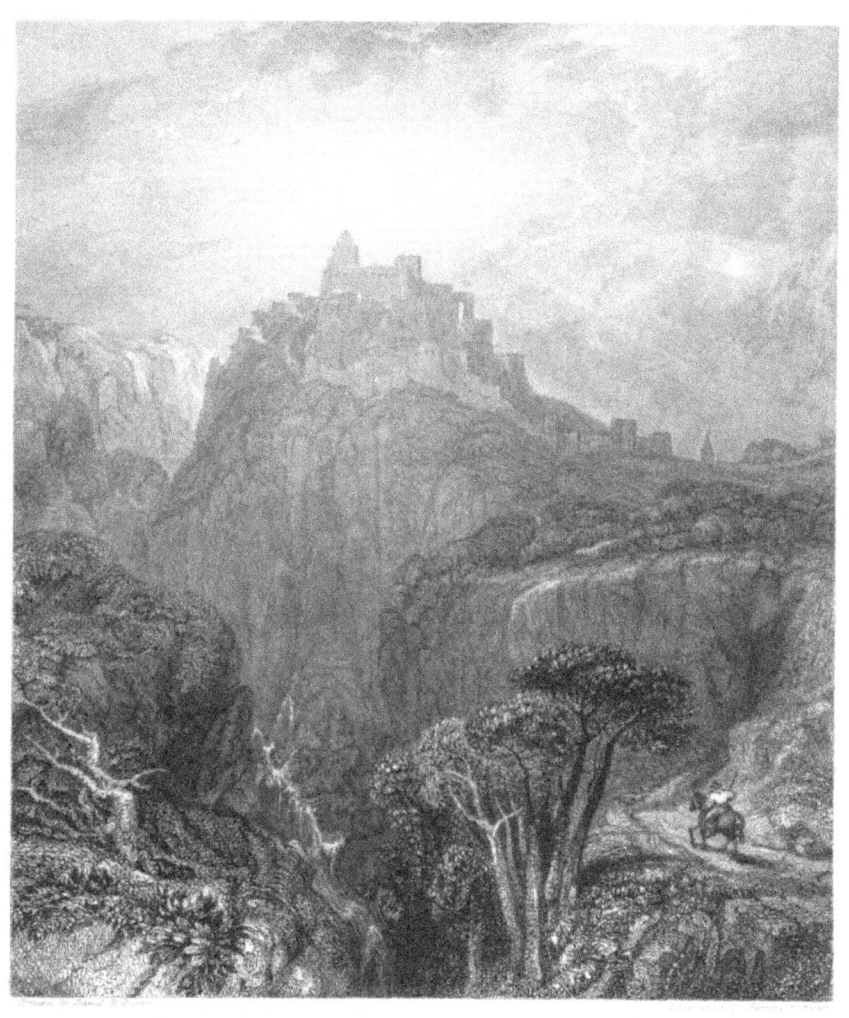

ANCONA IN PERU.

London Published by John Murray & Longman, Green & Co.

heroic consort, attended by the princes and the grand cardinal of Spain as far as the castle of Vaena, the same which had beheld Abu Abdallah a captive, belonging to the noble Count of Cabra. Moclin, the shield of Granada, was a prize worth contending for, and two armies were detached by different routes to make a simultaneous attack. One was led by Diego di Cordova and Alonzo di Montemayor, the other by the zealous Bishop of Jaen and the Master of Calatrava; while the king followed with the main force. Threading the mountain defiles, the count next day halted under some cliffs overhanging the bed of an ancient torrent, and calculated the hour when he was to reach his destination. Informed by one of his scouts that El Zagal had sallied from his capital, he scarcely

lies up a steep declivity, rendered more dangerous from the neglect to preserve this portion of it in the least state of repair.

The time given by the artist to his view of this interesting monument is sunrise, of which it is difficult to convey an adequate impression. The town itself, with its ragged population, the wretched condition of its posada in which the artist sheltered himself, boasts nothing which can arrest the tourist's attention. He might say, indeed, with the artist, like the gentleman in *The Mountaineers,* on rising in the morning, " I am the best flea-bitten bully in all Andalusia !" but as he was to reach Granada that night, it fully made amends for any little inconveniences he had been put to on his route from Cordova. During the last wars of Granada, Alcala, one of those towns " like the living rock from which they grew," was commanded by the brave Count de Zendilla, whose signal successes in the border warfare greatly assisted Ferdinand during these memorable campaigns. His genius for ambuscades, and his various exploits against the Moors, have all the character of wild romance. He was the only one who could baffle Redovan and El Zagal.

allowed himself time to breathe, bearing down upon the city, eager to anticipate his coadjutors in obtaining once more a royal booty.

At night-fall, as he was winding through one of those tremendous ravines worn by the autumnal torrents, and walled in by high overhanging rocks, the startling war-cry of " El Zagal ! El Zagal !" burst upon the astounded ear. It was deep night ; they were in the gorge of a hollow glen, and the moon suddenly rising upon their burnished arms, revealed them to the enemy's view. Struck down by a storm of missiles, one by one the Castilian horsemen perished. Every jutting cliff and crag seemed alive with the turbaned foe. Little availed the heroic efforts of the chief, who beheld his young brother, Gonzalo, struck dead by his side. His horse shot under him, his arm disabled, the slaughter continued till it exceeded the worst of those fearful massacres among the mountains. As the attack grew fiercer and closer, the count, extricating himself from his steed and mounting that of his fallen brother, gave the war-cry of " St. Jago !" Wheeling round his broken and shattered columns, he fought his way through that dark and fatal pass, beset on every side as he was by his inexorable foe. Some sought refuge among rocks and ravines, only to perish by a more lingering death ; others rushed up the cliffs to die upon their assailants, and only a small remnant were rescued by the timely appearance of the militant bishop ; while the terrible El Zagal returned with his bloody trophies to meditate fresh incursions from the warlike towers of Moclin.

During this tragic scene, Queen Isabella is said to have continued with the aged cardinal—the chief director of the Spanish councils—at the castle of Vaena. They were looking from its turrets along the mountain-paths in the direction of the disputed fortress, expecting to behold some signal of victory displayed on the adjacent heights.

At length one of the adalids, followed by a solitary corredor, and, at still wider intervals, by cavaliers at full speed, fugitives and wounded, spread tidings of the disaster far and near. With loud cries and lamentations, bereaved mothers, wives, and children hurried towards the castle from every hill and hamlet round; for on that morn the choicest of their youth and border-warriors had gone forth under their chieftain's banner in aid of their religion and their king. The heart of Isabella bled at the sight; for she had beheld them in all the glow and vigour of existence rush down to meet the Moorish foe. It was now the saintly wisdom and eloquence of the good cardinal were exerted to soothe the mind of his royal mistress; and he dwelt on the rapid progress of their arms, and how many subjugated cities of the Moors gave earnest of yet greater conquests to come.

But on tidings that Alhama was threatened, the venerable prelate offered to lay aside his crosier for a season, and advance at the head of some three thousand chosen retainers to its relief. Such evidence of vigour on the part of the holy church, at an age too " when the crutch is held in more esteem than the sword," was highly consolatory to the pious Isabella,

and convinced her she had no grounds for despair.
Meantime, Ferdinand had passed the frontier within
three leagues of Moclin.   It was then he first learned
the extent of the disaster ; but like his magnanimous
consort, he rather excused than reprobated the conduct
of the count.   While engaged in council, advices came
from Isabella which determined the king to adopt the
policy of a retreat, and content himself with making
an attack upon some less important strong-holds of
the Moors.   There were two castles situated upon the
frontiers about four leagues from Jaen, surrounded by
mountains, in the gorge of the valley of the Rio Frio.
They were connected by a bridge thrown across the
river from rock to rock; and, while they commanded
the pass, they held dominion over the road, so as to
become the terror of the whole of the good bishop's
territory, levying continual contributions on all its
valuable products.   To this feeling and patriotic
appeal he was no way insensible, and like so many of
his turbulent age, became a true church militant,
girding on the sword of the flesh in defence of his
territorial comforts.

But the vigilant El Zagal, who had so often dashed
the hopes of the boldest of Spain's veterans, came
flushed with victory, eager to gather another harvest
of death.   The van of his army under the heroic
Redovan, who had deluged the passes of Malaga
with blood, burst like a thunder-cloud upon the main
body of the Castilians, penetrating even their camp,
and putting all to the rout.   Moclin was free ; but he
pursued his victorious career to Velez Malaga, now

strongly invested by the foe. Carried away by his resistless ardour, he attacked the Spaniards in their intrenchments, without waiting the arrival of the main body under El Zagal. In the first desperate onset he carried all before him, till the Castilians, perceiving the smallness of his force, with a strong reinforcement, rallied and turned the tide of battle against him. The Moors in turn were completely routed, and such was the consternation, that it spread to the ranks of El Zagal, who came up at the critical moment. Spite of his efforts to retrieve the day, his army, seized with the like panic, joined the fugitives, and only helped to swell the triumph of the enemy.

But a few hours before, the Moors flushed with victory scoured the plains in all directions; now a feeble and scattered few, it was with difficulty they succeeded under the too brave Redovan in throwing themselves into Velez Malaga. El Zagal hastened to seek refuge in Granada, but tidings of his defeat having produced a sudden change in the feelings of the people, he found the gates closed against him. Knocking furiously with the hilt of his scymitar at the portals, he was answered only with threats and maledictions. The walls swarmed with the fierce mercenaries of Abu Abdallah, and yielding to the torrent, with strange indignant feelings, a king and a conqueror till this evil day, he departed with his fallen fame from the capital which had welcomed him to its throne with thunders of applause.

While brooding over his wrongs, his more fortunate rival, now undisputed master of Granada, was compelled to take up arms to defend himself against his imperial ally, who seemed no way inclined to pause in his career of conquest.   Vainly did he endeavour to convince Ferdinand that he was making war on a friend, devastating his plains and capturing his cities in violation of the treaty they had entered into.   The Christian monarch was deaf to his remonstrances, declaring that the cities in question were disaffected, and in favour of El Zagal, whom by the tenour of their compact he was bound to attack; that as a vassal to the crowns of Arragon and Castile, he called upon him to appear with his retainers in the field.   Roused to action by this galling and insulting reply, and the formidable preparations making at Cordova for another campaign, Abu Abdallah swore to decide the question of empire once more in the open plain.

Happy in possession of the object which lay nearest to his heart, whatever he possessed of noble and amiable in his character now came into fuller display. As he rode at the head of his warlike tribes through the vast and fertile vega, he gazed back with pride on that splendid city with its golden palaces, over which he held unresisted sway.   While he paused for a moment, there suddenly appeared on the edge of one of the heights above the Darro, near the spot where he reined his fiery barb, a gigantic form, wild and terrible in its looks, as if springing from out the dark, shaggy steep; and waving its arm with an air of command, it addressed itself in a harsh, hollow voice to the ear of the startled king.   There was something hardly human in the ominous voice and wild gestures of that dark being on whom care and fasting might well have conferred that superhuman faculty ascribed to the anchorite of the desart by the more credulous and fanatical among the Moors. " Was it the evil prophet who had so long predicted the fearful days to come?" was the inquiry. No; it was one mightier than he; of an order of saints more venerated,* who by long fixed contemplation and excessive maceration learned to penetrate the veil of time, and communed with the mighty prophets on the mysteries of eternity and the final destiny of man. Yet there was much in the grandeur of his air and looks, expressive less of religious awe than the high-bearing of a prince. In a deep sepulchral voice, with frenzied eye and waving arms, " Listen, oh King Abu Abdallah," he cried, " to the words of a worshipper of Allah, the Avenger! the searcher of secrets not come to light, a santon of the great Prophet, a dweller of the holy mountain. I am an echo of the dead; of the lost, forgotten language of the mighty of old time; the wisdom of the hallowed; the enshrined saints, that speak to thee from the ground. Listen, and tremble! for hast thou not broken the laws of the faithful and the resigned? cloaked thy soul in the darkness of the secret sinner? made spoil of the innocent? revelled in forbidden joys, till the dark spirit of Eblis and his angels hath become as the light of thy eyes? Hast thou not requited with the soul's bitterest torments the services of the just and good? Fore-doomed! the

---

* They were called saints, or santons, of the sect of dervishes, and their places of retreat were considered holy, as the holy mountain of El Santo.

dark star of thy birth hath ruled, and shall rule thee
to the end! Ignobly shalt thou perish in the battle
not fought for thee or thy country; an exile far away,
thou who didst refuse to stand that country's friend in
the hour of her bitter need. Oh, calamity of thy people
and thy age! thou hast leagued with the enemies of
thy faith; and beware! for I see near and more near,
the judgment-sword of the Prophet suspended above
thy head! Away! to the destiny which is written for
thee, written in blood and tears, for thee and the country
thou hast betrayed!"

As the solemn denunciation fell on their ears, horsemen and foot, alike rooted to the ground like so many
statues, motionless and voiceless with surprise, gazed
upon the king. After a momentary struggle, Abdallah
was the first to break the fearful spell; uttering an
exclamation of anger as the strange figure disappeared
from view, he dashed impetuously forward, followed by
his glittering host. Still, he could not shake off the
weight of these repeated prophecies which, doubtful
and undefined as they were, produced a secret, mysterious dread, an anticipation of some future deferred
evils, the fearful looking for of which is far more trying
and terrible than any existing woes, however keen; for
then the powers of action and knowledge of the worst,
assume a tangible shape which man can cope with or
endure. How far more tolerable than darkly to behold
the destiny foretold from his birth, the illimitable
gigantic fates of the future which stretch their distant
misshapen shadows before and around him,—haunting
him with sights and sounds he knows not how to in-

terpret, to what to refer! Such were the dark thoughts
of Abdallah; but shaking them off his spirit with a lion-
energy he knew how to exert, he hurried forward,
eager to measure weapons with the Christian host, and
vindicate his title to a throne.

The scene of action lay near Loxa, against which
Ferdinand indulged a vindictive hatred which he
sought in vain to disguise. Thrice had he been beaten
with ignominy from its walls, and he now resumed the
siege with a relentless fury which had levelled the
castles of Cambil and Albahar with the dust. The
town of Zalia was also surprised by the knights of
Calatrava, and the approach to Granada became daily
more open and practicable. It was less exposed to
those sudden and desperate onsets for which the Moors
were so distinguished, and which long baffled alike
the caution and the heroism of the best Castilian
leaders.

The Moorish king entered at an inauspicious moment
on the new campaign. In the early spring,* Ferdinand
had summoned the grand united armies at Cordova,
consisting of the power of the border chiefs and nobles,
in addition to increased numbers of the regular and
veteran troops. The rich valleys of the Guadalquiver
resounded with louder peals of war. The emulation of
the nobles and their retainers gave renewed splendour
and spirit to the scene. The magnificence of these
armaments, the wild, stirring enthusiasm of that chivalrous period, the light brilliant pavilions, the gold

* Previous to the grand siege of Granada, which continued
upwards of nine months.

and silken pennons variously formed and decorated,
the costly taste and richness of the several equipages,
gave to the whole encampment the appearance rather
of a public spectacle than the stern panoply of iron
war.   The luxuries and elegancies of courtly life, still
preserved in the heart of the fiery conflict, were scarcely
inferior to those of their gallant foe.   And such was
the high esteem they entertained for each other, that
Moorish and Castilian leaders were frequently connected by ties of friendship, gratitude, and affection.
Rich services of gold and silver adorned their tables ;
the housings of their steeds were of fine cloth and bro-
cade, embroidered with silk and golden tissue.   The
decorations of the tents resembled those of brilliant
drawing-rooms rather than the dwellings of war.

Then splendid cavalcades and processions by torch-
light, which cast a more novel splendour on their burnished arms, nodding plumes, embroidered scarfs and
trappings, with national games and festivals, filled the
various intervals and pauses of battle during a succession of brilliant and eventful campaigns.   And with
the proud Castilians mingled the chivalry of surrounding nations, attracted to the scene by the fame of a war
unequalled in exploits, in generosity, and magnanimity
notwithstanding its deep, religious animosity, rendering
it the admiration of after times.   Add to all, a romantic gallantry, love of poetry, with high refinement
of intellect and art, which threw the lustre of their
charms round a period in the change of empires, which
exhibited human character and actions in their utmost
variety, brilliancy, and force.

The Christian army advancing against Loxa, encamped at the foot of a towering cliff, known as the
Rock of the Lovers, on the banks of the Yeguas. The
pavilions of the chiefs, each surmounted by its streaming pennon, were seen raised above the surrounding
tents of their several retainers. On still higher ground,
commanding the entire encampment, was seen the royal
pavilion, displaying the banners of Castile and Arragon, and the figure of the cross splendidly emblazoned
in front. Here Ferdinand held a council; for it was
rumoured that King Abdallah was in the field, doubtless with design of frustrating his attack upon Loxa.
It was resolved that one part of the army should
attack the tremendous heights of Santo Albohacen,
confronting the city; while the other proceeded by a
circuitous route, and fell on it from the opposite side.
Alonzo d'Aguilar, Diego di Cordova, the Count of
Ureña occupied the posts of greatest peril, and ere
the approach of the Moorish king, their Castilian
ensigns were seen waving over the heights, threatening
the great city in its most vulnerable points. At this
sight, the Moors, transported with rage, clamoured to
be led on to the assault. " By Allah!" exclaimed the
king, " let it be done. I offered to hold my towns in
fealty and alliance : see! he hath come with a storm
of war upon my faithful Loxa ;—the treason rest upon
his head !"

In the front of his guards, followed by an army of
foot, the Moor then attacked the advanced parties of
the enemy; and having detached a division to cut off
their communication, he made a vigorous effort to

carry the heights ere they could concentrate their
columns. Their cavalry was still in the valleys below,
when the brazen throats of trumpet and clarion proclaimed the imminent attack, mingling their terrific
din with the report of firelocks, the shock of shield
and spear. The blackness of dust and darkness,
resembling the sudden irruption of a volcano over
those green and blooming declivities, involved the
whole field. Every where confronting the perils of the
battle, the Moorish king sought to dislodge the foe
before the arrival of the Castilian horse, evincing a
bravery and devotion which more than redeemed his
errors in the eyes of his admiring troops.

Suddenly a cavalier, arrayed as a Castilian chief,
spite of the utmost efforts of his guards, rushed upon
the royal Moor; and wounding him, and repeating his
blow with resistless rapidity, laid him prostrate in the
dust. The king was borne from the field; and with
the same undaunted vigour, that dark knight cut his
way through the battle and disappeared. But soon
the absence of the Moorish king was more than supplied by a band of the Abencerrages, headed by an
impetuous chief, borne on the same steed, with the same
device, and wielding the same sweeping falchion in
his hand. As the Count de Cabra, at the head of his
squadron, entered the field, he beheld the Moors conveying their favourite monarch towards the gates of
the beleaguered city. The combat still raged with
unabated fury;—at the head of his savage veteran
Gomerez, rode a dark-plumed gigantic knight upon a
huge black charger, clearing a path through the foe.

The noble Hammed El Zegri had flown with a band of his old garrison of Loxa, and renewed the assault to gain the heights. It was there fought Ponce de Leon, Alonzo d'Aguilar, his young brother, Gonzalvo, Garcilaso de la Vega, famed alike for his chivalry and song, with Fernando Cortez, whose united efforts hurled back their fierce assailants, dashing them down the declivities and rocks. The Count of Ureña, and his bold retainers, marked their recollection of the dismal day which had deprived them of the young Master of Calatrava, by raising to him a hecatomb of the slain.

Fresh succours from the city joined the Moors, and on all points along the groves, and gardens, and blooming orchards of the suburbs, separate parties engaged in deadly conflict,—the Moors struggling to cut them off, the Spaniards to join the standards of their lords. As fresh divisions cleared the valley, fresh bands also of the Moors rushed from their mountain holds and hamlets towards the heights of Albohacin, with fierce intent to rescue the key of all Granada from the infidel's grasp. Galled as they were by cross-bows and missiles from the cliffs, the Spanish leaders fought hand to hand and foot to foot with the enraged Moslems. The stern encounter of d'Aguilar with their great champion, El Zegri, the most celebrated of the single combatants of that great campaign, excited both armies to deeds of incredible daring, in which the body-guards of the royal Moor covered themselves with glory worthy of the Khaleds and Tarikhs of old times.

M

But strong reinforcements from the castle of
Gaucin, * and the adjacent territories, seen approaching in full march under Ferdinand, must decide
the fate of the day.   Surrounded by his princely
retinue, he took his station on a hill which commanded a complete view of the battle.   The chivalry

* Once a noble town, situated in the midst of steep
mountains, Gaucin overlooks a deep valley, fertilized by rich
streams, which irrigate it on all sides.   The adjacent convent
and domains of the Franciscan friars, while contributing to
adorn the landscape, offer a strange contrast to its former warlike character, towering 'mid arcs and obelisks, and domes
and towers, when it reflected back the radiance of the west
upon the sunny vega, which its rocky fort so well defended.
The monks have uniformly shown judgment in selecting such
situations, and in the high cultivation of the surrounding
territory, though after the expulsion of the Moors it appeared like a forsaken region, black and desolate.   To the
distance of two or three leagues beyond Gaucin, the road runs
along the sides of the hills through vineyards, which cover
them from their very summits to the centre of the valleys.
The country afterwards becomes still more uneven, as far
as Ronda ; it consists entirely of lofty mountains, in the defiles of which winds a ruined and rugged road.   At various
intervals you discover miserable villages, which hang as it
were on the sides of naked rocks.   Their position and their
names, Guatazin, Benali, and Atajates, seem to show that
they were built by the Moors, who sought in the bosom of
these almost inaccessible mountains, retreats where they
might be secure from the attacks of the Christians.   They
have since often become the haunts of robbers and smugglers.
After passing Atajate, the tourist enters on a ridge of lofty
mountains, from the summit of which he beholds, for the last
time, the rock of Gibraltar, with the Barbary coast in the distance.   Like other Moorish castles of this description, Gaucin
is now in ruins ; but is still imposing from its bold commanding situation, which defended one of the passes of that high

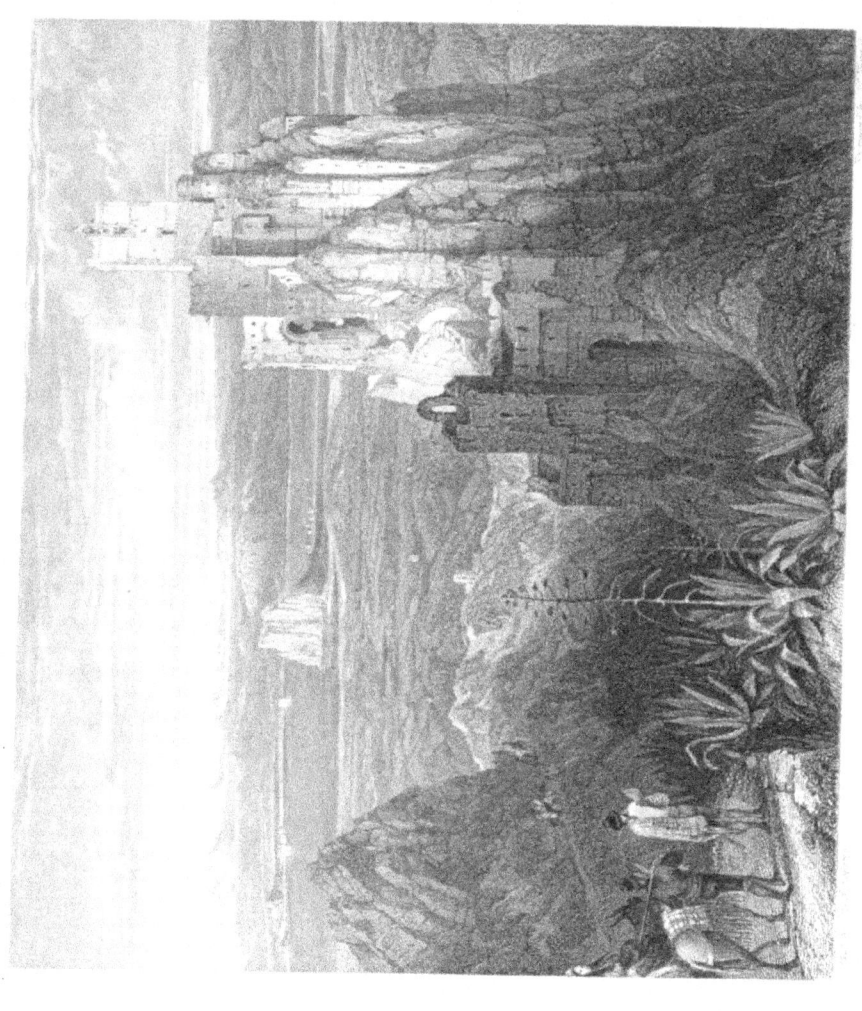

of other nations also swelled his ranks. The gallant
English knight, Lord Scales,* among others stood
near the king, eager to behold for the first time a
Moorish battle-field. The sudden onset—the shouts
of the horsemen—the feigned retreat—the hidden
ambuscade, with the quick wild careering, the hurling

chain of mountains called the Sierra di Ronda, and in the
midst of which lies the city of that name. Nothing can exceed
the beauty of the panoramic view from this height, looking
towards Gibraltar and the African coasts. The ocean-rock
is seen rising proudly from the bright blue, southern seas, and
the most callous spectator cannot but be struck with a warm
admiration of the mighty power which, sweeping from its
northern home of waves, made that grand sea-mark of the old
Moors its own. It is then, as the English tourist gazes round
him, that he feels proud of the country which gave him birth,
and it is an object of as bitter envy to the Spaniard. Directly
facing it, on the opposite coast, he beholds what were the celebrated Pillars of Hercules ; on the extreme left of the picture,
on the Barbary coast and connected by a narrow neck of land,
is Ceuta, a place of banishment for Spanish criminals. It is
almost the only possession retained by Spain on that coast. In
the little bay to the right of the view, is situated the tower of
Algesiras,—the rival port to Gibraltar ; while the high chain of
mountains in the distance, forms the lower range of Mount
Atlas. It was while defending the former of these noble citadels of the sea, that the brave governor, sooner than surrender,
beheld his son put to death by the enemy before his face, even
throwing them down the dagger with which they perpetrated
the deed. Nor did he less greatly distinguish himself as the
alcayde of Gaucin, here before us, in the defence of which
and of his religion, he gallantly fell.

* The chronicler calls him Conde de *Escalas*, or *Escalia*, Lord
Scales, Earl of Rivers ; not Lord Calais, as some writers have
chosen to interpret it. For much of the romantic spirit connected with the battle and capture of Loxa, the writer is
indebted to the admirable work of Washington Irving, in
addition to the accounts of the Spanish and Arab writers.

of the spears, the swift whirling scymitars, and then the close deadly strife with rapier and dagger,——on steed—— on foot—in the final grasp,—all stirred the blood of the brave Englishman : his eye began to glisten ; he grew uneasy; his hand was on his sword, and with stern brow and heightening colour, he asked the king's permission to breathe himself a space with his strong yeomen in the motley fray.   " On the next reinforce- ment to the Albohacen," says the ancient chronicler, " armed with simple morion and breastplate, did that stalwart knight bring up his body of merrymen, (so called, perchance, from their grave and solid looks— their bold, steady step, or the weight of their arms and axes).   He had a lusty band of archers, with feathered shafts of a cloth-yard's length and bows of the tough yew tree.

" As that staunch and dread-nought lord fought his way into the thick of the fray, he turned him to his bold liegemen ; ' And, remember, my merrymen,'' said he, ' where you are,—in a foreign land ; and that the heart of Robert the Bruce,* being borne hither on its way to rest in the holy shrine, did make fearful havock of

* Bruce thought of going upon this expedition when he was in despair of recovering the crown of Scotland ; and now he desired his heart to be carried to Jerusalem after his death, and requested Lord James, of Douglas, to take the charge of it. Douglas wept bitterly as he accepted this office,—the last mark of the Bruce's confidence and friendship. The king soon afterwards expired, and his heart was taken out from his body and embalmed. Then the Lord Douglas caused a case of silver to be made, into which he put the Bruce's heart, and wore it round his neck by a string of silk and gold. And he set forward to the Holy Land, with a gallant train of the bravest

these infidels. Carried by the Christians into the
battle, it so braced their spirits with that vigour I
would have your living hearts now to display, that
Mahound was fain to flee !' With that they raised the

men in Scotland, who, to show their value and sorrow for
their brave King Robert, resolved to attend his heart to the
city of Jerusalem.

In going to Palestine, Douglas landed in Spain, where the
sultan of Granada, Osmyn, was invading the realms of
Alphonso, the Spanish king of Castile. King Alphonso received Douglas with great honour and distinction, and people
came from all parts to see the great soldier, whose fame was
well known through every part of the Christian world. King
Alphonso easily persuaded him that he would do good service to the Christian cause by assisting him to drive back the
Saracens of Granada, before proceeding on his voyage to Jerusalem. Lord Douglas and his followers went accordingly to
a great battle against Osmyn, and had little difficulty in de-
feating the Saracens who were opposed to them. But being
ignorant of the mode of fighting among the cavalry of the
east, the Scots pursued the chase too far ; and the Moors,
when they saw them scattered and separated from each other,
turned suddenly back, with a loud cry of *Allah, illah Allah !*
and surrounded such of the Scottish knights and squires as
had advanced too hastily. In this new skirmish Douglas saw
Sir William St. Clair, of Roslyn, fighting desperately, surrounded by many Moors, who were hewing at him with their
sabres. " Yonder worthy knight will be slain," Douglas said,
" unless he have present help." With that he galloped to his
rescue, but was himself surrounded by many Moors. When he
found the enemy press so thick round him as to leave him no
chance of escaping, he took from his neck the Bruce's heart,
and speaking to it as he would have done to the king had he
been alive,—" Pass first in fight," he said, " as thou wert wont
to do, and Douglas will follow thee or die." He then threw
the king's heart among the enemy, and rushing forward to
the place where it fell, was there slain. His body was found
lying above the silver case, as if it had been his last object to
defend the Bruce's heart.—*Sir Walter Scott.*

old cry of St. George, and the doughty earl and his
men fell to it with right good will, laying about them
with manly and trusty brands ; wielding aloft their
axes like woodmen in a forest, they did astound the
mountaineers of Navarre by their deeds of hardihood
and strength.   And, albeit, the knightly spirits of
other lands did vie with each other in giving example
of old Europe's prowess, yet in valorous obstinacy
none could outdo these stout and lordly islanders."

At length, Hammed El Zegri fell covered with
wounds ;—and disputing every inch, the Moors were
driven back upon the bridge, though they fought
again within the suburbs.   King Ferdinand coming
up, the English earl followed the Moors almost to the
gates, and into the streets.   " But being smitten," says
the chronicler, " by a large stone in the teeth, he was,
per force, carried off by his men from the spot."*   Yet
he sturdily planted his standard where they stood, while
the king took up his position on the other side, nearer
to Granada ; the heights of Albohacen being occupied
by the great Alonzo d'Aguilar.   Here the Christians
soon began to prepare batteries, and to beleaguer the
city according to the rules of war.

* Pulgar.   He adds, that Ferdinand sent him magnificent
presents, and visited him in his tent.   Upon condoling with
the English earl on the loss of his teeth, the latter replied,
that he had cause to thank God, since it had brought him a
visit from the most powerful monarch of all Christendom ;
that as to his teeth, he thought little of them, for it would
be strange if he were not willing to lose two or three in the
service of him who had given him a whole set.

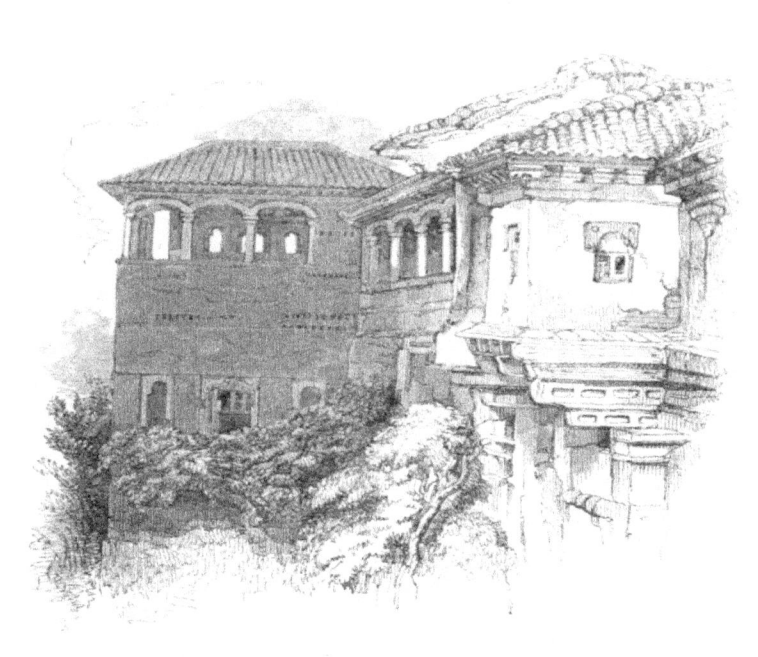

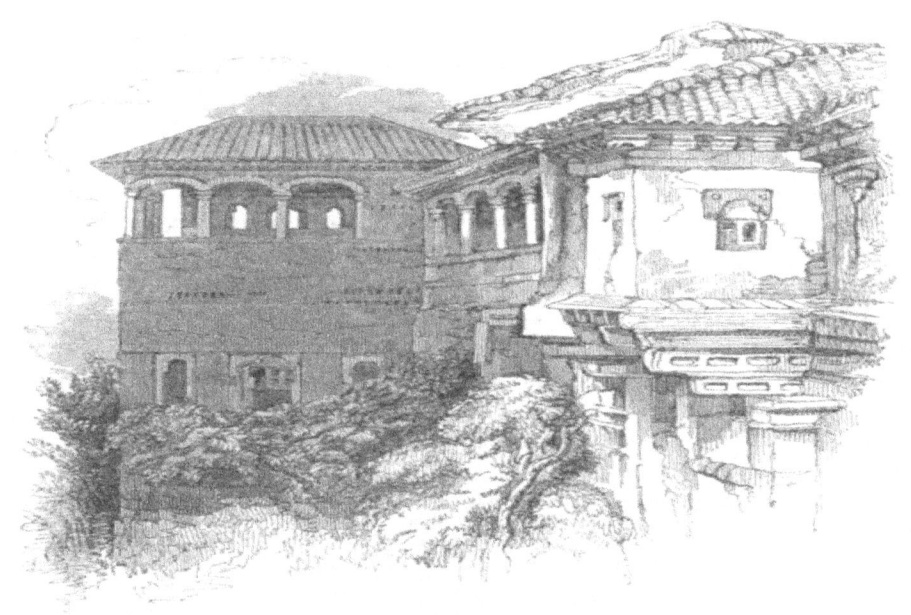

CHAPTER VII.

Green are the myrtle leaves that glow
On beauty's bright and polished brow;
But greener are the wreaths that shine,
And round the sword of freedom twine!
Those have flourished by the fount
On Cythera's golden mount;
These have drunk a richer flood
From the perjured tyrant's blood.

POEMS BY W. S. ROSCOE.

THE defeat of Abu Abdallah, and the failure of all his efforts to relieve the fortress of Loxa, spread consternation throughout Granada. That splendid capital now lay exposed to the victorious career of the Christian foe. It presented, at this juncture, the singular spectacle of a throne without a prince, an army without a chief. The king had been carried wounded into Loxa, and in this exigency the Moors bitterly lamented their long and deadly feuds, the rash confidence they had reposed in their favourite prince, and the precipitancy with which they had spurned the veteran El Zagal from their walls. They saw their fatal error in contending for rival monarchs, instead of flying to defend their mountain-barriers,—taking their stand in those impregnable forts and passes where they might have annihilated the enemy. While trembling for their very existence as a people, a cry was heard from the watch-towers of the Alcazaba; and soon the distant tread of horse, coming thicker and faster till it thundered upon the ear, startled them from their dreams of terror and suspense. Tower, and mosque, and minaret, teemed with dark, eager visages; their sharp features and flashing eyes bent over the spacious vega, while the tocsin of war sounded from the Viva Rambla along the banks of the Darro,—from the gate of Elvira to the gardens of the Generalife and the ancient Albaycin.

But, ere long, the distant gleam of the scymitar, the glimpses of the green turban, with the golden banners of the crescent reflected in the rays of the setting sun, produced a shout of exultation from the crowded walls and battlements. A gallant troop of horse drew up at the Elvira gate, and thundered for admittance. The cry of El Zagal rang through the streets as he rode, accompanied by Muza Ben Gazan at the head of the Alabez, through the gates of the capital. Brief as was the period since his rejection, the air resounded with acclamations of the warrior-king, who had thus magnanimously returned to offer his breast as a bulwark against their fierce invaders.

The chief authorities were soon compelled to reinstate him in his royal privileges; and it was then he was informed of the events which had taken place in the capital,—the inauspicious marriage of Abu Abdallah, the wrongs and sufferings of his noble rival. At this announcement, his brethren in arms,—the remnant of that faithful tribe, ever in the van of battle,—burst into the loudest expressions of grief, throwing down their arms, trampling their turbans, and casting dust upon their bare heads. They accused themselves of ingratitude and neglect in not remaining near him, or bearing him along with them upon their bucklers to the field. But the sorrow, the indignation of Muza Ben Gazan, and the emirs and elders, his old companions, and peers of Ali Atar, though silent, was still more deep.

" Whither," was the mournful inquiry, " had he bent his steps ? With what sad, dark purpose, and to what distant bourne ? Had he flown to the desarts of his revered forefathers to brood over his wrongs, to seek consolation in the rocky hermitages of the santons? or departed, a lonely pilgrim, to the Prophet's sacred shrine?" All was mystery; and as they stood and talked, the tribe again gave vent to their vehement ebullitions of sorrow for the fate of their favourite chief. They recalled his splendid deeds to mind, the generosity with which he had shared and relieved their sufferings,—their friend, their counsellor, and their shield before the foe.

Suddenly, they recollected the strange apparition of the Castilian knight, who, with resistless vengeance, had tracked Abdallah through the fight and had as swiftly vanished. Again, whose was that small serried band of heroes, at whose head a Moslem chief had displayed more than human prowess, spreading dismay through the Christian host,—till, charging through their camp, he doubtless fell a martyr to his country's honour?

On the evening of the royal Moor's re-entrance into the capital, there might be seen, as the deep silent shades of twilight stole over the groves and fountains, the figure of a bowed and aged man, attired in pilgrim-weeds, wending his weary way along the walls of its palace gardens. Wretched and haggard were his features, his air strange and wild, as with uncertain and varying step which bespoke the agitated mind, he bent his way towards the low wicket postern opening into the gardens of the Generalife. As he stooped down, it seemed to open at his touch, and with the familiar air of one acquainted with the scene, he stepped within its precincts. But all of fragrance and of beauty, in that soft night-hour, seemed to fall on his dreary spirit like the bloom of faded flowers on the urn of some beloved being whom he was consigning to the shades of death. Smiting his bosom as he went, he passed along the embowered vistas and shrubberies of palm and cypress, where—vainly to his eye—luxuriantly blossomed the myrtle and the rose, bright silvery fountains sparkled up; for he heard a voice borne on the still, evening breeze, so strangely and deeply sad, mingled at intervals with

the low breathings of the Æolian lyre murmuring to
the winds, as filled the soul of that Moorish pilgrim
with an ecstasy of sorrow he could not control.   No
longer master of himself, he gave way to expressions
of the most fearful and frantic grief.   Harsher than
the sound of death-knells came the wild murmured
sounds of that old Moorish melody on his soul,—the
song he had heard in other days,—poured from the
breaking heart of the lost Maisuna, wedded to the
monarch whom she could not love :—

> The russet suit of camel's hair,
>   With spirits light and eye serene,
> Is dearer to my bosom far
>   Than all the trappings of a queen.
>
> The humble tent and murmuring breeze
>   That whistles through its fluttering walls,
> My unaspiring fancy please
>   Better than towers and splendid halls.
>
> Th' attendant colts that bounding fly
>   And frolic by the litter's side,
> Are dearer in Maisuna's eye
>   Than gorgeous mules in all their pride.
>
> The watch-dog's voice that bays whene'er
>   A stranger seeks his master's cot,
> Sounds sweeter in Maisuna's ear
>   Than yonder trumpet's long-drawn note.
>
> The rustic youth unspoilt by art,
>   Son of my kindred, poor but free,
> Will ever to Maisuna's heart
>   Be dearer, pamper'd king, than thee.*

* Maisuna was a daughter of the tribe of Calab, remarkable
for the number of poets it had produced.   She was married

Directing his agitated step towards the myrtle bowers whence the sounds seemed to proceed, he suddenly paused, aware that it would be death thus to break upon the object whom he sought.   He now repeated in low and plaintive accents, the words of another favourite air, well understood by her for whose ear it was intended :——

> The boatmen shout, 'Tis time to part,
>   No longer we can stay ;
> 'Twas then Maisuna taught my heart
>   How much a glance could say.

whilst very young to the Khaliph Mowiah.   But this exalted situation by no means suited the disposition of Maisuna, and amidst all the pomp and splendour of Damascus, she languished for the simple pleasures of her native desert.

These feelings gave birth to the simple stanzas, which she took the greatest delight in singing whenever she could indulge her melancholy in private.   She was unfortunately overheard one day by Mowiah, who was of course not a little offended with the discovery of his wife's sentiments.   As a punishment for her fault, he ordered her to retire from court.   Maisuna, taking her infant son Yezid with her, returned to Yemen ; nor did she revisit Damascus till after the death of Mowiah, when Yezid ascended the throne.   Mowiah, however, hardly deserved her reproach, for he displayed as many virtues when in possession of the khaliphat, as he had shown talents in acquiring it ; and after a glorious reign of nineteen years, died at Damascus universally regretted.   The last public speech he made to his people is still preserved : " 1 am like corn that is to be reaped," said the dying monarch.——" I have governed you till we are weary of one another ; I am superior to all my successors, as my predecessors were superior to me.   God desires to approach all who desire to approach him ; O God, I love to meet thee ; do thou love to meet me !"—*Specimens of Arabian Poetry.*

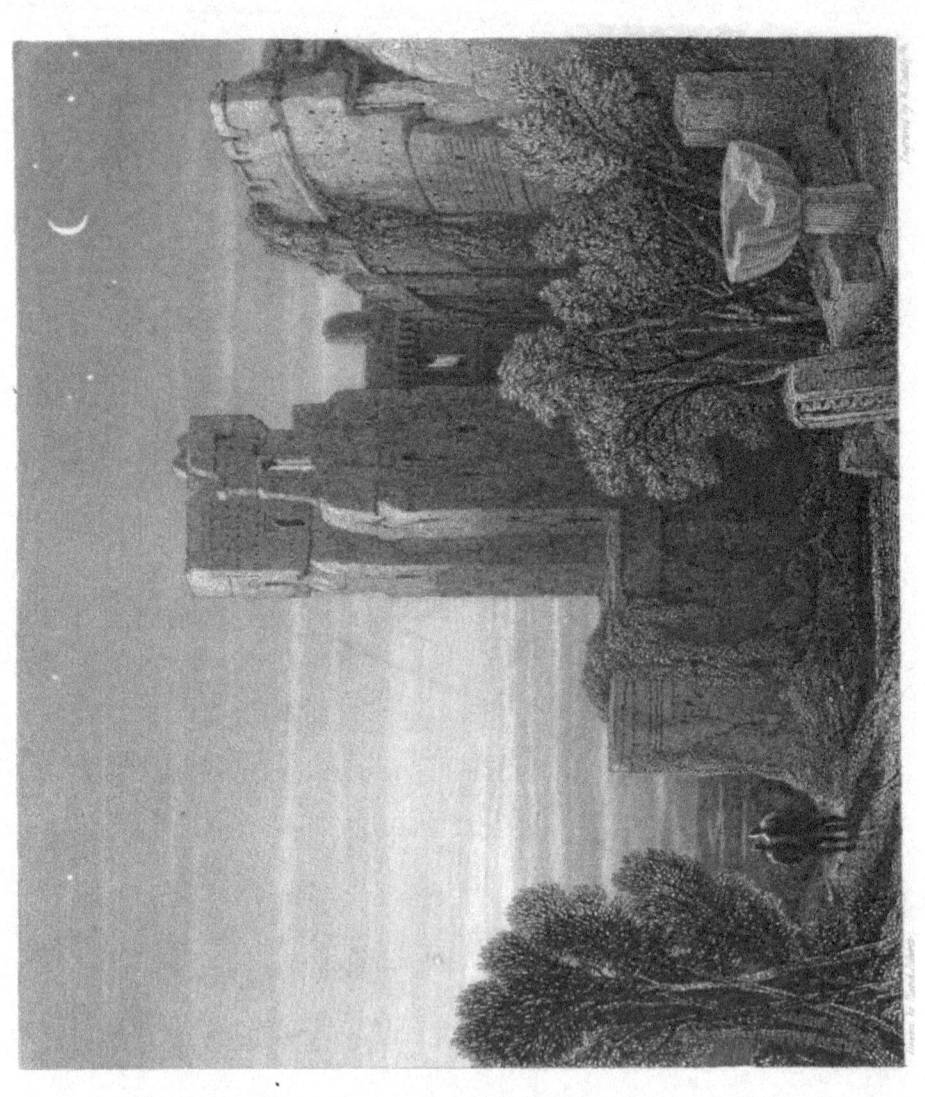

With trembling steps to me she came,
  Farewell! she would have cried;
But ere her lips the word could frame,
  In half-formed sounds it died.

Then bending down with looks of love,
  Her arms she round me flung;
And as the gale hangs on the grove
  Upon my breast she hung.

My willing arms embrac'd the maid,
  My heart with raptures beat;
While she but wept the more, and said,
  Would we had never met!

At the close, one low stifled shriek and the sound as of some one striving to fly, smote upon the heart of the lone stranger; and the next moment the chief of the Abencerrages clasped to his bosom the beautiful sultana of Granada. She lived! and the rush of overwhelming tenderness permitted him not to imagine that she was other than the bright reality of a love which had swayed every thought and impulse of their beings. He had indeed dreaded the worst, as he kept his lonely vigils in the Seven Vaults,*——

* Little beyond the wreck of this once massive and magnificent structure now remains, though the old religious traditions characteristic of the mind of the Moorish populace have survived in all their primitive vigour and freshness. Upon the French retiring from the fortress, it was undermined and blown up; and huge fragments of the walls are already covered with the rich vegetation of the spot, or mouldering under the shadow of the fig-tree and the vine. The arch of the gateway, however, though injured, escaped the general shock, adding perhaps to the sombre and picturesque impression associated with the ruins of human empire which every where force themselves on the eye and the mind. It was

that she was lost to him,——that to escape a more fearful
fate she might have herself closed those precious eyes
in the sleep of death.   But the idea of a renunciation
of their heart-chained vows, of her resigning herself a
victim into the power of a triumphant rival had never
for a moment possessed his soul.   To him, the cer-
tainty of again beholding her, was a conviction of her
perfect innocence and truth : and no exterior show,
no royal gauds and trappings had power to startle him
from his dream of blissful confidence in the enduring
spirit of their loves.   She lived ; she was folded to his
breast,——it was the bright realization of his long hopes
and dreams,——all of lovely, enchanting, and heroic,
which played round his heart in the dear-remembered
haunts of his youth.

In such scenes had he drank rapture, had their souls
mingled in all the delicious illusions of a high ineffable
love, and a smile of delight irradiated his features, as
his eyes rested on her whom he had believed lost

through these vaults that the weak and unhappy king quitted
his crown and kingdom for the last time, when proceeding to
lay down the keys of Granada at the feet of his Christian conqueror.   Taking his melancholy way over the hill of Los Mar-
tires, and along the garden of the now adjacent convent, he
thence struck into the hollow ravine, pursuing his way till he
arrived at the Puerta de los Molinos, or Gate of the Mills.
Passing these, he continued his route, following the course of the
Xenil till he reached a little Moorish mosque, which has since
assumed the name of the Hermitage of San Sebastian. Here it
is recorded in a tablet on the wall, that " On this spot the king
of Granada surrendered the keys of his capitol to the Castilian
sovereigns."   After this sad humiliating interview, the royal
exile proceeded to rejoin his family at a village across the
vega, whither they had departed the previous evening to shun

to him for ever. Feelings akin to those of the far-travelled pilgrim, when through thousand perils and sufferings he beholds at last that shrine of his revered master's rest, filled his heart as he still held her enfolded in his arms. Alas! that he should be destined to wake from such a dream to the bitter truth, terrible as the annihilation of the holiest hopes of the faithful, of the dying trust of the martyr and the patriot in that brighter land of the future promised to the just by the sages, the mighty prophets, and saviours of the world.

From the moment she uttered that piercing shriek, Zelinda had lain breathless in the young prince's arms. Too happy had she never breathed more,——never gazed upon the glorious aspect of nature, now involved in one dark shroud of woe. She, the idolized being of his thoughts, must now appear like some dark malignant power, or with the brightness only of Eblis and his angels,——the evil genius tracking his footsteps, till the triumphant gaze of the enemy, and being witnesses to such a scene of trial and degradation. At length, the fallen prince reached the edge of a chain of barren hills, which form a ridge of the still loftier and wilder Alpuxarras. It was from the summit of one of these that the unfortunate monarch beheld the beloved city of Granada for the last time ; and it bears to this day the emphatic name of the " Hill of Tears." The wretched exiles thence took their way across a dark barren tract, and their route is still traced along paths which must have been made immeasurably painful from the contrast with the scenes they had left. Upon descending from the last of these rocky heights, which still bears the name of the " Last Sigh of the Moor," his heroic mother, turning towards him, uttered that memorable and well deserved reproach, too well known to be here repeated.—*Chronicles of Granada.*

they be lost in the fiery dust and ashes of some heavy and precipitous doom.

But the heaving of the bosom, the mantling of the cheek, the start, the scream, the shrinking back into herself, gave evidence that she yet lived. A deeper shudder ran through her frame, as she recognised her lover, and with a strange sympathy of terror he caught the same wild despairing look as he gazed upon her. And his frame began to tremble, and his heart to quail like hers; as if some deep-seated instinct of his being, anticipating the shock, threw before it the black shadows of calamity over his spirit,——unfolding by degrees the secret of his coming fate, lest it cast down the flood-gates of life, and stop the ruddy current at its fountain.

Thus with looks of breathless anxiety, they continued to gaze upon each other, longing yet dreading to speak, as if struggling with some strange presentiment, till his eye shrank from the despairing woe of that beloved face, resting upon the emblems and decorations of a queen. "It was here," he lowly breathed, all pale and trembling with emotion, "in this your favourite bower, that we first exchanged our vows, our sacred oaths of endless love: here too we last met. Repeat, my love, the words you then spoke of truth and constancy till death."

Deep sobs were her only reply, as in the phrensy of her woe she tore her auburn tresses, cast away her bridal wreaths, her gem-spangled diadem, and trampled the brilliant plumes in the dust. Then bursting into a flood of lamentations and tears, she threw herself upon her lover's neck: "It was for thee, for thee! thy dear and sacred life that I am thus! My only beloved! light, too precious light of my eyes; it was to see again my Ibn Hammed, to hear his voice,—to be clasped in his arms once more, that I consented to wear these hateful trappings which my soul abhorred. But I see thee, and I shall die happy now,—for death, death alone now thou art saved—"

"Saved! and thou,—who and what art thou? for by Allah! thou lookest strangely, fearfully upon me! speak quickly, I conjure!"

"No, fly me, Ibn Hammed! let me not breathe a word! it is death, only death to *me*. Fly, ere thou art seen; and forget there was such a being as the lost, fallen, and soon—perished Zelinda."

"Why speak you in mystery and dread? there is guilt in thy looks and words. Oh speak!"

"It is! it is the most guilty, abhorred, impious of sacrifices! but save thyself; let it not be *all* in vain! Wilt thou not fly? I am the wife of Abu Abdallah! Now fly!"

The chief started from her as if he had held a scorpion; then, surprise and horror chained him to the spot,—the indignation of a spirit scorning longer to cope with calamity, mingled with so much dishonour, indignity, treachery,—all of so black a dye! But soon he gave way to the passionate vehemence of his grief, smiting his bosom, tearing his turban, and casting the dust upon his head! "Allah! Allah Achbar!" he exclaimed, "the great, the terrible God! not the merciful, the gracious, the director of our path;

N

but the mighty avenger, the swift in wrath, record the crime of mine enemy! Draw on him thy sword of judgment; vindicate thy glory as the one just and all-conquering God! Smite thou the traitor with its terrors, till he feel the weight of his heavy sin upon his own head!" Then turning to that woe-stricken girl, " Ah weak, faltering, and faithless to our honour, and to our God, as to all our wretched love! what is death, what a thousand deaths to the agony of one life such as thou hast made it? Ah, Zelinda! and wert thou but a glorious vision of all that was bright and pure, which my young imagination pictured; a dream fleeting as the dews of the flowers at the touch of the young morn's orient beams?

" Why, why did we live to see this hapless day! if indeed thou hast not wished to wear Granada's diadem! For sure, had thy love been holy and lofty as I deemed, thou hadst gloried in seeing me die,—yea, in proving the immortal truth and purity of a love such as ours,—in the ordeal of a fiercer trial than any which the impious and the bad could impose. Then none could have injured us ; our sacred honour, our unsullied love, pure in the eyes of Allah, triumphant over death! But feeble and fickle, thou hast sold thyself to evil; limned thy soul in the golden meshes of sin; and the lustre, the beauty of our life, the path of light and truth for ever faded and gone! I thank thee not, sultana, for a worthless life thou hadst done better to deprive me of; else why not bid me," he added with a look of withering scorn, "to the marriage festivals of the young sultana of Granada! despoiled, scorned, and abject, in the midst of all her pomp, as the lowest of her slaves ! "

The harsh, wild-despairing language of the chief, pierced the wretched Zelinda to the soul. Pitiable were the stifled sobs and sighs which shook her gentle being, in anguish which could not weep. They were the last drops that filled to overflowing her bitter cup, and drawing a dagger, she aimed it quick as light at her beauteous bosom ; but with yet swifter arm was it dashed, as it already pierced the folds of her rich-gemmed robe, upon the earth.

That sight produced a sudden, strange revulsion in her lover's feelings, which not all her tears could have done. It tested the depth of their passion ; voiceless, as he still held that trembling hand, they gazed into each other's eyes ; and full of eloquent meaning was the pause. And as their hands and eyes thus met, a wild fascination seemed to bind all their faculties in one delicious spell, which spite of all earthly ills and agonies told them they were still immeasurably dear to each other. Softer thoughts soothed the burning anguish of Ibn Hammed's soul ; he felt how intensely he was yet loved ; that it was the very excess of that love which had deprived her of the power to behold him die. He too had now experienced what she must have felt, when the sword was brandished above his head ; for he yet trembled with terror at the peril she had run, and he no longer arraigned the motives of the agonizing sacrifice she had made for his sake.

With hands trembling in each other, and eyes that seemed never to drink enough of delight from the restored looks of each other's love, as if all the dread interval between their last parting were but a fearful dream, they started from that trance only to rush into a wild embrace. Clasped to each other's bosoms with a passionate strength and energy of undying love, it seemed to compensate by its very excess for the agonies of wretchedness which they had previously endured. They felt that they still possessed Heaven's charter to preserve their heart's love inviolate, spite of all exterior injuries and wrongs;——they felt that let fate do her worst, there were moments of bliss of which no earthly power could deprive them. The delicious consciousness of perfect, supreme affection, which had sanctified their union in the eye of heaven and which no ulterior events could set aside, had now restored them to each other.

How strange and mysterious a thing is human nature, how inexplicable the secret links and workings of our human hearts, with all those hidden, antagonist springs of action too finely and awfully constituted for us to comprehend, but which with wonderful balance preserve those due alternations of power, which prevent the current of our being from bursting its banks and from utter stagnation in its channels.

The two beings who had just before met under all the terrors and agonies of a woe too deep for tears, had by one fearful attempt been rescued from utter despair; and in proving they were still every thing to each other, had drank far deeper of rapture than if the heavy hand of calamity had never pressed upon their hearts.

And now with words of enthusiastic tenderness, of absorbing joy, too exquisite long to last, they tore themselves from each other's arms. Often and again they pledged themselves by all that was dear and sacred, soon to renew their sweet but perilous meetings,—as if joys like theirs were more than a summer dream.*

Meanwhile, events were rapidly approaching a crisis in the progress of this chivalrous, but exterminating war. For though the Moors in the van of civilization, learning, refinement ;—in hospitality and magnanimity of character, had been the benefactors of Spain and the tutors of Europe, the superstitious ignorance and ferocity of the lower orders of both nations, conjoined with difference of habits and of religion, had at length rendered it a system of war to the knife.

Among the more cultivated and ennobled, however, sentiments of mutual honour and esteem, often founded upon congeniality of sentiment for what was great and disinterested, had knit the high Castilian and Moorish knights and gentlemen in bonds of chivalrous brotherhood. Their friendships often arose from singular, romantic incidents in battle, in captivity,† not unfrequently by sympathy of mind, studies

* One of the khaliphs, reflecting on the pleasures which the rich and fortunate enjoy in this world, exclaimed—" How sweetly we live, if a shadow would last ! "

† It would seem as if hospitality and magnanimity in distress were almost hereditary virtues in the character of the Arab, extending to all of the same blood. During Napoleon's expedition to Egypt, a French officer, taken prisoner by the

and pursuits, lofty traits of conduct, and impassioned
attachments to the lovely countrywomen of each other.
To all these was added, in many instances, the tie of
intermarriages, formed during various long periods
of peace ;——when but for the bad ambition of their
leaders, there was every appearance of these two noble
nations gradually blending into one great and happy
people.*

The Count of Cifuentes was thus rescued from
death by the brave Redovan Ben Egaz, and not only

Bedouins, had remained several months a prisoner, when the
camp of the captors was attacked during the night by the
enemy's cavalry.   Tents, flocks, herds, baggage, provisions
fell into their hands; and the scheikh with much difficulty
effected his escape, accompanied by his prisoner.   Next day,
wandering in the desart, isolated from his friends and deprived
of all resources, he drew forth a piece of bread from his abbu,
and, presenting half of it to the officer, observed,——" I know
not when we shall eat bread again ; but it shall never be said
that I refused to share my last morsel with my friend."

* It was not however till a chivalrous and cultivated period,
that this spirit of mutual respect and courtesy began to be felt.
In olden times, " they laid on load " with lusty epithets of
reproach, as well as weapons ; witness the author of the ancient
Legend of Sir Bevis, who glories in showing his hero's antipathy to " Mahound and Termagaunt."   He loses all sense of
gallantry in his religious zeal ; returning the following dis-
courteous and grumbling answer to the invitation of a fair
Paynim princess, who sent two Saracenic knights to invite him
to her bower :——

> " I wyll not ones stirre off this grounde
> To speake with an heathen hounde ;
> Unchristen houndes, I rede you fle,
> Or I your harte bloud shall se."

They then with equal politeness return the compliment,
calling him a " Christen hounde."

acts of mutual courtesy, but of sterling service and
devotion marked the esteem with which they regarded
each other. The conduct of Narvaez and the Moorish lover was no rare example; and it was, perhaps,
surpassed by that of a Moorish knight on occasion of
an appeal to arms by the noble Diego di Cordova
and Alonzo d'Aguilar, to whom the royal Moor had
granted the use of his territory to witness its decision
in the open lists.

On the appointed day, Don Diego appeared in arms,
but d'Aguilar was prohibited by his own sovereign
from entering the arena. Upon this, he was proclaimed by the umpires of the field conquered in
single battle. A knight of Granada, related to the
royal Moor and a personal friend of Don Alonzo,
could not witness the imputation of such indignity on
the fame of the absent hero; and, rushing armed into
the lists, he declared that the Castilian was too loyal
a knight willingly to fail to make good his word;
and he would maintain it with his sword. Muley
Hassan, however, overruled his plea, on the ground
that it would be an open violation of the safe conduct
obtained for the Castilian knight. The Moor nevertheless persisted, and the angry monarch gave immediate orders for him to yield up his sword. On this
chivalrous friend offering a determined resistance,
Muley Hassan called out for his guards to surround
him, and bring him his head. But Diego of Cordova, struck with the magnanimous act of his noble
rival, threw himself at the king's feet, and obtained
the remission of so harsh a sentence.

To return to Abu Abdallah ;——unfortunate in all he
undertook, pressed by his royal ally, he now began to
reap the bitter fruits of his rash confidence in a foe,
who altered his course of policy whenever he found it
expedient.   Under pretence of an infraction of the
treaty, he prosecuted the siege of Loxa* with redoubled
vigour.   He cut off its communications, and prevented
the sorties of its garrison by destroying its noble
bridge, while he constructed others to concentrate the
operations of his united camps.   Such was the tremendous fire of the heavy ordnance, that it opened
vast chasms in the walls of the leaguered city, through
which might be seen the blazing edifices, and the
terrible efforts of the Moors to quell the flames, which
had reached their houses.   Women and children were
seen rushing into the streets, where indiscriminate
slaughter from fire-arms, clouds of missiles, arrows,
and red hot shot threw additional horrors over the
scene.

* The city of Loxa, or rather fortress, situated upon a rocky
height in the defiles of the mountains of Granada near the
frontiers, on the Xenil, and commanding the entrance to the
vega, was considered as the key of the Moorish capital, and as
such its possession was disputed by the Moor with the desperate
courage and energy of despair.   More than once it had repulsed
the enemy, even commanded by Ferdinand himself, from its
walls.   Here it was that the famous Ali Atar carried terror
into the adjacent districts, until he sallied forth in that fatal
expedition with Abu Abdallah, and in which he fell.   Though
built among the rocks, the place is surrounded by meadows
and gardens, extending a considerable distance along the banks
of the Xenil.   It has been observed by Mr. Irving, that the
people seem still to retain the bold, fiery spirit of the olden
time.

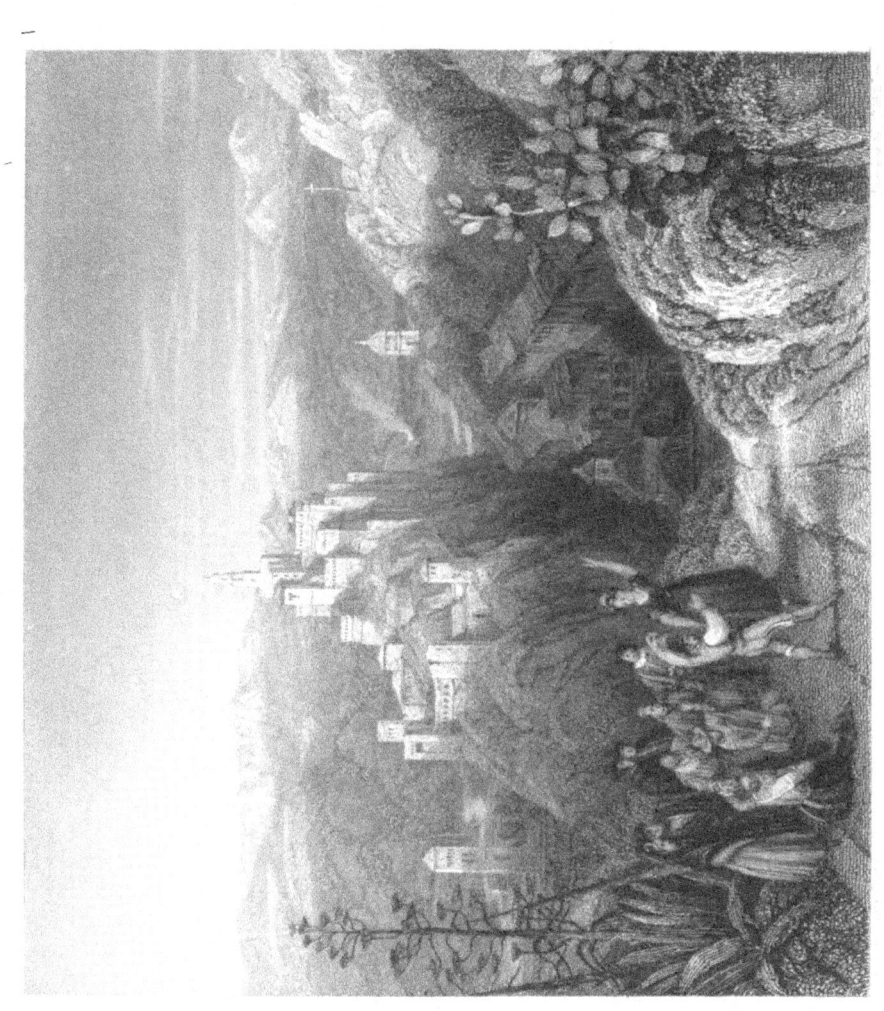

As fast as the brave Moors attempted to repair their loss, renewed peals of the heavy lombards poured on their devoted heads; and, in their despair, numbers of them dashed into the suburbs, and fought hand to hand in the trenches with their assailants. Even the religious orders, the alfaquis, the santons, and the pilgrim-dervish, armed with javelin, scymitar, and dagger, roused the old fanaticism to its highest pitch, and they fell with exulting shouts, glorying in their defiance to the last, as they beheld pictured to their closing eyes the ineffable delights of their Prophet's paradise. During two days, the assault continued with unremitting fury; for the Moors fought beneath the eye of Abu Abdallah, and the Christians were animated by the presence of their pious sovereigns. The Moor was already wounded, his chief alcaydes were slain, and the ramparts were fast becoming a mass of ruins. Soon, the leading citizens grew clamorous for a capitulation; the contest grew more hopeless, and terms were proposed to deliver up the fortress. To the number of Christian captives in the city, the inhabitants were, perhaps, indebted for their own safety: they were permitted to depart with as much property as they could carry with them. The valiant and generous Ponce de Leon was appointed to escort them to their places of refuge in Castile, Arragon, and Valencia.

Again a captive, Abu Abdallah was required to renew his oath of fealty and depart, in order to excite afresh the civil dissensions of Granada. The brave alcayde, El Zegri, with his principal captains, and the sons of the deceased veteran, Ali Atar, remained as hostages in the conqueror's hands. Few and broken, the old garrison marched through the Castilian camp, nor could the enemy withhold their tribute of sympathy and applause at the sight; some of the more distinguished opening for them a passage, and offering every token of their respect. They were followed by the women and children of Loxa, whose sighings and lamentations on quitting their homes and country to find an asylum in the land of their conquerors appealed to the sternest hearts, and moistened many a veteran eye which had shone undaunted on the fiercest horrors of the war.

Pursuing his victorious career from the heights of Albohacen, Ferdinand beheld the city of Moclin become a heap of ruins; while the humbled Moor, not daring to strike at once for the capital, retired to Priego, and next to Velez El Blanco. Here he first received tidings from the sultana, his mother, at Granada:—— "Are you not ashamed," wrote the high-spirited Aixa, " to desert a lovely bride and hover round the borders of your kingdom, while an usurping uncle sits upon Granada's throne? Strike quickly, ere honour die; the gates of the Albaycin will open to their monarch. Strike for your throne or fill a grave; there is no other resource for the man who has once swayed a sceptre."

With the sudden impulse of weak, irresolute minds, the Moor started as if from a dream, put himself at the head of his few faithful retainers, and inquiring if they would follow him to win an empire, his old guards laid their hands upon their scymitars, and in-

spiring the others with a shout of admiration, bid him
to lead them on.

As the shades of twilight gathered over hill and
plain, a single cavalier was seen urging his Arab
courser across the mountains which stretch between
the borders of Murcia and the Moorish capital. At
some distance a light troop of fifty lancers held on his
track; and on the summit of every height he paused,
and turned his eager glance in the direction of Granada. From their costly equipment, the splendour of
their armour, it was evident they were of no mean
lineage; and at the dead of night they approached
near, and rode under the dark wing of Granada's walls
till they first reined in their panting steeds at the outer
portals of the old Albaycin. Their chief's scymitar
was heard loud upon the gate, and to the sullen inquiry
of the warder,——" Open your gates; it is your king !"
was the commanding reply.

In humble guise, not unprepared, the guards obeyed;
and spurring at once to the mansions of the military
authorities and other inhabitants, the horsemen soon
roused the whole quarter of the city. It was the
cause of their favourite sovereign ;——and the flash of
javelins, the din of the tambours, first told Muley El
Zagal the startling truth. The old warrior-king instantly sallied forth at the head of his guards, to arrest
the insurrection in its bud. But he was driven back,
and a fresh encounter soon took place in the square of
the grand mosque, where, it is recorded, that the royal
relatives engaged with relentless fury hand to hand.

As their numbers swelled, by mutual agreement

they issued forth to decide the contest in the plains.
At night-fall they separated on nearly equal terms,
eagerly looking for the return of dawn.   The leading
chiefs and nobles fought for El Zagal, but they had
for rivals the hard veteran soldiers inured to blood and
toil, with all the mercenaries and the lowest dregs of
the people.   At the head of the Abencerrages shone
once more the noble Ibn Hammed, burning to avenge
his wrongs.   As he led on his few remaining brethren
in the van of El Zagal, he pointed to the rival tribe of
the Zegris with Abu Abdallah at their head, and burst
into a bold martial strain, at once in derision and
anger at the sight of the tributary and oft-captive
king.   As he appeared, the eyes of Abdallah shot forth
a malignant fire, and he trembled with rage as he imagined he could detect the secret exultation of his air,
and thought on his own long absence from the palace
gardens of the Generalife.

As he rode to the charge, the fiery prince infused
new ardour into his followers by addressing them in
the spirit of the old khaliphs, who rushed into battle
celebrating the beauty whose colours and device they
wore.*

> *   I saw their jealous eye-balls roll,
>   I saw them mark each glance of thine,
>   I saw thy terrors, and my soul
>   Shared every pang that tortured thine.
>
>   In vain to wean my constant heart,
>   Or quench my glowing flame they strove;
>   Each deep-laid scheme, each envious act
>   But waked my fears for her I love.

In this high-tempered mood, partaken by all his brethren, did the daring prince advance to storm the towers of the Albaycin; and in the stern encounter no quarter was either given or accepted. In the reiterated assaults to carry the Albaycin, the forces of El Zagal were repeatedly repulsed, but as often returned to the attack. Foreseeing his discomfiture, Abu Abdallah applied to his Christian auxiliaries; and the politic Ferdinand directed one of his generals to advance with a strong force towards Granada. At the same time, dreading treason, he was enjoined carefully to reconnoitre the proceedings of the conflicting kings, and to beware of the old Moorish ambuscades. But the Spanish commander soon saw enough to convince him there could be nothing feigned in the terrific encounters between the uncle and the nephew.

The Castilians, now joining the ranks of Abu Abdallah as their ally, added to the horrors and ferocity of such a contest; and for the space of fifty days the city of the queenly Granada continued a prey to the madness of a civil war, which deluged the thresholds of her noblest children with kindred blood.

'Twas this compelled the stern decree,
 That forced me to those distant towers,
And left me nought but love for thee
 To cheer my solitary hours.

Yet let not Abla sink deprest,
 Nor separation's pangs deplore ;—
We meet not ;—'tis to meet more blest,
 We parted ;—'tis to part no more.*

 * By Saif Addaulet, Sultan of Aleppo.

But the scenes of domestic calamity which followed in the train of Abu Abdallah, exceeded even the darkening hues of her public fortunes, fiillng Granada with tears and lamentations bitter as those of a captive mother over her offspring, ere she clothes herself in the slave-garb of her haughty master.   She had beheld tribes and kindred arrayed in the death-strife against each other; ties the most tender and sacred riven with the remorseless hate of her rulers; passions which impelled fathers, sons, and brethren to deeds which struck even the enemy who beheld them with astonishment and dismay.   Never, at any period of her deadliest feuds, had the flames of rival antipathy burned more strongly than between Muley El Zagal and his nephew : their continued hostility may be said to have formed part of the campaign of Ferdinand, to have fought his battles in the heart of the capital itself, hastening the downfal of the last kingdom of the Moors.   But now, driven from the capital, El Zagal once more betook himself to his fortune in the open field, holding at bay the fearful numbers of the foe—— often from his strong fortress-towns and castles carrying destruction and dismay into the very camps of his fierce invaders.

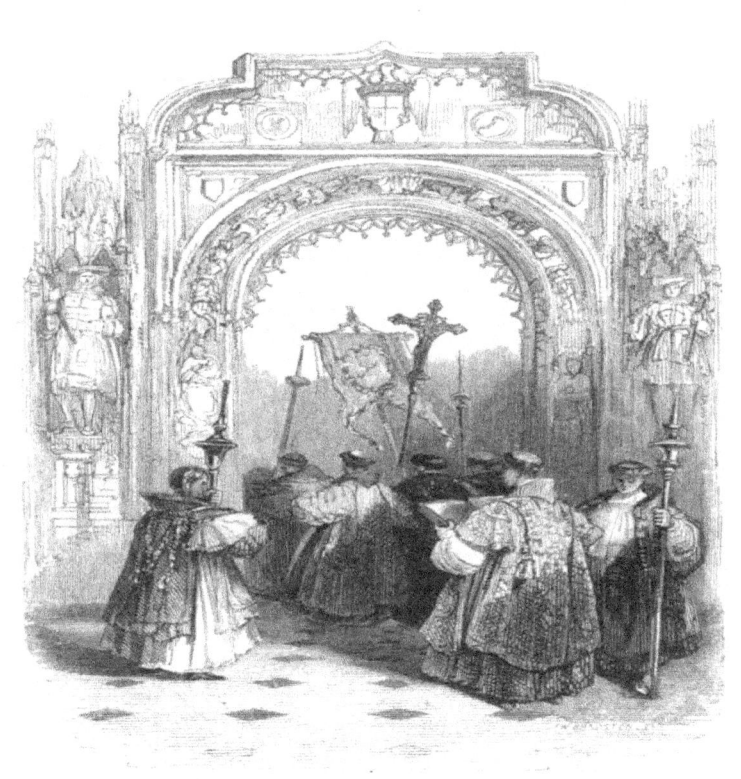

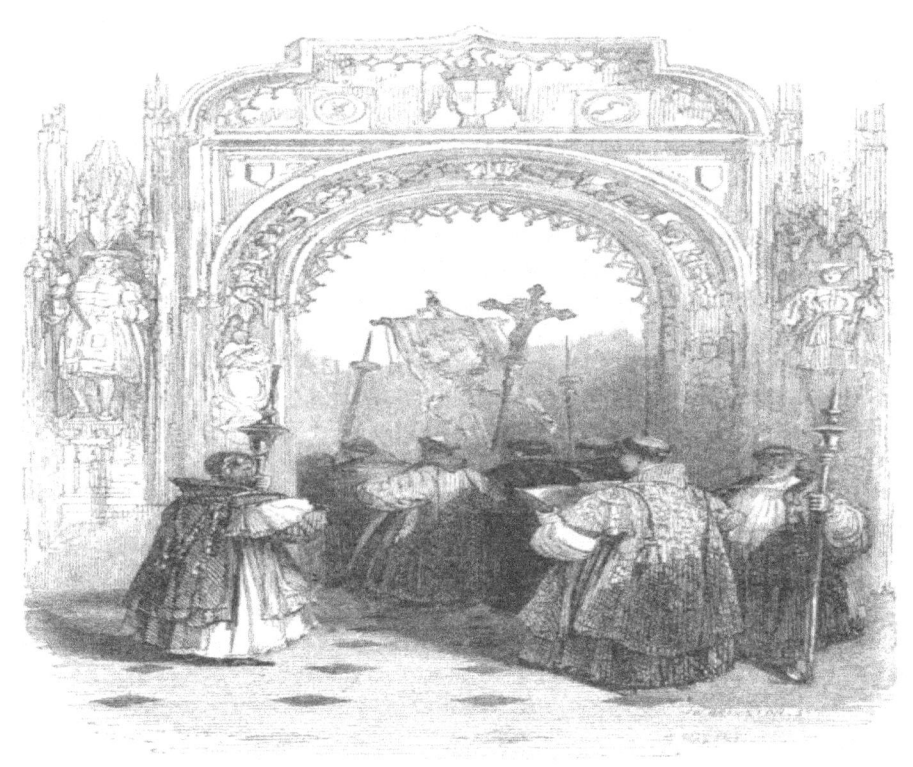

CHAPTER VIII.

From our distended eyeballs flow,
  A mingled stream of tears and blood ;
No care we feel, nor wish we know,
  But who shall pour the largest flood.
                    ALABIWERDY.

IT was during the foregoing conflict that an event
is believed to have taken place, which has stamped so
mournful an interest upon the spot.   The secret and

sanguinary character of the deed,* as it is popularly represented, naturally gave rise to the tradition of its having left indelible traces of its perpetration on the surface of the alabaster fount, which ran with blood.

In spite of his Christian auxiliaries, Abu Abdallah was daily losing ground; such were the heroic and persevering efforts of the Abencerrages and their adherents, animated by the voice of a chief whose chivalrous valour was sharpened by a sense of injured honour and thirst of revenge. But perfidy achieved for Abdallah what his open efforts against his enemies had invariably failed to do, startling the minds of all, inured as they were to the dark vicissitudes of this eventful and extraordinary war.

The golden light was fading in the west, tinging the Alhambra towers, and spire, and minaret, as it sank in one luminous flood of glory reflected from the deep azure waves, and shedding over hill, grove, and stream that dying radiance which may be seen and felt, but cannot be described. It now played through the shadowy vistas of those delicious walks, the deep retreats of fragrant garden bowers, which rendered Granada one sylvan palace of delights.

Sweetness and silence ushered in the blissful hour which drew the hearts of the two wronged, yet passionately devoted beings, lingering amid its old cypress groves, still close and closer to each other. The love that ruled their destiny, resistless and constant as the

* It has more recently been strongly questioned if it ever occurred; but we are taking the popular and romantic, not a strictly historic view of the fall of the Moors.

waves to the mystic influence of the moon's beams, had absorbed every feeling of anxiety or terror in one overwhelming and all-daring confidence of living only for each other.

They had met and parted,—that word so often spoken to trusting affection for the last time, still vibrated on the chords of their inmost spirits, like sighs of the dying night-gale on the mourning strings of the lyre; when the sudden rush of feet, and clash of arms fell on the startled ear of that sultana, ere she reached the palace balcony of the Generalife. Though brief withal, it was a wild and fearful sound; and she clasped her hands in an agony of undefined horror, as she fancied it came from that rose-bower overhung by the lofty palm and cypress branches which had but now breathed their melancholy music in the ear of love. How eagerly gazed she through that airy vista, where in the sudden, awful silence that succeeded, she saw but the bright silvery fountain playing in a thousand light eddying circles from its green marble ground; while lit up with a softened brilliance from the dark blue sky, the deepening shadow of the hills shed a mellower lustre on the dim and solemn groves that stretched around. She heard but the clear, wild note of the nightingale,—not an object or sound gave token of what those strange voices and sudden clash of arms might portend.

But more dark and silent was the scene of which she dreamed not, in another spot. One by one, as the gathering gloom seemed to hang over that proud and splendid saloon like a heavy pall, and the night-

winds sighed through its shadowy courts,* did the
victims follow each other to meet a sudden and untold
doom.   And there stood the stern inexorable judge
with jewelled diadem, and a chaplet of myrtle in his
hand,——there the three dark forms of the accusers, and

* On passing along the graceful, airy arcades of the Court
of Lions, you enter to the south a lofty apartment, in which
a marble fountain in the centre diffuses its refreshing coolness.
It is the Hall of the Abencerrages, famed alike in history,
by tradition and by song.   There is little in unison with the
unhappy associations it awakens in the gorgeous splendour,
the beauty, and refined taste which burst upon the eye in a
sudden flood of light from above, exhibiting its admirable
form, the elegant cupola, the exquisite design and painting
of the decorations, with the brilliant stucco work ; every
combination, in short, adapted to produce a species of fascination—the strange illusion of some delightful dream.   Yet
in such a magic, soul-inspiring retreat, it has been supposed
that King Boabdil executed that atrocious treachery of
secretly assassinating the noblest of the Abencerrages, commanding their heads to be struck off, one by one as they
entered the place, into the marble fountain.   The idle tradition of sanguinary traces of the dark deed needs no re-
futation ; but after long, patient research and inquiry by the
ablest writers, the deed itself continues involved in much
the same uncertainty and mystery as they found it.   The
effect of the ceiling on the eye is remarkable, displaying a
series of grottoes from which depend stalactites, painted of
various colours.   The intricacy of the lines crossing each other
in a thousand forms, and uniformly returning after a variety
of windings, is not surpassed by any mosaic work of antiquity.
     At the extremity of the court are two apartments, sup-
posed to have been employed as Tribunals, or Audience
Chambers.   Here are seen three historical paintings, executed
with considerable vigour upon the ceiling, though the heads
and figures are not equal to the composition.   One of these consists of a cavalcade, the other the entrance of some princess,
and the third a council, or divan.   It is not clear to which the

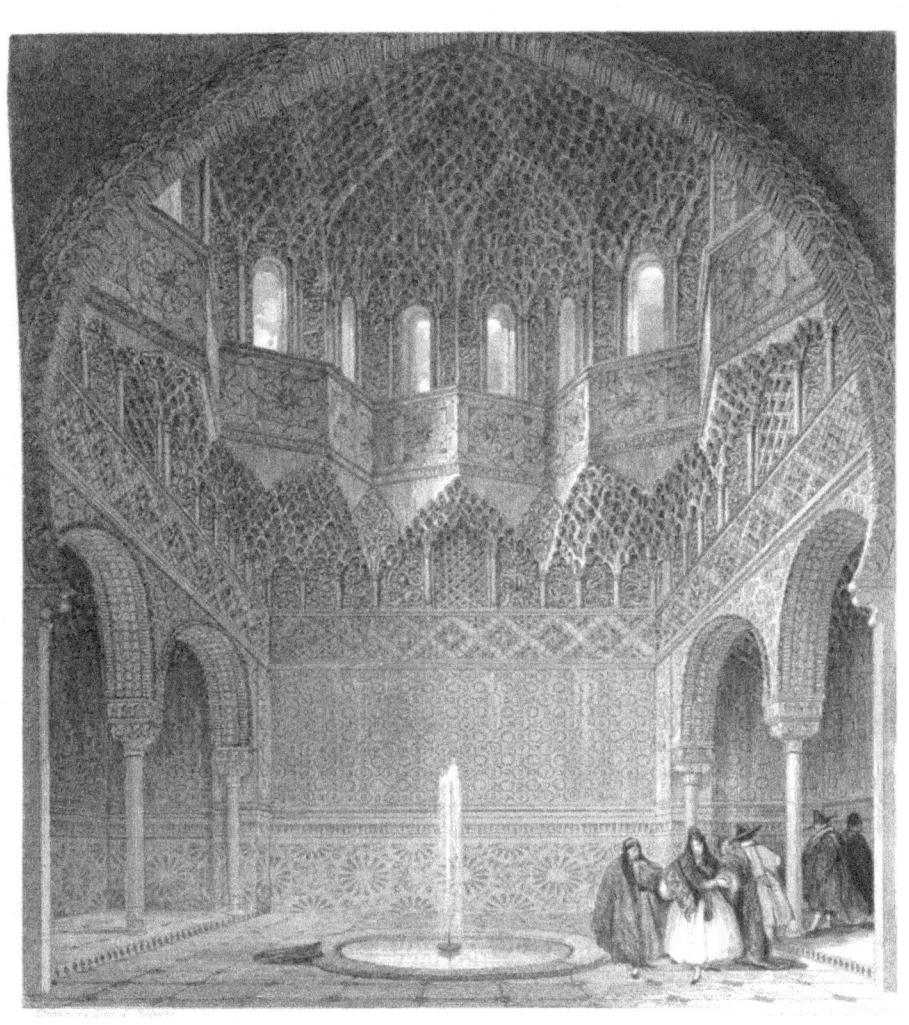

HALL OF THE TWO SISTERS. ALHAMBRA.

a single headsman with gleaming scymitar, which shot
portentous light upon that secret conclave of hate and
revenge. Silent they stood, and in a silence which
threw double horror on the soul, was each feast-bidden
guest hurried to the marble fount which received his

subject refers, but they are given, by popular belief, to the
sultana of Boabdil and her four Christian knights. Whether
painted contemporary with the supposed events to which
they refer, it is difficult to say; for though the Koran prohibits
the representation of living animals, the lions of the great
fountain, and the effigies of various kaliphs on their coin,
show that such a law was little closer observed than were
those against tobacco and wine. There is one fact which
seems to favour the idea of their genuine character; they have
been traced back to the close of Ferdinand's reign, and it is also
difficult to believe, that any painter so near the period when
so many witnesses must have survived to detect him, would
have boldness enough to invent the incidents of a trial and
ordeal of arms, more probably suggested to him by some
recent events. Whatever the truth may be, the popular
rumour so well grounded on the weakness and licentious
cruelty of the king, affords ample authority for assuming the
more romantic aspect of the story in a work chiefly descriptive and imaginative, and of such humble pretensions to
historical research as the present. It may also be worth
observing, in reply to those who have taken the unaccountable
fancy of vindicating Boabdil throughout a reign of weakness,
treachery, and crime, that few princes who have deserved well
at the hands of posterity, have had their memory maligned,
though so many who have pursued a dark career could boast
adulators during their lives, and vindicators of their memory
when dead. If to this consideration we add the severity of the
Moslem law, and of the Koran, with regard to filial duty and
obedience, the power given to the fathers,—in particular
where those fathers occupied the station of rulers, the conduct
of the usurping son would seem to display any thing but a
weak or amiable disposition. It required a bold and reckless
spirit, as well as the darkest treachery and deceit, to grasp

blood.   Withering was the look of hate and scorn shot from the eyes of those rival Moors, as the triumphant Zegris heaped on the noble chief the names of traitor and paramour, and the furious Abdallah held forth that fatal myrtle crown.   Baring his neck to the scymitar, the sceptre of a warlike father at the moment he was engaged in a severe struggle in open field with the common foe.   That he chose that moment also, during a brilliant and successful campaign, when Alhama was on the eve of being recovered by the arms of his royal sire,—giving thenceforth a disastrous aspect to the war, showed a base cunning, an audacity spurning at all ties perfectly consistent with his subsequent actions with regard to Ferdinand, and those imputed to him by the public voice relating to the assassination of the Abencerrages, the trial and condemnation of his consort, the sultana.   The drawings from these curious specimens of art in Murphy's work are very incorrect, being, moreover, only detached portions of the pictures.

When at Granada, Mr. Roberts carefully examined the three paintings alluded to, and has no hesitation in saying that they are of the same date with the rest of the ornamental work by which they are surrounded.   Taking into consideration the hard and stiff manner in which they are delineated,— the fresh and brilliant appearance of the colours,—the faithful and minute detail of the various costumes of the numerous characters introduced,—their close resemblance to which is still practised in China and the east,—and their total dissimilarity to any thing of the same kind to be met with in Spain, there can be no doubt after fairly examining the subject as to their being genuine, and perhaps the only existing specimens of the degree of excellence to which the Moors had arrived in cultivating the fine arts.   Here, as in other matters, it is probable, indeed, that the two people were long and mutually beneficial to each other ; the Moors communicating to Spain their earlier acquisitions in science and art ; while they borrowed on the side of European chivalry, moral feeling and a truer estimate of the rights of humanity and of the dignity of woman.

the prince dashed the turban from his brows, replacing it by the flowery chaplet with an exulting air of defiance and derision to the last, which stung his enemy with pangs of unsated revenge, even as that heroic head rebounded thrice from the ensanguined fount, the eye yet flashing, and the lip curled with supreme, ineffable disdain. As head after head resounded on the cold alabaster banks of that stream of blood, each successor marked with recoiling eye the features of some friend and brother, or the still nobler traits of his beloved chief.

Fast, and yet faster, poured the tide of life, as at the feigned summons of their leader, each brother of that lordly tribe hurried to share the same strange fate; and as, singly, he entered through the small secret portal to welcome his comrades, was seized and borne into the hall of death. Six-and-thirty had already dyed its waters with still ruddier deepening hues; when one faithful page, following the steps of his master, recoiled with horror as he caught a glance of the tragic scene enacting within,——eluding the grasp of the savage arm ready to clutch him as he started back with affright. Throwing himself at the feet of the next devoted brother hurrying to a like doom, with blanched cheek and quivering lip, he could only point towards the entrance, and cling to the knees of the Abencerrage.

The fearful tidings flew with death-winged rapidity through the tents and dwellings of the soldier-tribe; captains and men, arming with hurrying speed, rushed in small serried bodies up the steep avenues of the

Alhambra, and beating down the guard at every point, opened a path to throngs of followers, till they burst upon that fearful spectacle of death. And next the Alabez, with all their adherents, the emirs, scheikhs, and alcaydes, mingled in the rush of battle with the common herd, eager alike to solve the appalling mystery of secret treachery,——the sudden massacre of the brave in the heart of their own citadel, at the hour of peaceful twilight, afar from the field of the foe.

As the shrill Moorish horns sounded along the dim courts and groves, again the insatiate furies of discord, newly awoke to havock, shook their serpent locks, inciting the hearts of their victims to deadlier struggles, as they scattered their firebrands to the night, and swept through that wild, doomed city on the black thickening clouds of war. With loud shouts of rival brethren, re-echoed by shrieks and cries which rent the veil of silence, gathering over the far plains and hills, they met in the fierce shock which fell like a hurricane on that mighty fortress,——filling its halls, and towers, and palace gardens, with the sound of its desolating career, till the high-vaulted dome and deep hollow donjon alike trembled with the hideous din.

Long and desperate was the conflict,——bitter the revenge,——terrific the havock in the best and noblest of Granada's ranks. And the morrow beheld her again bathed in her own blood and tears ; and as the shades of another evening fell, the proudest and bravest of her children wept as they gazed on a self-banished and shattered band of brothers, urging their chargers through her gates, to re-enter them no more.   They were the Abencerrages,——abandoning the ungrateful city of their kings, where they had beheld the chief and nobles of their kindred,——victims to the fury of their royal feuds,——fall unhonoured, not for their country, ——their fame in the open field. Darkly and sad they passed into the plains, taking their way to the towers of Almeria, still ready to meet the common foe under the banners of the warrior-exile, El Zagal.

His vengeance still unappeased, and fired even with maddening jealousy of the dead, Abdallah turned his wrath against his unhappy and ill-fated queen. The dark accusations of the Zegris now impelled him to crown his previous crime with another of a yet darker die. Summoning a grand council of his chiefs, he explained his reasons, grounded on the evidence of the Zegris, for passing summary judgment upon the Abencerrages. Witnesses were not wanting, however deeply perjured, to attest the guilt of his unfortunate consort with the most solemn of oaths. They had met to consider of a punishment due to the supposed commission of so rare and flagrant an offence.

The sentence, solemnly pronounced in presence of the chiefs and elders was, that the adulterous queen should suffer death by being burnt alive, if within twenty days she could not produce four knights to vindicate her aspersed fame. On the proclamation of this fearful doom, the sultana's friends,——those who honoured the memory of the noble Abencerrage, and the brave Ali Atar, indignantly drew their scymitars in the Hall of Audience, and openly declared that they would resist such a mandate to the death.

But as they flew to her rescue, the noble Muza threw himself before them, entreating to be heard. Appealing to them with a commanding eloquence surpassed only by his heroism in the field, the chief of the Alabez besought them to consider, " that though by valour they might protect the sultana, it could prove only injurious to her honour in the eyes of Granada, and of the world. If they dared not to submit her cause to the great ordeal of battle and the justice of the Supreme, how came they so boldly to impugn the equity of her `threatened doom ? Nor would the princely lady," he maintained, " accept their proffered swords on terms that must condemn her in her own eyes and those of the people."

Listening to the suggestions of the valiant and wise chief, they hastened to enrol their names as her champions——a numerous list, from which she might select the bravest of the brave. Already a captive within the walls of the Comares, this proud testimony to her merit and her misfortunes was no alleviation to the bitter sorrows she endured; while full of gratitude for their noble-minded offers, she felt such insurmountable horror at the treachery of the Zegris, that she could not behold any of their nation stand forth to vindicate her honour in the lists. No ! she would throw herself upon the gallantry and generosity of the Christian foe.

She knew the high esteem long entertained for him she had lost by the great d'Aguilar, and the gallant knight, Don Juan de Chacon. He was lord of Carthagena, and to him she appealed for succour ; nor did

she appeal in vain. With the generous spirit of their
age and of their country, the gallant leaders replied
in terms of the tenderest condolence such as might
have breathed from the lips of sisters or mothers,
rather than the most famed and terrible soldiers, bred
amidst those fierce frontier wars. All of courtesy and
magnanimity mingled in their high resolve to champion the cause of the lovely and the oppressed, even
unto their death; nor did they less burn to avenge
upon the heads of the traitorous and cruel Zegris the
loss of that heroic chief, whom they had all learnt to
honour and esteem.

A few of them, indeed, were knit in closer bonds
of friendship, having imbibed the most impassioned
attachment for a sister of the noble prince, and the
lovely daughter of Aben Kassim; while the youthful
hero of Cordova, Europe's famed captain, was yet more
enthralled by the charms of the Moorish princess,
with whom those high-born beauties and the now
grief-stricken Zelinda had been companions from
their tenderest years. Deep and touching then was
their sorrow, and that of their noble Castilian lovers;
who in many a sweet and oft-stolen interview, and in
the pauses of the dread campaigns, had with soft-
breathed vows and sighs, and, ah! not rarely with
tears, smoothed the stern, iron aspect of horrid war.

But the mad ambition of bad princes, of fawning
favourites, and mitred, evil counsellors, uprooted from
that glorious soil the mingling growth of all nobler
virtues and high qualities, of gentler thoughts and
sweetest passions, even the old courtesy and gallantry

itself; and planted in their ashes the bitter seed
of murderous discord, persecution, and superstition,
through whose Moloch fires the best and noblest of
two great people were condemned to pass.

And now the fearful hour was fast approaching,
when bright honour or ignominy, with its fearful
doom, should spring from the swords of the champions or the accusing chiefs. The lord of Carthagena
had selected his three brethren in arms, and submitted
their names to the approval of the lovely accused.
They were accepted, for they were those of Don Alonzo
d'Aguilar, Don Diego di Cordova, and the generous
Ponce de Leon, lord of Cadiz. Never at any moment
of her destiny had Granada evinced so lively an interest and excitement as on this extraordinary and
affecting occasion, when the appointed day drew nigh.

But as the Moors were preparing the lists, the war-
cry of San Jago resounded at their gates; and blinded
as he was with jealous rage, the fears of the vain
Abdallah for his crown,——not for his country or the
honour of her arms, compelled him to prolong the
hour of vengeance, and rouse to action against the
foe. The mountain bulwarks of the queenly Granada,
her fairest towns and provinces had fallen under the
thunder of their new engines of war. She was doomed
to struggle with her fate alone. Moclin followed the
fate of Illora;——Zagra, Baños, and other strong-holds
sent in their submission, for vainly had they sued for
aid from Abu Abdallah, wholly absorbed in the idle
conquest of the Alhambra, and the delight of reigning
alone over the ruins of a once mighty empire.

But as the evil hour drew on, the old fiery spirit of the Muselmāns could not behold with apathy the sun of their splendid career sinking for ever in the waves of the west. Forming a league with the princes of Barbary, Bajazet II. prepared an expedition against Sicily,—whole squadrons of fierce native tribes poured down upon the African coasts.

Ferdinand, at the same time, with a brilliant host, marched from Cordova, laying waste the Moorish territories in his course, while the Christian squadron swept the neighbouring coasts. Investing the great sea-port of Velez Malaga, he took up a strong position which commanded the city; but the Moors making a sudden onset, he was not only driven back, but in extreme peril of his life. At that moment Ponce de Leon, at the head of a strong force, followed by the heroic Lara and other knights, extricated him from his dangerous situation, and enabled him to resume the siege. Still the Moors from the nearest forts and castles attacked their convoys, surprised their divisions,—harassing the foe with an incessant guerilla warfare, which left not a moment's repose.

Vainly was the city summoned to surrender; from every hill and lofty sierra the fierce mountaineers bore down upon the invaders; they were supported by sorties of the garrison,—the conflict raged on all sides, till finally the Moors were repulsed with immense loss.

Velez Malaga shared the general consternation, on learning from the brave Redovan the rout of the army marching to its relief. He exhorted them to a bold defence, till the terrible array of artillery on the

heights, and evident preparations for an assault, convinced the inhabitants of the necessity of surrender,
though the heroic alcayde wished to bury himself
beneath its ruins. It was fortunate that he was there;
his noble treatment of the Count Cifuentes was now
appreciated, and he obtained for him milder terms
than could have been expected, while their generous
friendship continued unbroken to the last. Once
master of that noble sea-port, Ferdinand was eager to
attack Malaga itself. Its surrounding forts and strong
holds fell in rapid succession.

The deputies of forty towns appeared to do homage
before the victorious Ferdinand; while his possession
of Marbella and Ronda to the west of Malaga, of
Antiquera, Alhama, and Loxa to the north, and Velez
to the east, rendered the position of Malaga almost
untenable. Still it was a city of immense strength,
fortified both by natural bulwarks, with a strong
citadel and towers, and a warlike garrison. Then its
delicious site, its fair and fertile vega, its wealth, its
splendid edifices, its noble territory teeming with
productive streams, groves, and hanging gardens,
could not be surrendered by their possessors without
a severe struggle. But after bitter experience of the
horrors of a long siege, a wealthy townsman, Ali
Dordux, seconded by the chief inhabitants, became
eager to enjoy the privileges of surrender granted to
other fallen towns. The famed tower of Gibralfaro was
becoming a heap of ruins; and the commander, Muza
Ben Conixa, sought to gain time by entering into
negotiation. But the fierce African bands, imagining

that he was about to betray them to the enemy, rushed to possess themselves of the fortress of the Alcazaba, putting to the sword its garrison and its gallant commander, Muza's own brother.

The negotiation was broken off, and Moors and native bands vied with each other in deeds of the most daring character, making the most desperate sorties, and repeatedly forcing the enemy's intrench-ments. But famine soon completed the work of the sword; Ali and his friends despatched a secret mes-senger to the Christians, offering to admit them into the fortress by night, unknown to the fiery Africans. He was already in the act of returning with Fer-dinand's guarantee of life and property, and Dordux and his friends beheld him from the walls.

A party of the Moors, however, taking him for a spy, seized upon him, and the whole transaction was on the point of transpiring; when, by a sudden effort, the envoy burst from their hands, and fled for the Christian camp. He was closely pursued, and we may imagine the feelings of the inhabitants during that awful sus-pense; their lives would pay the penalty of discovery. As he crossed the boundary line, the nearmost pursuer fired, and hit him between the shoulders; yet, mortally wounded, the faithful Moor held on till he reached the camp, and fell dead as he entered the royal pavilion.

At the dead of night, the Spaniards were introduced into the castle of Gibralfaro; they opened the gates to their followers, and a fearful scene of carnage ensued. The lives of Ali Dordux and the inhabitants, were spared; but the brave garrison were put to the sword.

Ali was commissioned to collect the ransom of the
unfortunate citizens; many were led into captivity,
while the abject Abdallah sent to compliment Ferdinand on his conquest.*   As if to outrage the feelings
of his suffering countrymen, he had actually intercepted the forces hurrying to its relief under El Zagal,
and driving him back, left open the path to the capital,
madly dreaming, by such dastardly treason to his
country, to propitiate the wily conqueror.

Her proud invader could now proceed at once to
invest Granada, or attack the remaining cities belonging to El Zagal.   With his usual crafty policy,
he adopted the latter course, and summoned Baza,
Almeria, Guadix, Vera, and other strong-holds, ere he

* During the siege, Ferdinand had nearly fallen a victim to
the fanaticism of a Moorish prophet or santon.   With a body
of four hundred men, chiefly the Gomerez, whom he had
inspired with a like zeal and fury, he concealed himself in the
mountains above Malaga; and, in the dead of night, rushed
down upon the most vulnerable quarter of the Christian camp.
Falling on the sentinels, they forced their way into the
intrenchments, and filling the camp with slaughter and consternation, two hundred of them succeeded in entering the
gates of the city.   But this was not the sole object of the
"Moro Santo."   Placing himself in a situation where he knew
he should be taken, he was found wrapped in prayer; his
haggard features and wild air, his white grizzly beard, and
tattered mantle (called albornoz) inspiring a sort of awe, even
in the enemy.   On being questioned by Ponce de Leon, he
declared that he was a saint of the holy mountain, to whom was
revealed the approaching destiny of the Moors.   He knew the
day and hour when Malaga was to fall, and the empire of Mohammed crumble with the dust.   He came commissioned to
direct Ferdinand in the right path, and to his ear alone could
he breathe the dread secret of coming events.   He was then

fell upon the capital. Vera, Mujacar, Velez-le-Roux, and other towns opened their gates, terrified at beholding the slavery and ruin which had fallen to the lot of Malaga. El Zagal, meantime, made fearful struggles to maintain his dominion; he defeated the Christians before Taberna, was equally successful on the side of Huescar and Baza, and in one of these terrific encounters slew the Grand Master of Montesa, nearly related to the royal house of Castile.

Enraged at this sudden check in his triumphant career, Ferdinand had marshalled anew armies after armies to prosecute his great object. In 1489, he marched from Jaen at the head of fifty thousand foot and twelve thousand horse, at the same time entering into stricter bonds of alliance with Abu Abdallah.

introduced into a tent, where imagining that a noble and one of the ladies present were the king and queen, he drew his dagger, struck Don Alvaro, and then attempted to stab the Countess of Maya. The attendants threw themselves upon him, and several nobles, rushing forward on hearing shrieks from the royal pavilion with drawn swords, hewed the assassin into pieces. His body was then thrown from a catapult into the streets of the beleaguered city; while, to revenge the death of their holy santon, the Moors executed one of their chief captives, and binding the corpse on an ass, drove it into the Christian camp.—*Cura de los Palacios.*

An instance of rare magnanimity is also on record. In a night sortie, led by a fanatic dervish, Zenete, a noble Moor, pierced into the Christian tents. There were a number of pages and youths, roused from slumber, whom he might easily have slain; but contenting himself with striking them with the flat of his sword, he exclaimed. "Get home, get home, children, to your mothers;" and, on being reproached by the savage recluse, he only replied, "I could not kill them, because I saw no beards."—*Ib.*

Such was the Moor's abject submission, that he even
consented to receive a Spanish garrison into Granada
the moment he should have subdued the cities which
owed allegiance to El Zagal.   Dreading lest the
conqueror of Baza and Huescar should return and
deprive him of his crown, he preferred the downfal
of his country to the sight of a successful rival.   The
Cid Yahia, a prince of high and estimable qualities,
held Baza for El Zagal, with a garrison of ten thousand
veterans.

Ferdinand attacked it with his whole force, and the
siege was long and bloody.   But feats of hardihood
and heroism not to be surpassed, failed to preserve
the city from the hands of the enemy.   At the expira-
tion of six months, the cid wrote to his uncle with
information that famine had begun, the inhabitants
threatened revolt, and he must capitulate if he did
not receive instant succour.   Fully appreciating the
valour and talents of the prince, El Zagal grieved
that he was no longer enabled to relieve him.   Brilliant as were his efforts, they were paralyzed by
Abdallah ; and, in reply, he could only conjure his
nephew to make the best terms in his power.   Baza
was filled with lamentation and despair.   The alcayde,
Mohammed Hassan, was sent by the cid with propo-
sitions to the Christian camp.   He obtained for the
inhabitants that they should be admitted as subjects
of the Spanish crown, and preserve their liberty and
their religion,—words of promise to the ear, which
raised the unfortunate city from the abyss of despair,
and induced other towns to follow its example.

The interview of the prince with Ferdinand and Isabella is curious and interesting; such indeed was the respect they inspired him with, that he swore never more to draw his sword against the Christian cause; and accepting a large jurisdiction in towns and lands, declared that he would do every thing in his power to bring over his kinsman, El Zagal, to the same views.

His reasons had only too much weight with the veteran, but now broken monarch; and he at length convinced him of the inutility of carrying on a campaign at once against the Christians and his own countrymen. "It can only," he observed, "hasten the general ruin. Better to appeal to the generosity of the sovereigns, and no longer seek to oppose the destiny which presided over the birth of Abdallah. We believed it fulfilled when he was made prisoner at Lucena; but what calamities followed! what may not the future yet inflict! For myself, I bow down before the will of Allah; he hath united the thrones of Arragon and Castile; he it is who wills that the crown of Granada should adorn the brows of Ferdinand. It is so written; and will you not believe, and resign yourself as a follower of our holy Prophet?"

With deep sighs, and after a long and mournful silence, El Zagal despairingly exclaimed, "*Alahuma subahana hu!*—I see, my kinsman, that Allah's eternal decrees are against us; for by the fire and hate I yet feel in my heart, this hand had vindicated our freedom, had not the God of our Prophet made known that it must not be! Let us treat, then, with the enemy, for it is the will of Allah—not mine!"

Together the two princes hastened to the camp of Ferdinand near Almeria, and were received with the respect which their extraordinary and brilliant efforts to save their country had so well merited.* El Zagal was presented with ample domains, and still permitted to bear the title of a king. The inhabitants of Almeria and Guadix, like those of Baza, were admitted to the privileges of Castilian subjects, and exonerated from heavier payments than such as they had been wont to make to the kings of Granada.

* Not a few instances of still greater magnanimity and patriotism are recorded of the noble Moors. The veteran Ali Fahar, had defended the towns and castles entrusted to him, till their garrisons would no longer second his heroic efforts. He took his way to the Christian camp, where he found a number of other alcaydes, who had come to deliver up the keys of their respective fortresses, and he saw them depart loaded with gifts and treasure. Ferdinand, sensible of the importance of the places he had surrendered, ordered ample remuneration to be made him; but he persisted in rejecting the whole of the treasures spread out before him. " I came not hither," he replied, " to barter what is not my own, but to yield what victory has made yours. It is no voluntary gift; for had others supported me in my efforts, death should have been the price at which you should have had my fortresses, and not the bribe of gold, which is not mine." Struck with his greatness of mind, the Castilian sovereigns sought to attach him to their service. " Is there nothing," insisted the queen, " that we can prevail on you to accept as a token of our high regard?"——" Yes," replied the Moor eagerly; " in yonder towns and valleys which I yield up, are my hapless countrymen with their wives and families, and they cannot, like me, become exiles from their native homes. Give me your royal word that they shall preserve their religion in peace!"——" We pledge our word for it," said Isabella; " but for thyself, what dost thou require?"——" Nothing," replied Ben Fahar, " but permission to pass with my horse and arms into Africa."— *Pulgar.*

So rapid was this strange vicissitude in the fortune of the Moors, as to astonish even the Christians. We may imagine the surprise and consternation of the people of Granada, and its immediate towns and territories. But the new subjects of the Christian monarchs congratulated themselves upon their escape from the fierce scourge of war; nor was their example without its influence upon their neighbours—numerous towns hastening to send in their submission and oaths of fidelity to the camp of Almeria.

The grief and terror of Granada, on hearing the extent of the evil, knew no bounds. The discontent of the populace, as in all times, soon found vent in murmurs of revolt. Abu Abdallah was now a faithless Muselmān, a renegade to his religion, a traitor to his country. With mutinous cries and brandished weapons, they rushed towards the gates of the Alhambra. The scheikhs, the alcaydes, and the faquirs threw themselves before the exasperated people, but they could barely give time to Abu Abdallah to intrench himself within the walls of the fortress.

While they prepared to besiege him in his palace, he contrived to give intimation of his danger to his Christian allies. It was their policy to take advantage of so fortunate a conjuncture, and Ferdinand having united his frontier forces, marched to the relief of his trembling satellite and slave. He ravaged with impunity the richly populated towns and hamlets in the fertile territories of the capital; and the thundering appeal of this new invasion wrought all the effect upon the mind of the populace, which the eloquence and

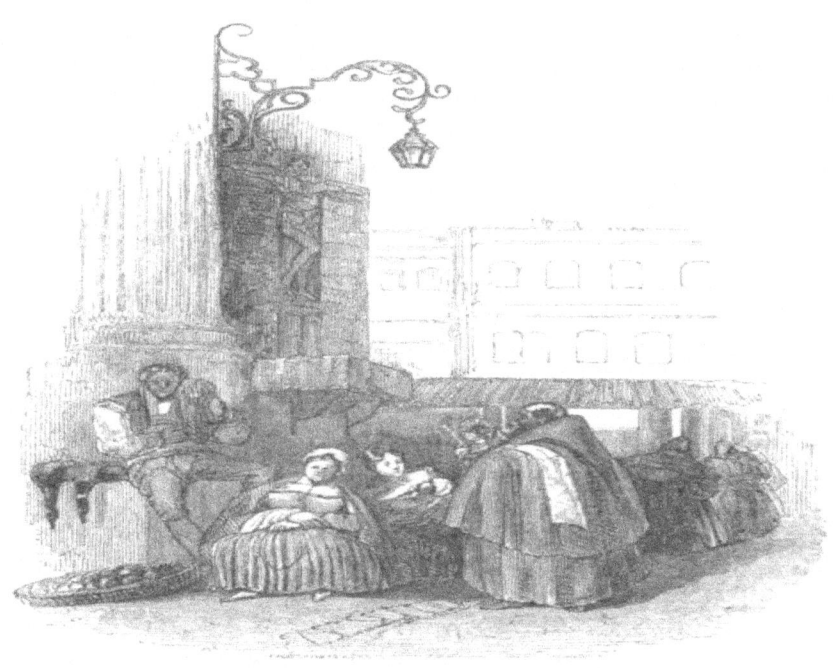

CHAPTER IX.

Mortal joys, however pure,
  Soon their turbid source betray ;
Mortal bliss, however sure,
  Soon must totter and decay.

Ye who now, with footsteps keen,
  Range through hope's delusive field,
Tell us what the smiling scene,
  To your ardent grasp can yield ?

THE KHALIPH RADHI BILLAH.

SINCE the lamented fate of the chief of the Abencerrages, all eyes had turned with hope to the chivalrous Muza Ben Gazan. Idolized for his daring

valour and skill in all the exercises of arms, he also possessed talents, as a commander, surpassed by no leader of the day. The terror of the foe, his lofty qualities, his fine person, and strikingly handsome features made him the theme of the lips of beauty, and of the heroic, romantic strains of the Andalusian poet.

On the reiterated demand of Ferdinand that the people should yield up their arms, and admit a Spanish garrison into Granada, his eyes flashed, his lip quivered with indignant scorn. His feelings were partaken by all the emirs and chiefs of tribes, by all the veteran warriors and heads of noble families illustrious by lineage as by their deeds. "Are we old men, and do we handle staffs? or are we women and play with distaffs," cried their gallant leader with bitter irony, "that the king of Castile should address us thus? Were we not bred to wield the scymitar—to hurl the spear—to draw the bow? Is it not our nature? or will he teach us how to career the steed and direct the onset of battle? Here are our arms, why comes he not to take them? To me a grave beneath the walls of Granada were dearer far than a couch of down in her luxurious palaces, purchased by crouching to the infidel foe."

The generous patriotism of the Moor was caught by all ranks, and Granada awoke to battle from the spell of torpor and terror, like a giant refreshed with wine. Every street and avenue resounded with the din of war; the scheikhs and chiefs, with Muza at their head, assumed the direction of the public

council, and the inhabitants, down to the lowest populace, burned to signalize themselves and meet the
insulting requisitions of the Castilian monarchs by
deeds of proof. The indignation against El Zagal
and the renegade Cid Yahia, whose banners were seen
displayed with those of Arragon and Castile, knew no
bounds. It exceeded all they had before felt towards
Abu Abdallah; whom, though the real cause of that
disastrous submission, it now became their policy to
support. They respected him for the position he had
dared to assume; their new leader Muza took advantage
of the popular feeling to reconcile the interests of the
sovereign and the people, and render them unanimous
against the foe.

Incessantly in action, he appeared to live and
breathe only in the exploits of the field. At the
head of the noble youth of Granada, the squadrons of
every tribe, and followed by an army full of confidence and admiration of his brilliant deeds, he now
shone with a lustre which made all exclaim that had
he earlier appeared and led an unanimous people to
the field, he would have revived the noblest days of
the Moslem fame. As it was, he was irresistible in
the onset of his brave chivalry, and was generally
avoided by an equal number of the foe. So signal
indeed was his success over a far superior force, that
Ferdinand was compelled to issue an order that no
challenges to single combat should be accepted,—no
skirmish or detached encounters courted by his cavaliers and commanders, under severe penalties. Muza's
indignation at this unknightly mandate was extreme;

and he lamented it as a sign of degeneracy and decay of the old chivalrous courtesies and usages of heroic war.

To the honour of the Castilians, the royal edict was not seldom broken; and while he despised the base commissariat spirit of the monarch, calculating his losses to a fraction, the illustrious Moor displayed in victory the utmost liberality towards his chivalrous foe.   Even the infantry of the Moors followed him to the most hazardous enterprises, and again Granada sent forth her legions which scoured the plains and hills up to the walls of her captured cities, returning loaded with booty and triumph to her grateful capital.   Captives and banners were borne with loud acclamations through her gates ;—the blended ensigns of Arragon and Castile were seen waving from her mosques and towers.   The Elvira gates which had before been cautiously closed, were thrown open by the orders of the gallant chief ;—the guards, the scouts and adalids were all in active duty, and squadrons of horse were held ready equipped to pour down at a moment's notice in masses upon the plains. On all sides, indeed, the name of Muza became the dread of the Christian van-guards; and Ferdinand with his customary caution withdrew, ere the close of autumn, into his intrenchments to await fresh supplies.

Another spring of this eventful war again beamed forth ; the glorious vega bloomed in all its pristine luxuriance, now sacred from the foot of the spoiler. Ferdinand still delayed to renew the fearful contest,—

he knew the chief and the chivalry with whom he had to contend. "We must weary, and ravage them," he observed, "till we can draw our toils closer, and let famine and our artillery do the rest!" To this politic object he had directed all his strength and energies during the wintry season, and in the intervals of the dread campaigns.

Nor had Muza Ben Gazan,—the soul of action, the protector alike of the sovereign and the people, neglected to array Granada in the iron panoply of imposing war. When all was prepared for the field, he sent forth the holy faquirs and dervishes to rouse the enthusiasm of the faithful, and impel them to still hardier deeds by visions of that delicious paradise, of which they boldly declared, "that the famed gardens of Irem, and the golden palaces of King Shedad were but a feeble type." * The old spirit of the Mus-elmāns responded to the appeal, and the conquered towns and provinces threatened to throw off their new allegiance. Guadix was in revolt, and the dominions of the wretched slave-king, El Zagal, rose and com-pelled him to take refuge in the Christian camp.† Nor were the gigantic preparations of Muza—now

* The paradise of Irem this,
  And that the palace pile
  Which Shedad built, the king.
                                    SOUTHEY.

† He there entreated Ferdinand to relieve him of his petty sovereignty, to take back his fatal gift, and enable him to reach the African coasts. He resold it for a large sum, and with a few faithful adherents he arrived in the kingdom of Fez, whose monarch seizing upon his treasures, threw him into a

as eagerly promoted by Abu Abdallah, restored to the favour of the people, completed, ere they were called into active display.

Enraged at having been so long foiled in his grand attempt, Ferdinand poured down upon the vega in a sudden storm of war, desolating towns and hamlets in his career. Twice had his ravages extended to the gates of Granada; and, in the last sweeping hurricane, he left not a vestige of life or fertility in all its blooming territory, which bore the aspect of one vast desart,—harvests, flocks, herds, and herdsmen being involved in one indiscriminate ruin.

But the great Moorish chief prepared to take signal vengeance on their fierce, ruthless destroyer. He appeared with the king before the chiefs and tribes, and in the presence of the entire Moorish host he announced that their favourite monarch—no longer the ally of the perfidious Ferdinand—would once more lead them to the field. The air rang with acclamations, and the sudden return of Muza's squadrons with ample spoils and banners of the enemy, appeared to crown the happy augury of unanimity and success.

dungeon, and deprived him of his sight. Blind and poor, he was afterwards set at liberty, and, like the aged Belisarius, was compelled to beg his bread on the highway, during his last painful pilgrimage through the world. In this abject, forlorn state, he traversed the regions of Tingitania, till he arrived at Velez de Gomera. Its king compassionately gave him food and raiment, permitting him there to drag out the remnant of his wretched days. He continued to live upon alms, and upon his breast he bore a placard, on which was written in Arabic, "You behold the unfortunate King of Andalusia." —*Pedraza.*

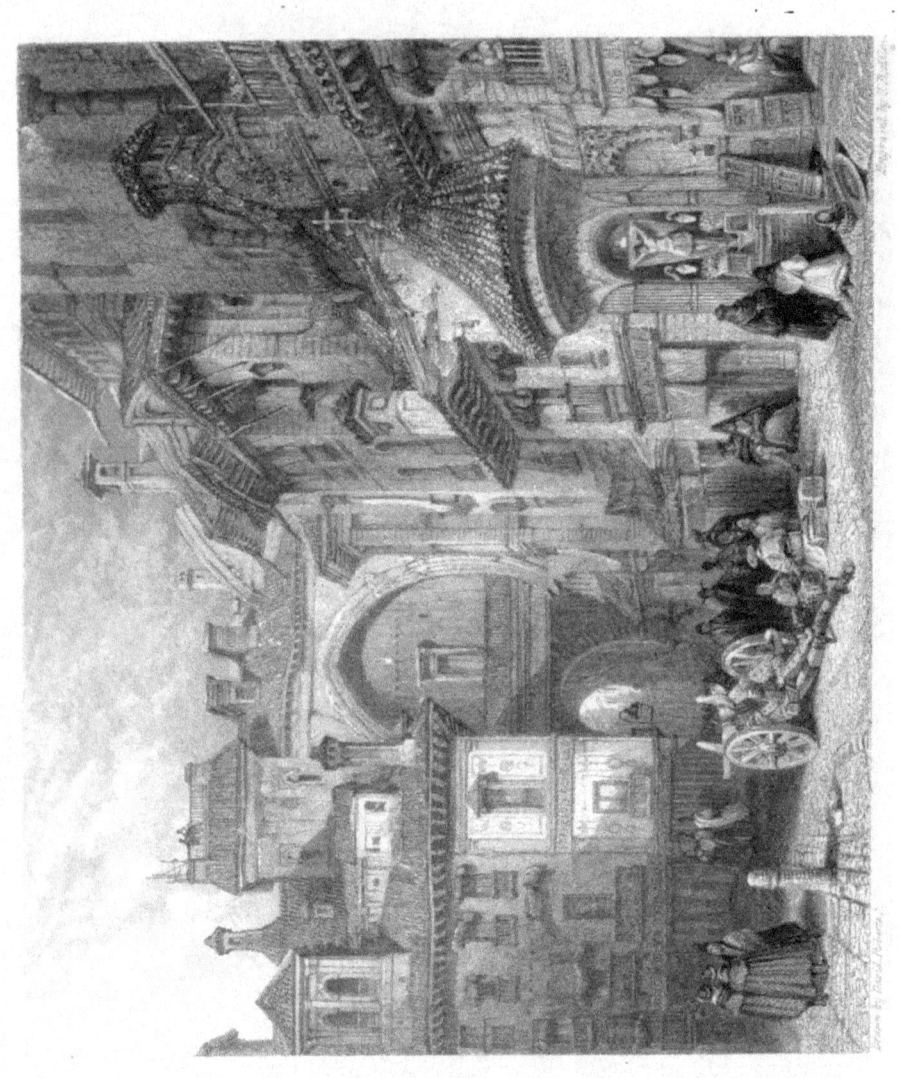

All breathed the soul of fiery action, and enduring war; of a campaign more terrible and decisive than any yet recorded in the annals of Moslem sway.

But ere hurrying to avenge their desolated plains and hamlets, came the hour destined to decide a cause of so much woe to Granada, in the sad fortunes of her peerless sultana and of that heroic chief she had too early lost.

The die was cast; the fatal decree had gone forth; the jealous rage of Abdallah, and the honour of the queen alike forbade its revocation. And now the magnificent square of the Viva Rambla,* arrayed in all the solemn pomp of chivalric justice peculiar to the Moorish battle-ordeal, gave forth its loud-repeated summons, heard far along the banks of the Darro, to assemble on the field of honour, to grace this strangely exciting but mournful spectacle.

* It was through this gateway, it is said, that the Castilian hero rode, when he nailed a challenge upon the door of the mosque, which occupied the site of the present cathedral on the opposite side of the square of the Viva Rambla, and returned again whilst his followers were engaged in mortal combat with the Moorish guards. The small niche with a representation of the Crucifixion, is one of those small chapels to be found at the corners of every street in a Spanish town; and it is almost constantly surrounded by a group of devotees. The figure of our Saviour, the Virgin, the Infant Christ, or one of those numerous saints with which their calendar abounds, is generally decked out with mock trinkets and tawdry dresses; it being no uncommon thing to see the Infant Saviour in an antique court-dress, satin-flowered waistcoat, knee breeches, silk stockings, square-toed shoes and buckles; whilst on the other hand, the Virgin is represented in a satin gown and flounce, wide hoop petticoat and hand-

For on that morning the capital offered a singular contrast to the gay, gladdening ceremonies of the old joust and ring. No joyous groupes, no rich emblazoned colours with the thousand fluttering devices of love and honour, ushered in the fearful day. Instead of the flaunting of the crescent pennons, the royal splendour of warlike costume, ominous silence and trouble hung like a heavy cloud over that devoted city, and cast a deeper shadow on the soul. With restless step and anxious eye, the superstitious Moors marked the fearful santon mingling with the throng; and as they drew nigh the entrance to the lists, their agitation rose into a thrill of terror and entrancing awe; for as if maddened with the terrific spirit of the revealed future, his wild, ghastly features assumed a deathlier hue; his appalling eye seemed to rest on some object no other eye could see; while the emblems of frail mortality which invested his brows, and the magical characters traced upon his face and

some Leghorn bonnet with artificial flowers, necklace, fingers covered with rings, &c. &c. Wax lights are kept constantly burning before them, a person being appointed and paid for that purpose, by the inhabitants of the street to whom the saint belongs. Near the side of the little chapel delineated in the drawing, is a small cross, which marks the spot where a murder has been committed. This is a regular memento throughout Spain; and, in towns, a small board is fixed beneath the cross with the name of the "unfortunate wight," and the day and year in which he fell. In some streets, especially where it is a low neighbourhood, these crosses are so numerous as to cover the walls. It may be as well to mention that this gateway is called the "Arco de los Orejas," from the ears of those unfortunate Moors who had committed any state crimes, having been nailed to its gates.

forehead, threw a fiercer supernatural terror into every word and look.

Pointing to a high scaffold, surmounting the funereal pyre overhung with sables,—the gloomy trappings of departing life,—his knees began to tremble and his lips quivered, while he muttered certain unknown, cabalistic sounds, as if in dread communion with some invisible thing, on which his eye was still fixed in a sort of prophetic phrensy which shook every fibre in his frame.

"*Alahuma subahana hu !!*" was the cry which broke from him in an accent of the wildest grief and dismay ; "Woe! woe upon us, and our race—doomed, evil-doomed, to run the career of sorrow, and crime, and death! But what is death? happy were it only to die; but thou shalt live, oh child of Allah, predestined to slavery and sorrow,—live to feel many lingering deaths,—and ah, worse than deaths, the fear and the fate that shall surprise thee as a sudden storm midst the desolate hills. Ah! that blasted were my eyes, and life's ruddy current stopped at its fountain, so that I beheld not the triumphant genius of your fate,—the prince of terrors, the mightiest of chiefs over the powers of evil, who glows more freshly youthful and vigorous with time,—with toil and stratagem more unweariedly subtle and overreaching, with vengeance and hate but more eager in his thirst of blood. He triumphs, and will triumph,—Eblis, the dreaded Eblis,—the prince of the air ;—nor only of the air, but of the earth—the waters,—and the fires which are never quenched.

" Once I have beheld, and I now again behold him —exulting—on the wings of his death-winds—and through land, and sea, and air, hurrying with those wild huntsman's cries his shadowy steeds to their appointed goals of time. He hath reached us, and there he sits enthroned in dim, dread majesty over that sad funereal pile, on a throne of enduring and surpassing glory which proclaims him indeed a king —a crown that encircles eternal sovereignty—and in his hand a spear that levels the palmy splendour, and knighthood, and beauty of ages with the dust. Oh Eblis! my eye is upon thine—thy eye is upon us— upon us—for thou exultest in our approaching woe. Turn whither I will, thy hand is in every work,— thy foot upon every soil : the poison of thy spirit leaveneth the living mass of the world, and thy destruction keeps pace with creation in the great primeval impulse—the career of eternal doom.

" I behold thee busy in thy works while it is yet day ; and to thee night is the brightest of days, in which thou appearest in darker splendour —more fearfully terrific to the soul. I see, with recoiling eye, the dim shadow of the deed thou art now tracing in the soul and the brain of love's unhappy victim ; I see the steel—I hear the shriek—and to my eye and to my ear are present thy triumphant look, thy mocking laugh—heard above the appalling cry of ' Woe! woe to Granada !' and the night of ages of chains, and of tears, and of blood on blood." And with the same heart-sickening howl of despair as when he rushed into the crowd, he strangely disappeared from all eyes.

Then, as with searching glance and eager question they turn their faces from the symbols of death, another, nor less thrilling spectacle, burst upon their view. In weeds of pall—long sable mantles which swept the earth, came nigh in sad and dark array, the mournful procession of the condemned. Preceded by bands of those fierce Africans long devoted to Abdallah, it was led on by the judge and umpires of the lists. And next, surrounded by the few and faithful friends of her youth, and her weeping attendants—not one of whom had forsaken her, was seen the heart-stricken object of all that panoply of woe,—her lovely head bowed in sorrow too deep for tears, with pallid cheek, and wandering eye, and hands uplifted in the agony of prayer. On all sides the vast throngs, opening a path for the funereal car, bowed their heads in silence, not unmingled with grief and shame, as it passed the gates of the Viva Rambla and through the noble barriers into the open arena.

On drawing near the appointed spot, through ranks high overseen by ranks, till all Granada appeared spectatress of the stirring scene, the queen caught the sable hues and more terrific aspect of that funereal pile; and the deep shudder—and the recoil—followed by low stifled lamentations, ran with electric speed through every beholder of that revolting sight. With still slower and statelier pomp of woe, the restless champing steeds, in their darkly-splendid housings, now passed up the great square, and stood before the fatal scaffold, where the judges appeared to conduct the accused to a seat of state, high overhung with the

same startling symbols of guilt and woe.   As she was
borne by the heroic Muza to that fatal spot, and threw
herself on her knees before the assembled people,
as if appealing to Allah, and to his children, for
redress and pity of her heavy wrongs, the air rang
with cries and lamentations, succeeded by deep low
murmurs such as portend the coming storm.

The judges proclaim the fearful sentence; and
though the great Muza himself presides, he is answered
by maledictions and groans.   But again, on beholding
the unconscious form of the sultana, who lay supported in the arms of the princesses and the noble
daughter of Aben Kassim, having swooned in the
aspirations of heart-wrung prayer, there burst a sudden
peal of admiration and applause, as if to attest *their*
belief also in the innocence of their queen.   Every
eye bent on that heart-appealing group,—woman and
beauty in bitter peril and distress; and every hand
grasping the nearest weapon—one simultaneous impulse made them start to their feet; and the next
moment they had rushed, as an insulted brother,
to the rescue of innocence and honour, when the
loud-swelling note of Moorish clarions broke on the
ear and arrested their step, as their eye was caught by
other objects fraught with an interest equally intense.
Even the judges, seated near the queen, bent forward
as if eager to catch some responsive note of war.

Armed from head to foot, mounted on high-mettled
Andalusian chargers, and clothed in burnished armour,
over which flowed the loose albornoz, with sashes
richly embroidered, and dark waving plumes, rode the

stern accusers through the startled throngs, up to the very head of the lists. On their splendid shields, surmounted by two blood-stained swords, appeared emblazoned the words, "For the truth we draw them!" A noble band of their kinsmen and adherents attended them to their respective stations within the lists. Saluting the judges and umpires, they seemed to turn their eyes from their lovely victim, as they darted swiftly to their posts.

In the long, deep silence that ensued, when every ear was intent on catching the first faint echo of the Castilian bugles in the distance, you might have heard woman's softest foot-fall—the slightest murmur of the breeze rustling in the palm and cypress leaves above their heads.

Hours wore on—the uneasiness and excitement had risen into murmurs and threats—all eyes were bent on the barrier gates ; and yet, and yet—no champions of the lost queen appeared. Two brief hours, and the fire, in default of rescue, must claim its victim ; —and at length it went forth, in fearful, muttered sounds, that, absorbed in her despair, the sultana had cared not to apprise her defenders of the appointed time. All was confusion and distress ; and, on the spur of the moment, the noble judges, Muza Ben Gazan and his friends, Ali Fahar, Azarque, and Almoradi, conjured her to accept their swords. But confiding her cause to supreme justice, and eager only to rejoin her noble lover in death, she heeded not the proffer, nor the increasing confusion and dismay of the imauns, the judges, and spectators around her.

Q

Hope itself began to fail, for six of the eight appor-
tioned hours had now elapsed, and loud and louder
the pity of the people rose into lamentation and
threats. Already they began to measure, with kindling
eye and ready hand, the strength of those fierce bands
that environed the fatal scaffold; five times have the
judges, at the four quarters of the lists, summoned
aloud the champions, and are again conjuring the
accused to behold in them her defenders — eagerly
waving their gleaming scymitars as they confronted
the Zegris with threatening looks—when the tramp
of horse is heard rapidly nearing the Spanish gate.
One shout of exultation—one rush of eager throngs,
and every spectator's eye bent towards the extreme
verge of the open barriers, attested the intense interest
awakened by the sound.

And soon, in full career, bounded four Turkish
horsemen into the spacious square. One of them,
reining in his fiery barb before the judges, addressed
himself to their chief, requesting permission to parley
with the accused lady of the lists. Kneeling at her
feet, he informed her, that he and his companions
were from the towers of Stamboul, in quest of adven-
ture; and having just put foot in the land of old
Moorish fame, to try their prowess on some of the
heroes of Castile, had heard of that strange solemnity, and first preferred to break their lances with the
enemies of peerless charms and pure fame, like hers.
It was their first essay of arms, he continued, and
as he spoke, he dropped into her lap the letter she
had sent to the Lord of Carthagena; for he it was,

attended by the famed Ponce de Leon, d'Aguilar, and Diego di Cordova, rejoiced thus to avail themselves of so noble an occasion to prove their chivalrous devotion at the appeal of innocence and beauty. Each of the combatants now stood confronting the Zegri he had selected as his opponent, with fixed eye and deadly lance in rest.

The judges having solemnly declared the queen's acceptance of their swords, commanded the twenty clarions to sound the charge. Furious was the onset, and long doubtful the result. The Lord of Carthagena at length bore the fierce Mahandon Gomel from his seat; Ponce de Leon wounded Ali Hammed El Zegri, while Don Alonzo, with equal fortune, overthrew and bound the arch traitor, Mohammed Zegri, the mover of that fatal plot. But Don Diego di Cordova was still engaged to disadvantage with the gigantic and terrible Moctader and would have fallen, when his gallant rival, Alonzo, rushed to his rescue; then, presenting his dagger to the throat of El Zegri, he called upon him to reveal the origin of the foul conspiracy, and to speak truly if he wished to live.

It was then El Zegri made confession, that private hate and jealousy had led him to associate in the dark design his brethren of the tribe, and to conspire against the queen's honour in order more effectually to compass the destruction of their great rivals, and win the exclusive favour of King Abdallah. Acquitting the injured sultana of all stain or reproach with his dying breath, the unhappy Zegri motioned with his hand to the king, and, with an upbraiding look and heavy sigh, as he gazed round on his companions, he expired.

But the presiding judge had taken his deposition, which he now proclaimed aloud, amidst thunders of applause. All prepared to celebrate the proud event of the queen's vindication and the detection of the conspirators with unrestrained festivity and exultation, as some relief from the anxiety and terrors of the day,—bursting into fresh plaudits as they beheld the court advance to escort her in triumph to the Alhambra. Deeply impressed with the result of this strange appeal, not less than by the voice of the people, the really penitent Abdallah fell at the feet of his injured consort, attempting with tears at once to atone for his faults, and to merit her forgiveness.

The action called forth reiterated applauses on every side—momentarily changed into shrieks of despair, as they saw the sudden gleam of steel, which as suddenly vanished, sheathed in the bosom of the beautiful object of their regard. One cry of fearful surprise, as she saw the monarch at her feet—one recoiling shudder—and the flashing dagger, seen but a moment in her hand, drank the pure life-blood of her heart. Murmuring the name of her fallen Abencerrage, and casting on that king, as he stood with blanched cheek and startled soul, the same wild reproachful look as the dying Zegri, she sank to rest in the arms of her weeping, youthful friends, amidst general sorrowing and lamentations, which recalled the strange santon's prophecy;—his threat of fast-hurrying doom.

But their grief and indignation were forcibly recalled

to other objects; a fleet, under the renegade prince, Alnayar, swept the coast of Adra, and with that treachery inherent in the soul of the apostate-traitor, he displayed the flag of his country. The inhabitants, in hourly expectation of relief from Africa, and shouting with exultation as they beheld the Moorish signals and costume, hurried to open their port; while his father, the Cid Yahia, rushed upon the city from the land. Startled by this two-fold treason of their countrymen, the garrison and inhabitants were for a moment thunderstruck; then, flying to arms, sold their lives and freedom dearly to their more than infidel destroyers. Castel-Ferruh, numerous towns of the insurgent Alpuxarras, and the territories of the departed El Zagal, shared the same ignoble fate; while the Castilian conqueror, with his whole united strength, bore down with increasing fury for the third time upon the heroic and devoted capital.

The strong castle of Roma, within two leagues' distance, fell a prey to the foul treachery of Ferdinand and his new allies. A Moorish force, with Christian captives, as if pursued by a superior enemy, made its appearance before the gates. At the sight of turbans and scymitars, the sentinels flew to the summons of a noble chief, loudly knocking for admittance. Once in possession of the courts and battlements, the shout of the tributary Moors gave signal of the attack of the Prince Yahia and his faithless followers. The keys of the castle were handed to Ferdinand, as the first offering of the dishonoured slave at the new shrine of his perfidious saint of Castile; while the bitter scoffs and maledictions of Granada fell loudly upon his head.

Abdallah could with difficulty believe that the plaudits with which he was welcomed were meant for him ; but after treason of so black a dye, he appeared with the heroic Muza, as the great champion of their liberties. When they saw him glittering in arms by the side of their beloved chief, throngs of hardy followers from the mountains and the cities hurried to his standard, and the great square of the Viva Rambla glowed with the legions of swelling chivalry, till they spread far up the spacious avenues and along the banks of the Darro. The whole region was filled with the din of war,——the shrill notes of the clarion, and the deep muffled thunder of the tambour announcing that the old tribes and families marshalled by the great Muza, and led by Abdallah, were marching to meet the deadly foe in the open plain. With forty thousand infantry, and ten of horse, Ferdinand had encamped at two leagues only from Granada, near the fountains of Guetar. For thirty years had the ravages of the Vega continued unavenged, and from the mountains of Elvira came the retiring sound of the Castilian trumpets, as the last booty was borne from its once blooming tracts. Near the Alpuxarra mountains rose the formidable castle of Alhendin, commanded by the valiant Mendo de Quexada, in a position extremely perilous for Granada. It was now become a continual source of annoyance and loss ; and once in the field, Muza fell upon it with tremendous vigour, resolved, spite of its massy walls, to carry it by assault. The governor beheld his brave garrison perish at his side, and it was only when it was about to be blown into a heap of ruins that he surrendered to the Moorish king. As the victorious chief directed his arms against the fortresses of Marchena and Bulduy, the bold mountaineers, marking his banners in the field and roused by the zeal of their dervishes and faquirs, hastened to swell the number of his ranks. Convoys and supplies were intercepted, ambushes and forays were renewed amid the hills and sierras, and the strong-hold of Alcalà la Real had nearly fallen by a *coup-de-main*.

Still Muza held the field, and the redoubtable seaport of Salobreña on its rocky heights, commanding a noble and fertile region, was the next object of the Moor's attack. Advancing by forced marches upon the place, he surprised and drove the garrison into the citadel, while the inhabitants rose in a mass on beholding the still faithful champions of their country. The governor of Velez Malaga and Fernando Pulgar, famed for his exploits, summoned the frontier forces to its relief; but beheld the Moor seated in possession of the town, with one solitary ensign of Castile displayed from the walls of the castle keep. At the dead of night, the Moorish camp was assailed by Pulgar at the head of a veteran body, part of which fought its way into the citadel, enabling it to protract its defence, till the arrival of Ferdinand at the head of an immense force threatened to cut off the Moorish communications with the capital. After a furious assault, Muza, with the skill of an experienced leader, turned the position of the enemy, and then striking at the dominions of the Prince Yahia and his son, Alnayar, he overthrew their commanders, and destroyed their chief fortresses. Taking ample vengeance for the desolation of Granada's plains and hamlets, he pursued his fearful career through the mountain-districts of the foe, till, enriched with spoil and treasure, he led his army through the defiles of the Alpuxarras to the gates of the capital.

After this brilliant march, in which he had foiled some of the ablest generals of Ferdinand, the grateful Abdallah addressing him as he stood surrounded by the chiefs and the people :—" You, you alone, are the last stay of the empire ; you and your generous soldiers can wash out our common injuries in the blood of the infidel ; restore its glory to our religion, its dignity to the throne, peace and honour to your wives, and hope to yourselves and your children. Oh Muza ! be thou then our dictator ; you and your honoured chiefs direct all your energies to the salvation of Granada,—the existence of our name and country."

On the instant the brave Muza justified the high eulogy of his monarch ; he distributed the several commands and stations with equal promptness and judgment, going rapidly into the resources and details of a defensive war. He himself assumed the most perilous post of directing the main sorties against the invader, with the valiant Redovan and Mohammed Ben Zaida at the head of their fierce squadrons. The bold prince Almanzor, the half-brother of the king, still led on the foot, while the terrible Zegri, Abdel Kerim, was to hold possession of the battlements. To

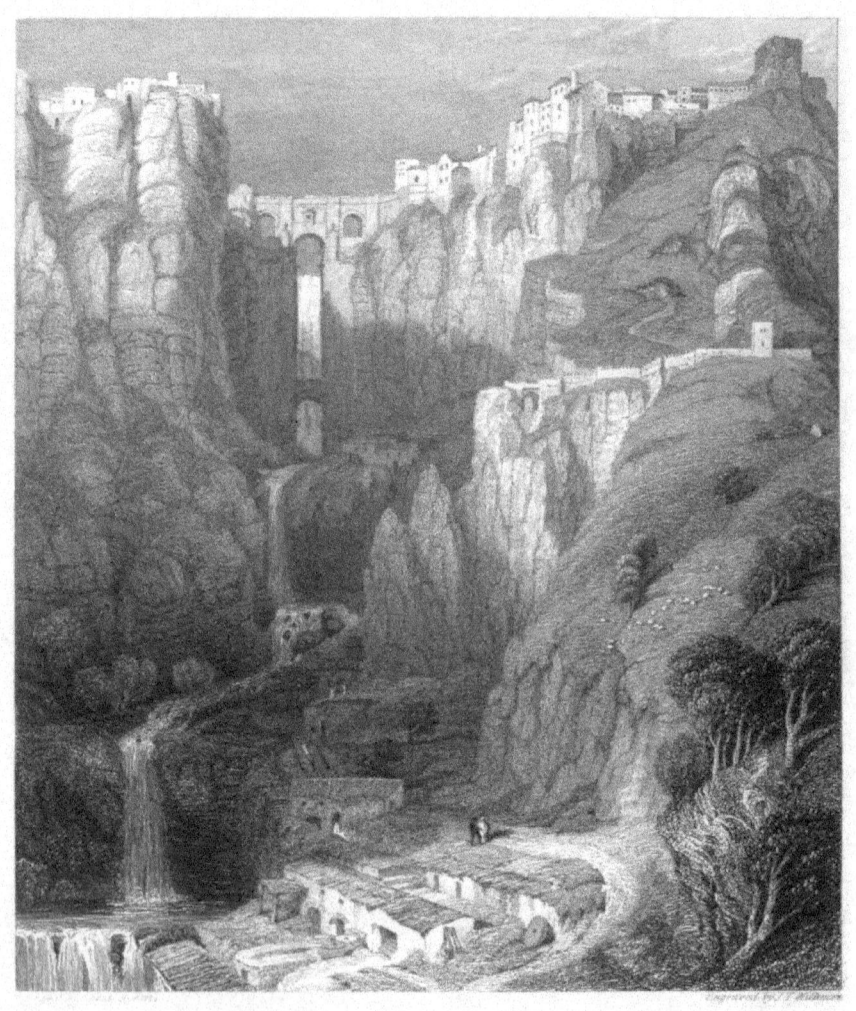

THE BRIDGE OF RONDA.

London, Published Oct 20 1837 by Robert Jennings & Co 62 Cheapside

Drawn by David Roberts.
Engraved by J.T. Willmore.
Printed by Lloyd & Hastings.

each governor of mark and likelihood was assigned
some particular fort, or tower, or quarter of the
capital. The munitions of war and the supplies,
next engaged his attention ; for to all minds it became
evident that the long-predicted, fearful siege was close
at hand. To the entire citizens, as well as soldiers,
offices of labour, of trust, and honour were appointed;
for at such a crisis every inhabitant is a soldier and a
patriot. It was decreed that on each day three thousand
veterans should issue forth under the eye of Mohammed Sahir Ben Atar, son of the old alcayde, his equal
in valour, surpassing him in consummate prudence;
and under his guard, with five hundred bold pioneers,
the supplies were to reach the city. The whole of
these arrangements, conceived with wisdom, were long
executed with heroic firmness. While Muza by his
terrific sorties,——for his great enemy had now enclosed
him with overwhelming numbers,——drew upon him the
full vigour of the enemy, the supplies and provisions
were gallantly escorted by the veteran Atar into the
capital. Many were the fierce skirmishes, the deadly
hostile encounters with intercepting detachments of
the foe, in the hills of the Alpuxarras and the moun-
tain-passes of the great Serranea di Ronda.* Often
was the contest for the bridge of the ruined town
renewed, till the echoes of the Moorish horn and
the shouts of the horsemen reach the camp of the
Spaniards and rouse many a sortie from Granada
to prevent his sending more aid to the mountains.

* See description of Plate, p. 131.

To such a height, indeed, was carried the confidence of the Moors in their great leader, that during many months of the stern siege, the gates of the Elvira and the Xenil remained constantly open. In the various rencounters, Ferdinand saw that the Moslems had the advantage, that he experienced tremendous losses by the sudden, vigorous sorties of their squadrons; and he was compelled not only to throw up fresh lines of intrenchments, raise fresh camps, but at length actually to build a town in the vega to protect his troops, and issue orders for none to venture forth without directions. It was then the high spirit of Muza inspired his troops to carry the war into the Christian intrenchments, inflicting severer loss than if the wily invader had made a gallant stand before the walls. Poor was the triumph when he began to surround his camp with solid walls and enormous ditches, till from the height of their new battlements they could better withstand the fierce shock of the Moorish sorties. Muza saw that it was the scythe of time on which Ferdinand relied as his great arm of war, and with a people like the Moors, how much were tactics like his to be dreaded! Their warlike ardour and exploits would fail for lack of fuel; and he now bent his active genius to mature some counter-plan, to foil the deep-plotting monarch at his own weapons. His vast influence rendered the attempt practicable, for it was no less than to besiege the invader in his new town of Santa Fe, and storm his very intrenchments.

Having marshalled the entire strength of Granada, he led his squadrons forth, and took up a position in

the open plain. Soon the shrill clarions and the heavy
rolling tambours gave note of the furious onset, but
his gallant enemy anticipating Muza's design, threw
an immense force into the intervening space, as if
eager to show it was no craven spirit which held
them within the precincts of their camp. The Castilians sustained the attack with firmness; fresh troops
were deployed on both sides, and the ravaged vega
became an arena of deadly and persevering conflict, in
which the chiefs brought all of skill and heroism to
their aid which could influence the dread decision of
the battle. The soul of Muza rose at the sight of the
Christians pouring into the plain, and the hot blood
of the Moors caught the heroic infection from their
leaders as they renewed each fierce assault. Terrific
was the shock of the hostile squadrons, as with the old
war-shout of *Allah illah Allah!* the Moors dashed
with the desperate energy of despairing patriotism into
the thickest ranks of the foe. The conflict became
general; all the spirit, and every stratagem of Moorish
warfare was displayed by the noble Muza; the attack,
the retreat, and the sudden onset during their Parthian
flight which annihilated the heroes, no regular battle
could subdue. Thus during the bitterest fury of the
action, the squadron headed by the chief himself,
suddenly turned and fled; when the next moment the
thunder of the Moorish artillery fell on the Castilian
horse in wild pursuit, and the new-formed squadron
charged them, half-broken and dispersed, with redoubled
vigour. The Spaniards fell back on the battalions
of Ponce de Leon; who, with the answering cry of

Santiago! rushed forward to their support. Enraged at having the victory thus snatched from their hands, the Moors exerted a more firm, persevering valour,— for brilliant it ever was, than had yet stood the brunt of the veteran charges of the Spanish infantry, so superior to that of their fiery foe. Nor was Muza alone; the king was every where to be seen in the action, bringing up successive charges of his African guards with a spirit not unworthy the eye of a Tarikh, or the bravest of the old khaliphs. Nor did his half-brother, Almanzor, less fulfil the duties of a true Moslem, exerting the noblest efforts to form, to rally, and to hold his wavering infantry firm before the face of the foe. In this awful suspense, the Christian monarchs knelt absorbed in prayer, in which they were joined by their court, the confessors, courtiers, and priests, headed by the aged and saintly archbishop, while his mitred brother of Jaen was as fervently engaged with the weapons of the flesh. Notwithstanding his heroic efforts, the resources of his genius and skill, and nobly supported as he was by the squadrons and tribes, the dawning victory of Muza was suddenly clouded by reverse.

Opposed to overwhelming numbers, and not equally seconded by the Moorish foot, he could not prevent the enemy from rallying and gradually extending their line so as to threaten his communication with the capital. He had more than achieved the action of a brilliant sortie, and still maintained the field, when his infantry, seized with a sudden panic, turned and fled. In vain did their princely leader, and the faquirs and santons who had mingled in their ranks, strive to incite them anew; some rushed headlong into the city, others to conceal themselves in the hills and woods. So strange and instantaneous was the terror which fell upon them, that the Christian prelates did not fail to ascribe it to the prayers of their sovereigns, rather than the arm of their lusty chivalry in the field.

And now, with feelings of indignation against his countrymen he sought not to repress, Muza was compelled to return within the gates of the capital, still, however, presenting a wall of scymitars in his disdain to close them upon the insulting foe. Though deeply incensed, Muza was never depressed; and Granada, the last retreat of Moorish honour and high-bred chivalry, assumed a yet bolder attitude in the day of her despair. Still fiercer sorties upon the intrenched camp, carrying its defences, and scattering slaughter and dismay through the interior works, marked the unsubdued heroism of Muza and his squadrons. Reiterated orders to avoid all skirmishes and partial engagements proved the terror which the Moorish horse inspired, while the arrival of Isabella and the court at the newly erected city of the Faith, evinced on the other hand, an obstinate determination to weary and starve out the patience of the heroic foe.

The Christian camp was one scene of exultation and festival, as the queen rode forth to survey the field; but the shouts were re-echoed in as loud a strain of defiance, while the gallant chief, turning to his young and fiery squadrons,—" Now I know you will fight," he cried, " for if we lose the ground we stand upon,

we must henceforth cease to possess a country or a
name." Then breaking through the intrenchments,
assaulting the suburbs of the Holy Faith, and casting
insulting challenges into the heart of the camp, he so
roused the Castilian blood, that spite of Ferdinand's
anger, he drew numbers into the open plain, who
mostly fell victims to their temerity, and the skill and
bravery of the Moslem chief. Often skirring the intervening field in sudden fiery clouds of horse, he
dashed up to the very barriers, and it was a trial of
prowess who could farthest send his javelin into the
interior of the camp. On it was fixed some challenge,
or other insulting missive, intended to provoke the
parties to come forth, and abide the shock of spears.

In these chivalrous encounters, none acquired a
more brilliant name than Prince Almanzor, the African
chief, Allamar; and yet more than all, a young chief
of the hardy Berbers, the most gallant of all the tribes
of the desert. Hassan Omar Fahar almost rivalled the
fame of Antar in his father's ancient tribe—bold as
that of Abs or of Adnan——being at once their shield
and their terrible spoiler of the neighbouring foe. But
when the African monarchs sent aid to their Moorish
allies, the "lion-facer" Omar was among the foremost
to lead his band to the southern shores of the beloved
Granada. Nor did he depart alone; the high-souled
heroine of his love, unlike the more timid Ibla of the
slave-warrior,——bred to hardy exploits in the chase of
the panther and the lion,——clothed herself in dazzling
arms, and vowed to share the fortunes of her lover
and her countrymen in the great Moorish wars. After

many brilliant efforts in the field, where they fought
side by side, the beautiful and heroic Zaida, spite of
her Omar's sword, became a captive of the Castilian
foe.   She fell into an ambush laid by the alcayde of
Loxa, who bore her to his citadel; and struck with
her lofty charms, refused all ransom, resolving to take
advantage of his fortune.   Her lover, equally bent
upon her rescue, approached the place in the dead of
night, disguised as a Spanish cavalier.   On his path he
met a knight; it was the device and armour of the
hated governor himself.   Swift as a whirlwind, Hassan
rushed upon his foe; who, after a brief struggle, lay
dead at his feet.   He loosed his morion, and the face
and flowing tresses of his own Arab maid met his view.
She had assassinated the governor in his secret cham-
ber, on the couch where he lay; and taking his armour
and pass-word, issued unmolested through the gates.

Next among the Moors who greatly signalized himself at these adventurous feats, was the powerful and
high-spirited Tarfe.   On one occasion he daringly
urged his charger over the barriers, and traversing the
Christian camp like the wind, actually hurled his
lance at the royal pavilion; and ere the fleetest of his
enemies could intercept his path, he had again cleared
them in the same chivalrous style.   On the javelin
being drawn from the earth, it appeared from the mes-
sage attached to it, that it was intended for the life of
the queen.

The indignation of the Castilian lords was now
extreme, and hardly to be repressed.   Fernando del
Pulgar, sirnamed from his exploits, made a vow not

to be out-bravadoed by the fiery Moor. He first beat up for some companions in the perilous undertaking on which he was bent; and having found them, he issued from the camp in the dead of night, and brought them to a low postern gate, guarded by foot soldiers, and looking out upon the Darro. While his companions engaged the guards, their leader rode in, and rushed at full speed through the streets of the city. At the entrance to the great mosque he first drew bit, sprang from his steed, and affixing the names of Ferdinand and Isabella on the portal, offered it to the Virgin, by a tablet nailed upon the door inscribed with "*Ave Maria*." The sudden act, and the astonishment at beholding a Christian warrior riding through the city, were favourable to his escape; and being seconded by his brethren in arms, he fought his way back, and was received with acclamation by the whole army.

What was the exasperation of the Moors, on next entering the holy mosque, to mark the sacrilegious insult nailed by a dagger to its doors! and to such a height did the spirit of chivalrous rivalry and honour, —of religion and of country proceed, that seldom a day passed over without being marked by some splendid action, some rare feat of arms, of devotion and magnanimity on the side of the unfortunate Moors, surpassed by nothing in the whole compass of Greek or Roman annals.

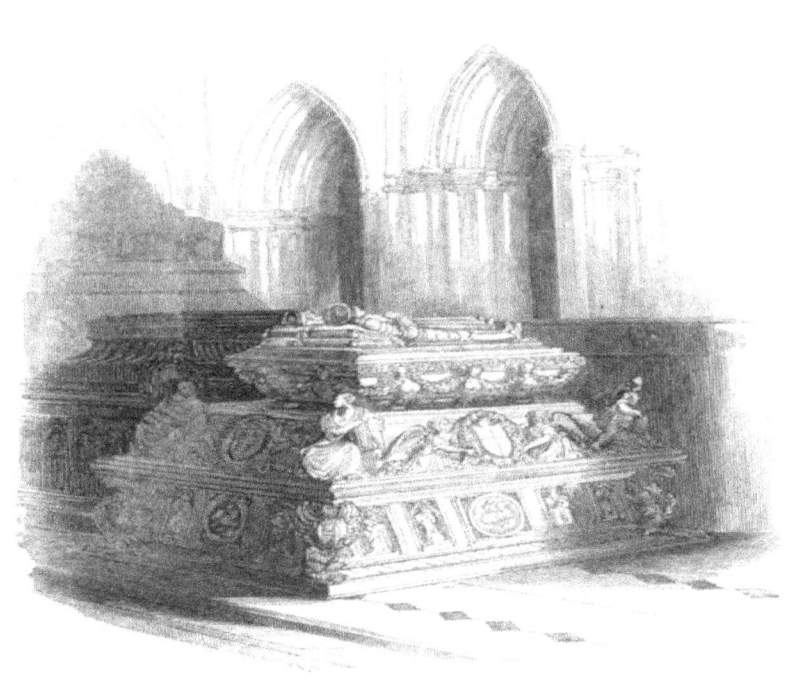

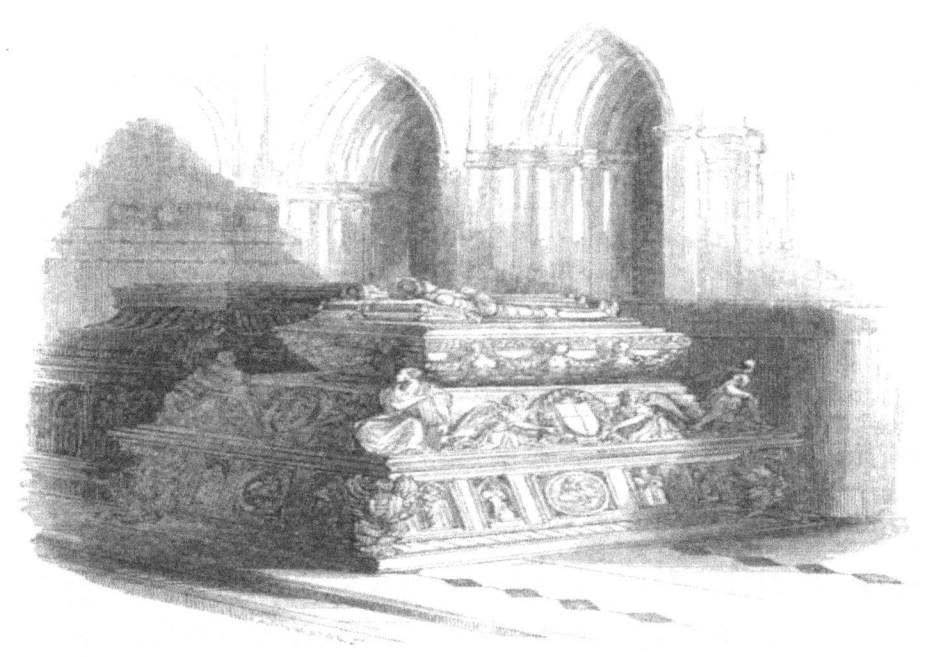

CHAPTER X.

Tyrant of man! imperious Fate!
   I bow before thy dread decree,
Nor hope in this uncertain state
   To find a seat secure from thee.

Think not the stream will backward flow,
   Or cease its destined course to keep;
As soon the blazing spark shall glow
   Beneath the surface of the deep.

ALY BEN MOHAMMED.

NEVER had unanimity and concord, such as now absorbed all hearts, been known to prevail in the Moorish capital. No longer confined to threats and

R

perils, the actual presence of fearful, impending
doom awoke that instinctive strength of desperation,
which makes the final struggle noble and heroic,
and life itself resigned with less regret in acts of
honour, devotedness, and courage. It is then, as the
guardian of some treasured trust,——of past fame,——
home, religion, and country, with all their associations
of time and circumstance, and some one dear spot
loved and revered beyond every other,——that the
patriot, like the martyr, glories in the fires of adversity with which he ascends into a purer and brighter
sphere ; for well he knows that the crown of true
honour, like truth, is eternal in the heavens,——that
nobility of the soul renews its lustre through all
time,——that the actions of the just and good " smell
sweet and blossom in the dust." And Granada prepared to undergo that fierce ordeal of nations which
precedes their fall,——her spirit strung to that high tone
of honoured martyrdom which buoyed up the elastic
soul, and spoke in every word and deed of the fearless Muza. He stood as one raised above the lowlier
impulses, the trials, and anxieties of our common
nature, with the looks and bearing of an Abdiel,
" faithful among the unfaithful found,"——the fortitude of the hero who eyes death as the last of vulgar
evils which falls to the lot of all, but which he, with
better fortune, can meet in the arms of glory,——on the
field of the generous brave who fall for their own,
their native land. Such was the high resolve of
Muza, which seemed to give him a charmed life, and
renewed elasticity and fire from every reverse. Dread

alone of him and his squadrons still held the crafty
Ferdinand at a distance, after months had rolled away
since the sword of yon white pavilions round that
usurping city of the vega,* had shorn the glowing
region of its strength, its wide blooming beauty,—
rearing on high that fearful symbol of persecution,
the fierce torturing cross,—as the dread precursor of
a people's doom.

Never had the capital of a powerful empire been
invested with greater fear and circumspection,—
clearly evincing the respect and almost awe with
which the Castilian monarchs gradually approached
the completion of their long and eagerly pursued
ambition. Only dimly could the form of Granada,
and the variegated lights of her spires and towers, be
discerned from the distance of leagues, in the respect-
ful position of the beleaguering towns and camps; and
when the royal personages moved forth to behold the
loveliest and most glorious of the imperial queens
that had exacted slave-tribute and homage from their
predecessors, they were defended by legions of armed
warriors, led forth in battle array to meet any sudden,
unseen stratagem of the fiery foe. Splendid too
and battle-proof was the princely cavalcade, as Queen
Isabel approached the gentle eminence near Zubia, on
the left of the city, to gain a view of the Alhambra.
Alonzo d'Aguilar, Marquis Villena, Count Ureña,
took up strong positions along the mountain-skirts
which commanded the hamlet; while Ponce de Leon,

* The town of Santa Fe.

the Count de Tendilla, Alonzo Fernandez, drew up their lines in the space below.   From the village thus environed with the strength of war, the Castilian court gazed with awe on the gorgeous towers of the Alhambra, and that long line of fortresses which cast a darker shadow on the doomed city of the infidel foe.

The gallant Moors, beholding this splendid parade of courtly chivalry and war, imagined it was a challenge; and bodies of Moorish horse swept through the gates of the capital magnificently arrayed,——the whole flower of Granada's youth, and at the head of these glittering squadrons rode their indefatigable chief.   At a distance followed the infantry——bodies of arquebuse and spearsmen,——of the artillery and the cross-bow, supported by the heavy armed troopers.

Suddenly, while the hostile squadrons gathered in stern array, surveying each other with flashing eyes eager for the dread appeal, there burst a shout of exulting joy; and a single horseman armed at all points rode out of the Moorish ranks, and careered along the lines of the Christian host.   Of towering height, his huge buckler, his long javelin, his Damascus blade and rich-gemmed dagger,——all proclaimed him a knight of no common note.   Soon the whisper ran that he it was who launched his rejōn at the queen's pavilion, with that insulting missive. Dragged in the dust at his charger's tail, was seen the Christian label affixed by the brave Pulgar to the portal of the grand mosque.   But burning as the Castilians did to avenge this indignity upon their religion and their honour, the queen, impelled less by

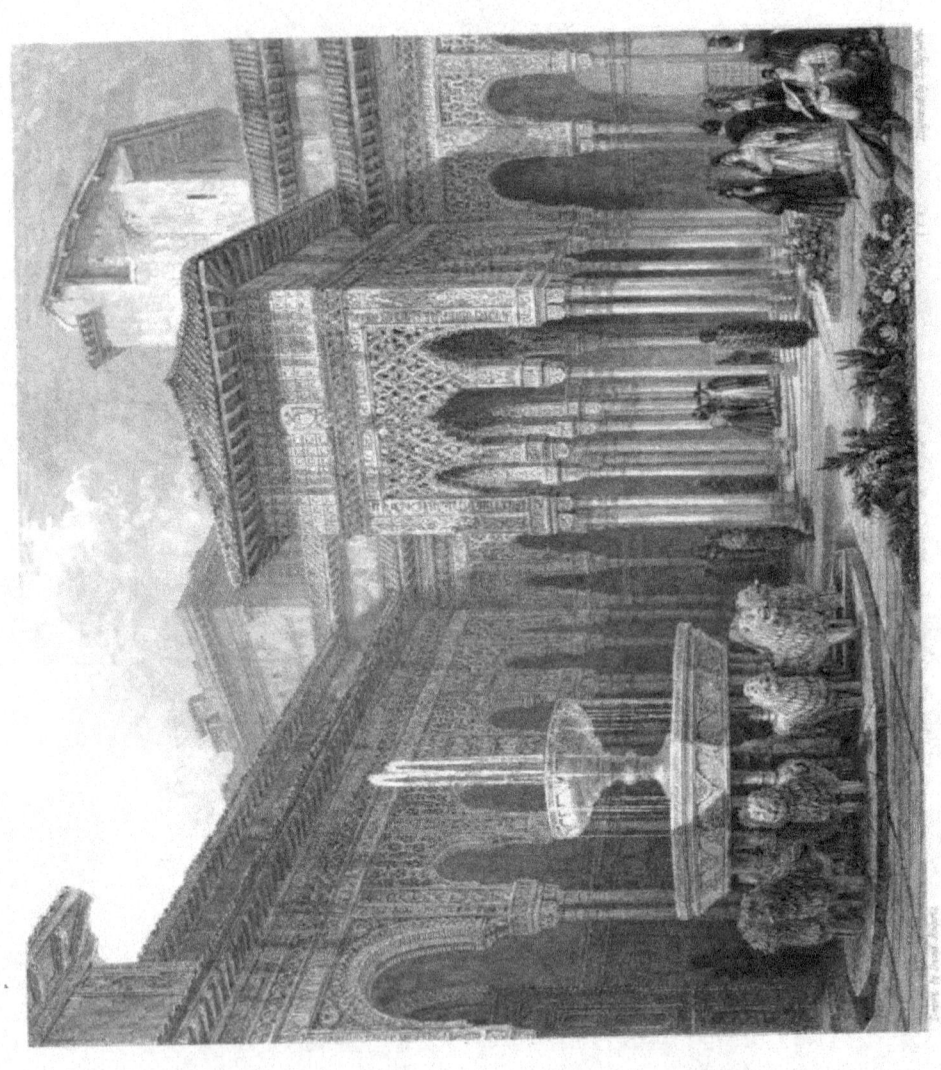

terror than by humanity, for she was heroic and
pious as her consort was crafty and insincere, had
given special command that no Spanish cavalier
should dare to provoke the attack.

Still, on beholding this bitter insult, the young
hero of the famed house of Lara, threw himself at
Isabella's feet, to solicit one exception in behalf of
their honour and their religion. It was granted; and
little dreamed the chivalrous Pulgar, as he lingered in
disguise at the cool umbrageous fountain of the Court
of Lions * with the Moorish lady of his love, that at

* The feeling of astonishment excited on first entering the
Alhambra, and crossing the court of the great bath with its
parterre of flowers and orange trees, is mingled with admiration and delight on beholding the palace-region of the Lions
and its splendid halls. A spacious oblong court, exceeding a
hundred feet in length by half as many wide, it is environed
with a noble sweep of colonnades seven feet broad and ten at
each of the ends. Two elegant porticoes at the extremities
project into the court, which is lined with coloured tiles, extending five feet from the ground, curiously inwrought in
blue and yellow. Both above and below runs a border of
escutcheons of blue and gold enamel, bearing the old Arabic
inscription, " There is no conqueror but God." The columns
supporting the corridors and roof are slight and delicate, the
peristyles adorned with a fantastic display of arabesques, knots
and festoons of flowers. They are about nine feet in height,
taking the base and capital, and irregularly disposed; in
general, two together. The arches above in the usual horse-
shoe form are four feet in the larger, and three in the lesser
spaces. The ceiling of the portico is a splendid exhibition of
the elaborate genius and intricate combinations of Moslem
art. The stucco ornaments are laid on with unrivalled skill;
the delicacy with which it is frosted in the handling of the
ceiling boasting intricate beauties altogether inimitable. The
capitals are of various design, richly decorated; but in the

that moment his youthful friend, so beloved for his martial hymns and soul-moving songs, was flying to the
encounter of the terrific Tarfe,—resistless as the thunderbolt in the single conflicts of that dread campaign.
As his fiery steed appeared to devour the ground; as
he flew to confront the proud insulting Moor, that
fierce Moslem, turning at the thundering sound, uttered
a shout of derision, caught up by his horsemen, as
he heard the purpose of the Castilian youth.   But
careering his steed with surpassing grace and power,
the Castilian gave little space for their idle taunts,

infinite diversity of its foliages and grotesques, there is
remarked not the slightest imitation of animal life.   The
arabesques around the arches have those borders, or rims,
appropriated to the usual purpose of eulogy, or moral and
religious inscriptions, chiefly in the Cufic character.   Arranged
round the centre of the splendid court are the figures of the
twelve lions, which support an enormous alabaster basin,
formed of a single slab, superbly decorated, out of which rises
another of smaller dimensions.   From this there perpetually
sprung an immense volume of water, which, being received in
vast aerial falls of fantastic yet symmetric forms into the
greater basin, thence passed through the lions, issuing forth
again at their mouths.   It lastly fell into a large reservoir,
which communicated by channels with the lesser cascades and
fountains of the surrounding apartments.   Round the sides
of solid white marble, richly carved and festooned, appear
among others the following mottoes :—

   " Seest thou how the waters flow copiously as the Nile ?"
   " This resembles a sea washing over its shores, threatening shipwreck
to the mariner."
   " This water runs so abundantly to give drink to the lions."
   " Terrible as the lion is our king in the day of battle."
   " The Nile gives glory to the king, and the lofty mountains proclaim it."
   " This garden is fertile in delights; God takes care that no noxious
animal shall approach it."

It has been supposed that this singular fountain was designed

and met the shock of his gigantic foe more than half
way over the ground. Shivered were their lances;
but sorely struck as he was, young Lara held his
saddle. As his steed careered anew ere he could
resume the attack, the Christians trembled for their
youthful champion, and the name of Pulgar was
bruited about the field, as the anxious squadrons
gazed with intense interest on the fearful odds. In
their next shock, they met with brandished falchions,
and the Moslem swept with the rapidity of a sand-
storm round his opponent, and every moment ap-

to imitate the brazen sea, one of the vanities of King Solomon,
which he ordered to be placed in the temple of Jerusalem.
　Of the stucco-work of the court, it is observed by Mr.
Murphy, " that the portion which is out of the reach of
hands is beautifully clean and white. Not a single spider's
web, nor insect of any kind, could the author discover in any
part of the court; while the stucco-work executed by order of
later kings was decayed and covered with cob-webs in various
parts." The wood work of the Arabs is also known to continue
free from worms and insects of every kind. Indeed no portion
of this truly royal fortress conveys a more complete idea of its
original beauty and magnificence, or appears to have suffered
less from the ravages of time. Still, in the centre, the tourist
beholds the fountain so long famed in song and story, and
listens to the murmurs of its waters. The alabaster basins still
shed their crystal drops, and the twelve lions which support
them cast forth their sparkling streams as in the days of the
last Moorish king. He still traces the same court laid out in
beds of flowers, surrounded by light Arabian arcades of open
filigree-work, supported by the same slender pillars of white
marble. The architecture too, like that of all other parts of
the palace, is characterised by elegance rather than grandeur;
and one side of the court, richly adorned in the same style
of elaborate art, opens into the lofty Hall of the Abencerrages,
with its white marble pavement.

peared as if it were his last.   But fast though the
flashing strokes succeeded each other, they were as skil-
fully and nobly parried; nor could his sharp-tempered
Damascus find an entrance through the double-
folded shield of Flemish handicraft, borne by his
youthful rival.   Soon the blood was seen streaming
down the armour of both; but the young gallant Lara
evidently retreated, having recourse in vain to his
utmost skill and coolness to counteract the superior
powers of the Moor.   Often indeed he rallied, and stood
up to his enemy with a storm of blows; more than
once he drew blood, yet every one saw he was the
weaker and more exhausted of the two.   Aware of his
advantage, Tarfe seized on him, and with iron grasp
dragged him from his saddle: but he clung to his foe,
and both rolled from their steeds upon the earth,—the
Castilian beneath his enemy.   Ere he could rise, the
Moor bounded from the ground after a fearful struggle,
and as the other rose to his knee, planted his foot
upon his breast, and hurling him back, brandished his
dagger to strike at his throat.

A cry of horror rose from every Christian spectator,
followed by a fiercer shout as Fernando del Pulgar
rushed breathlessly towards the spot.   He appeared,
as it were, just in time to witness the last terrific blow,
the expiring effort of his young-loved hero, which he
was seen to make as the dagger reached his throat.
At that instant the Moor loosened his fearful grasp,—
his arm fell,—his whole frame rocked and heaved,—
and then with the heavy, sullen sound of collapsing
death, he lay a lifeless heap upon the plain.

On closer examination, the thin keen dagger, bound by a golden chain round the wrist of the Castilian was found, snapped from its hold, slumbering in the bosom of the giant-Moslem.   At this sight, Muza, apprehensive of its impression on the troops, bade the trumpets sound a charge, and assaulted the division of Don Alonzo d'Aguilar.   In the conflict which ensued, the brilliant Muza and his squadrons charged and drove back the enemy into the very intrenchments; and had the Moorish foot shown half the spirit against the Spanish infantry, victory had not long remained undecided.   Perceiving the foot again wavering and giving way, Muza, covering their retreat with his dauntless squadron, retired slowly into the gates.   The queen and court were full of gratitude for this fortunate termination of their terrors.   The former made a vow on the spot to raise at Zubia a monastery to St. Francis; * while the chivalrous leaders gallantly attributed their triumph to the prayers of beauty and royalty in distress.

Ferdinand, after these partial successes, resolved to deprive the unhappy Moors of their yet unravaged

* This monastery is known still to exist, and in its garden is pointed out a laurel said to have been planted by the hands of majesty itself.   The house, too, from which the sovereigns viewed the battle, has not hitherto been destroyed.   According to that agreeable modern chronicler,—Washington Irving, it is in the first street to the right, when you enter the village from the vega, and the royal arms are painted on the ceilings. It is inhabited by a worthy farmer, Francisco Garcia, who in showing the house, refuses all compensation with true Spanish pride; offering, on the contrary, the hospitalities of his mansion to the stranger.

portion of the vega, by laying waste the whole of the
pleasure-grounds, gardens, and orchards which clothed
the sides of its two crystal rivers.   The autumn of
this wild, exterminating campaign, was drawing nigh ;
seven months had the beleaguered capital been thus
closely invested, and, save from the towers and battlements of the Alhambra, the banners of the cross every
where waved over the last kingdom of the Moor.
Still more desperate efforts were anticipated, as it
approached the closing night of its predicted doom.
The royal victor and his chiefs beheld the gathering
clouds and shadows of its destiny with anxiety not
unmixed with apprehension, like daring mariners about
to tempt some dark and unknown sea.   Still were
they onward borne by the impulse of mighty events,
which made them appear less like actors than mortal
agents in the fearful drama enacting before their eyes;
the final act which consigned the world-dictating empire of Mohammed to the insatiate tomb of conquerors,
and creeds, and kings.

As the Moslem crescent waned in the heavens before
the glorious light of the cross, the minds of men were
impressed with a mysterious feeling of solemnity and
awe at the extent of the eventful changes now in progress.   It was displayed in the more frequent councils,
and still oftener recurring ceremonies and celebrations
of religious faith.   With all its pompous and spiritual
observances, were conjoined those of an expiring chivalry, and the savage, iron institutes of religious hatred
and persecution by which it was to be replaced.   The
Christian camp, now constantly under arms, prepared

to meet the new contingencies and vicissitudes of the war, from whatever quarter they might arise.

Nor were the apprehensions of change of fortune, or some sudden reverse, unfounded. In the depth of night, amidst the silence and repose of the vast, wide-spreading camps, with their white pavilions glittering round the city of the Faith,—amidst all the splendours and luxuries of regal residence and sway,—the cry of fire went through the tents of the besieger, and soon the whole scene of the spacious vega was illuminated with the unnatural vividness of death-fires, which cast their baneful hues over tower, and hill, and stream. It rose with more terrific grandeur from the centre of the royal pavilions, fed by the thousand combustible materials supplied by the luxurious tastes and refined genius of that golden age of chivalry and art. The queen and court rushed from their prayers, ere they retired to rest, into the open courts, filling the air with their cries. A scene of confusion and dismay it is impossible to depict, added to the dread of a momentary onset of the Moors, distracted all hearts; and the intrepid Ponce de Leon at the head of a strong squadron advanced to cover the camps from any sudden stratagem of the foe. Yet the Moorish turban was to be seen only in the red glare which fell on the walls and battlements of the capital; along the gates and ramparts gleamed burnished helm and jewelled scymitar,—the alarm was rung,—and the tocsin beat to arms; yet not a Moorish horseman appeared in the plain. Both people and leaders suspected treachery in their foe, and each therefore forebore to strike at a moment which must have crowned with victory a vigorous onset of the besieged.

At length the fearful conflagration ceased to illumine the far horizon, gradually fading from the glowing peaks of the snowy sierra and from vale and stream, till again the darkening shadows stretched their dense masses over the fated city ; the terror and turmoil of its thousand human cares and sympathies died away with the heavy din of the tambour, and all lay hushed in strange and dread repose till the quick *reveille*. The fire of the Christian city was quenched in a heap of smouldering ashes,—the perished relics of the proud, the beautiful, and the gay, as the heroic Marquis of Cadiz, musing on the strange apathy of the Moslem, led his squadron towards the devastated camp.

The circumstance of the accidental fire, and of the prompt, high-souled Muza having failed to take advantage of it, encouraged Ferdinand to more daring acts of insult and aggression. The indignation of the chief, who had only been dissuaded from sallying forth by the king and his coadjutors, exceeded all bounds when he beheld the fate of the Christian camp, strewed with the wreck of magnificence and wealth ; and he soon poured down with his squadrons, hurrying to repair the error of his colleagues and his king. But at dawn, the drums and clarions had also summoned the Christians to arms ; and he saw their spreading lines and shining banners, amidst peals of martial song, taking up their bold positions in the plain. They seemed to behold the heaps of ruin which surrounded them, with as much joyous confidence as if they had befallen the foe ;—and now they dared even to advance nearer to the walls. The Moorish king, too justly entitled " The Unhappy," bitterly lamented his want of resolution, which had restrained the ardour of his chief, and by every exertion, and the most reckless bravery, he sought to repair his fault in the eyes of the people and the troops. Already was the foot of the Christian spoiler trampling the pleasure-grounds and orchards immediately surrounding the beloved capital, when, maddened with every incentive of insulted honour and violated homes, the Moors, ever fiery, fell on the advanced ranks with demoniac fury and thirst of revenge. In the heart of that one loved spot,—surrounded by the dear familiar objects of their childhood, the passions of their growing years,—they would have poured their life-blood in torrents had they held a thousand lives to cope with hand to hand, and exterminate their hated foe. And dearly did they sell their birthright to the Spaniard, as they fought at the threshold of their wives and maidens, under the eyes of the old men, warriors of another age,—of striplings and children who seized on the long-rusted arms, and rushed into the glorious conflict of their sons and of their sires, happy thus to die at each other's side.

That day, along the walls, and gates, and ramparts, on tower and mosque were to be seen only thronged groupes of women and infants, gazing down upon that battle-field with the breathless anxiety of dread suspense, never to be felt but in the crisis of such a war.

As fast as the troops of Ferdinand received fresh support,—the common artisans, the peaceful citizens,

old invalided soldiers, even to the muleteers, the
halt, and the infirm, seized their family weapons, and
hurried to take part in some of the thousand deadly
and close conflicts spread over a wide but interrupted
space of wood and thicket, houses, walls, grounds,
and hanging-gardens,—all the once delightful suburbs
of a great and splendid city.   It was here the struggle
for mastery grew most hot and desperate ; and here
the sudden onsets and ambuscades of Muza's squadrons mowed down whole columns of the enemy.
But it was in the more insulated encounters, in small
parties and single battles, the Moors proved their
superiority in this soul-appealing moment ; and every
hedge, and fount, and hillock,—each plot and clump
of trees was strewn with Christian corpses,—victims of
the infuriated people.   And now to their gladdening
hearts and flashing eyes, appeared in their aid small
bodies of hardy mountaineers and veterans of the old
Alpuxarras; who, as fast as Spain's border squadrons
were called into the general action, hastened from their
fastnesses to support their countrymen in the unequal
struggle.   The Moslem king, who had acquired wisdom and humility without losing his native courage,
was in every part, not now too proud to obey the impulse of the eagle-eye and lion-heart of a chief, who
had infused the intoxication of valour into the breasts
of all.   The favourite squadron of Muza swept the
field from side to side, ever prompt where hard-pressed
heroism sank under overwhelming numbers to throw
around its generous shield.   How often that well-
fought day did it excite to nobler feats of prowess

the fainting spirits of the children of the faithful, calling on their holy Prophet; and then with their beloved Muza raising their old war-shout of *Allah illah Allah!* as they rushed to die upon the sword of the infidel who polluted their soil. Even when wounded unto death,—wherever the brave chief appeared,—the dying Moor, forgetting all but his country, turned round his face to greet him with a sad smile and utter a blessing on his head, as with a feeble cheer, he pointed to the enemy and expired. Nor was this either rare or remarkable at such a moment of stern energy and excitement, when to die at the threshold of Granada's freedom was more eagerly coveted than to live a slave. Could valour alone have saved her, she had not fallen, nor was it by the sword of the Spaniard; it was the crafty policy of their leader,—it was their own destiny, their own consuming fire of discord and dissension,—which consigned them bound into the hands of the fanatic sovereigns of Castile.

From early morn till the dusk of evening began to steal over the plain, had the dire conflict been maintained, and every foot of ground yielded to the overwhelming superiority of the Christian was steeped in a more than equal portion of his blood. At last the cross-bow and riflemen who had held the suburb-towers, retired from their posts as others advanced to relieve them; but the Moorish infantry, conceiving they were abandoned, were seized with their old fatal panic, and fled with the impulse of one man. In vain Abu Abdallah sought to rally them, exposing himself with heroic indifference to every danger;—too late

flew the swift death-winged horsemen of Muza to retrieve the evil fortune of that one fearful flight. Rushing with panic-struck speed towards the mountains, or
through the gates of the city, the Moors were pursued
with desperate fury by the enemy; and Granada had
that day anticipated her dreaded doom, but for the
faithful squadrons who stemmed the tide of battle
before the walls. With slow, retiring rear and bold
conflicting van, the horse of Muza re-entered the city;
and then, for the first time, their chief commanded the
great portal to be closed and barricaded, as perilous
longer to entrust to a people who could desert their
bravest champions in the stern encounter, bearing the
brunt of their gallant foeman's charge.

From this period, rejecting their assistance in the
field, he ordered the infantry to the walls; and soon
the terrific volleys of artillery swept the plain, thundering along the vales and hills, and checking the
nearer approaches of the enemy. And the valour of
the tribes seemed still to rise with their ebbing fortunes; and all spectators who took part in that desperate contest applauded the unyielding heroism, the
ability, and wonderful resources of Muza and his noble
squadrons. But their ranks could not always continue
renewed with the best blood of Granada, which had
flowed in torrents till its heart waxed feeble, and its
limbs trembled under the oft-repeated shock. Like
the Phrygian rival of the Greek, she had for nearly
ten years sustained the horrors of this desolating war,
till she fought alone from the towers of her Alhambra.
" Their persevering energy, disputing every foot of

ground," says the old chronicler,* "proves how reluctantly they left the vega, which seemed a paradise and heaven to them, heedless of wounds, or conquest, or death itself." When no longer able to keep the field, they closed every avenue to their city with gloomy despair. Its rival, Santa Fe, soon drew from it the resources of commerce, with all its exterior connexions and support.

Desolate, and driven to the spot of earth on which they must yield or die, the unhappy Moors now beheld famine, and heard the dying cries of their wives and children, adding poignancy to their bitter woes. The lamentations of the old Moorish historians over this agonizing period of their fall are so truly pathetic, yet mournfully beautiful and resigned,—such is their tone of deep humiliation and distress, as to force tears from the reader's eyes, and fill his heart with a sentiment of grief akin to that which follows the last sound of "ashes to ashes, and dust to dust."† They vibrated on the spirits of the bereaved children of the Prophet like the final knell rung in the ears of the condemned, when called forth to meet their doom, surrounded by all the dread pageantry, the appalling aspect of a death, the spectators of which raise hideous shouts of mockery and insult at the startling sight.

* Abarca.

† " Alas for thee ! thou pride and gem of cities, how is thy beauty faded—thy glory despoiled ! Sweet land of groves and fountains—home of the happy and the faithful who died in thy arms—thou despairing and forsaken mother of heroes— shorn is thy greatness and thy strength ! Where are thy merchant-princes ? where thy tribute-cities, the sceptre of

Such was now the spectacle of that troubled capital, and thus exultingly did her bitter enemies and the world look upon her fate. A strange despondency, deepened by the spirit of their faith, seized on all hearts, and the faquirs and santons, casting dust upon their heads, were alone to be seen and heard in the streets. Again they harrowed up the feelings of the people, by ringing the changes of their destiny till it approached the sound of its dreaded fulfilment,—all they had predicted at their king's birth, at the outbreak, and through all the stages of that long, disastrous war. Often excited to a pitch of fury by these fanatics, they pursued them howling through the streets, attacking the tribes and nobles, and venting their wrath in maledictions and spoliation,—a popular convulsion not unfrequent at the hour of dissolution, ere mighty states and cities yield their last and lingering breath.

Then they relapsed into the same fearful gloom, smiting their breasts and trampling their turbans in the dust. Again, in nobler mood, they called with frantic eagerness to be led against their besiegers; and it was in these moments that the faithful Muza mar-

thy far-spreading sway? Where now the chivalry which swept thy plains, and filled thy spacious lists with the beauty and the joy of lordly war?—Hewn down as the young trees of the forest, fallen in the oft-bloody field! Thy proud Alhambra yet lifts its gorgeous towers to the sky, but silence reigns in her courts and halls; her marble founts flow unheeded, her garden-bowers are desart and sad, and her princes look from their lofty palace walls upon the ravaged land, where bloomed the yellow harvests of her glorious smiling vega!"

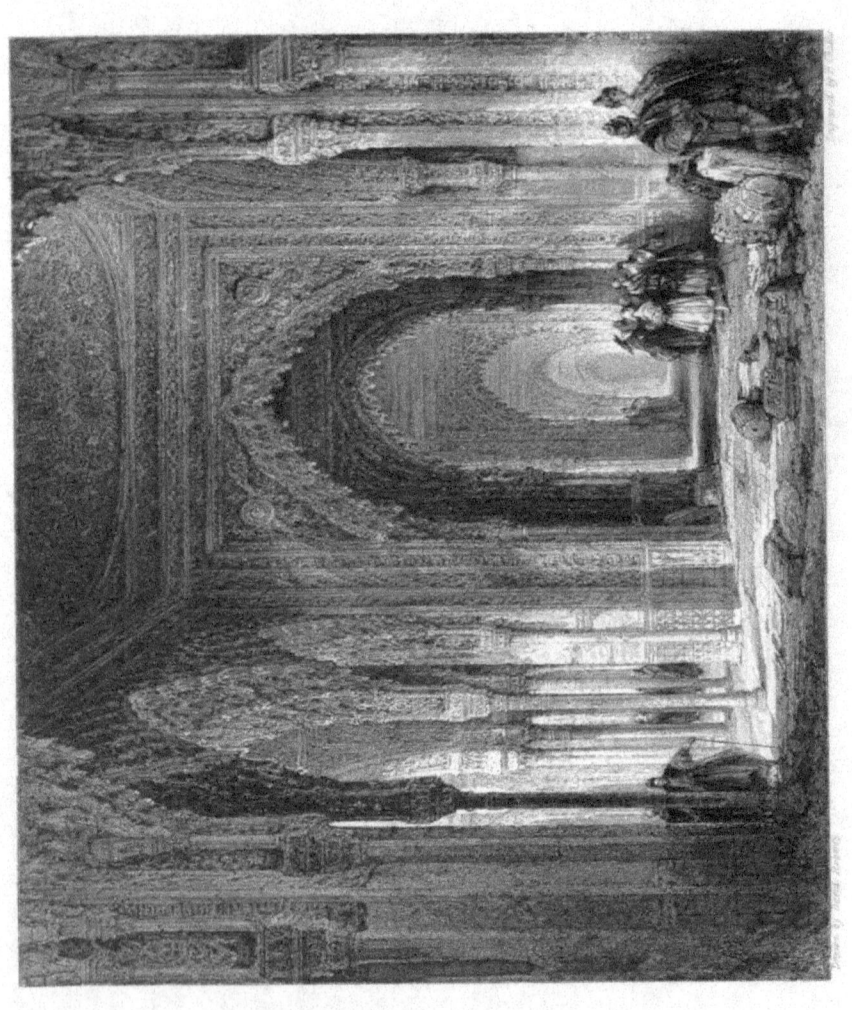

shalled his squadrons anew, and sallying forth took sudden vengeance for their accumulated sufferings and woes. By night and by day these fierce sorties carried slaughter and consternation into the Christian camp; but increasing famine and the sword palsied their generous efforts, and they returned to weep within their walls.

The fate of Granada was on the eve of a final decision, from which there could be no farther appeal. Neither the pride of royalty, nor the enthusiasm of patriotism could any longer keep hope alive. The melancholy of a resignation which, partaken by noble families and tribes, seemed rather to solicit the pity of the conqueror than the sympathy of the brave and great, now sat on every countenance. And when the last council of Granada had assembled in the Hall of Judgment* to determine on the measures to be pur-

---

* The annexed view is taken from the windows of the splendid Hall of the Ambassadors, and in it are contained the only remaining specimens of those curious paintings before alluded to, of which the subject and period of production have long engaged the inquiries of the learned and curious. The grand Hall of Audience, or of Judgment as it is more generally termed, is situated between the noble Court of Lions, the Hall of the Abencerrages, and that of the Two Sisters. It is a spacious apartment, thirty-six feet square, thirty-six feet high up to the cornice, and at least eighteen from that point to the centre of the cupola.

"Continuing your walk round," observes Mr. Swinburne, "you are next brought to a couple of rooms at the head of the court, which are supposed to have been tribunals or audience-chambers." After passing along the arcade from the Hall of the Abencerrages, the tourist is struck with the noble and symmetric proportions of the Hall of Judgment. In point of

sued at this eventful crisis, the dejected looks of the
prince and his most devoted adherents proclaimed at
once that the spirit of royalty no longer held its seat
in their bosoms.

After a brief discussion, in which, with a single
exception, every voice was raised in favour of submission, the hajib, Abil Omixa, was charged with a missive to Ferdinand, expressive of the readiness of the
king to yield to the necessities of his situation.   The

costly taste and magnificence, it rivals the elaborate splendour
and elegance of the adjacent halls, while it has a more sombre
and imposing air than is observed in the prevailing character of
Moorish architecture.   It is here, and in the adjoining halls and
courts, where the scenes of so many of the old associations and
traditions of the Alhambra have been laid by the credulity of the
people, more especially as they lie contiguous to the old fortress
of the vaults, since appropriated as a dwelling for the Catholic
curate of the city.   Strange tales are current, not only of
unaccountable sounds, but of sudden lights, and other more
alarming apparitions at the dead hour of night.   Shadowy
processions of the old Moorish warriors, and of those of their
singular successors, the Franciscan friars, have been seen with
long tapers in their hands, who salute the modern father,
without invitation, as he lies upon his mattress, and jump one
after another over his bed.   At various seasons, also, deep
groans and fearful outcries are to be heard in the Court of
Lions, from the indignant spirits of the Abencerrages, who
never cease to complain of the unjust fate to which they were
so suddenly doomed.   The region of the Seven Vaults, and
other parts of the Alhambra where the ancient treasures are
deposited, are the resort of spirits and necromancers, who
perform the most singular feats, particularly in the large
round tower near the ramparts of the great fortress.   You
may hear, it is stoutly maintained, the clash of arms; and if
you listen at the exact moment and keep a sharp look out,
you will not fail to hear the tramp of the armed tread, and
catch the dark shadows of the old Moorish squadrons.

only dissentient council raised against this humiliating proceeding was that of the noble-minded Muza. To him it appeared that while swords remained in the hands of even a few brave men, it was base to speak of surrender and slavery; that by courage and fortitude a glory might be won which would render even calamity prosperous, and confer an honour and renown which would be more than equivalent to the mere outward trappings of courtly luxury and dominion. While sentiments like these flashed momentarily in the eyes of the bold Moor, the heroism of his nature was poured forth in a torrent of expressions which shook the very souls of his auditors, and made them feel as if the angel of Death were already sweeping over the blood-stained threshold of Granada. But his words passed away like an empty sound; the council was dissolved, and Abil Omixa took his departure. On reaching the camp of the Christians, the Castilian monarch, in beholding him introduced into the royal pavilion, testified his respect for old age, by giving the bowed and sorrowing hajib a courteous and cordial greeting, as honourable to the passing feelings of the victor as soothing to the troubled Moor.

When the purpose of his mission was made known, the king at once declared not only his willingness, but the desire which he felt to save Granada and its inhabitants from the miseries with which they were threatened. Abil Omixa had conferences also with the chief ministers of state, Ferdinand of Zafra and Gonzales of Cordova; and the substance of the conditions which he bore back to his anxious countrymen

was to the effect, that Granada in two months should
be surrendered, if in the course of that time it should
remain without farther succour ; that the king and his
chiefs should swear allegiance to the crown of Spain,
but that the Muselmāns should preserve their liberty,
their arms, and possessions, the right of exercising
their religion, of being judged according to their
own laws, and that they should remain free from any
farther imposts than those they had paid to their native
princes.

But notwithstanding the favourable nature of the
concluding articles in the proposed convention, the
aged ambassador had no sooner made the result of his
mission known, than all Granada resounded with cla-
mours and lamentations.   Was the haughty foe to
trample the glory of their city under his feet ?   Was
the Christian to stand and scoff whilst they worshipped
in their temples ?   Were their matrons and maidens
to blush under the rude licentious eyes of the masters
of their lovers and their husbands ?   Indignation and
terror summoned up every thought that could gall
and madden the hearts of men, when it was found
how near and probable was the consummation of the
Spaniard's triumph.

In the midst of these loud but fruitless complaints
of the multitude, the voice of Muza rose like thunder,
or rather like a blast amidst a forest of saplings, which
it bends to the very earth as it sweeps among them.

" You shed tears ! " exclaimed he ;   " shed blood !
Gather around me, and I will lead you in the face of
death to victory.   Do you tremble at the thought of

death? Is not slavery more terrible than the destroyer? Is life to be purchased at the price of every thing dear to the soul? Will you purchase it with your honour, —with your liberty,—with the religion of your fathers, and be content with it, when to live shall be only to grovel in the dust under the feet of your enemies? But live thus, if it be your will. For me, I swear by Allah these eyes shall never look upon Granada— fallen, miserable, and captive! My head shall never bow to the scornful conqueror; my neck shall not wear his yoke, nor these hands wield a sword with which they dare not strike!"

It was thus the indignant Muza spoke in the midst of the assembly convened for the purpose of receiving Ferdinand's proposals. But there was no echo to his words: a deeper silence seemed to succeed his last sentence. Every face was pale with rage; many a heart swelled almost to bursting; but despair conquered every other feeling, and not a lip moved in reply to his heroic summons. Contempt, wild and bitter, flashed like a lurid light over his countenance, when he found himself thus without a single companion in the strife he waged; and darting from the place where he stood, he rushed out of the hall, flew to his mansion, and full armed and mounted on his favourite barb, passed through the gate of Elvira, and was never either seen or heard of more.*

* Numerous rumours and traditions, connected with the strange disappearance of the last great hero of the Moors, naturally arose; and both Spanish and Arabian chroniclers give their versions of so remarkable an event. One of these avers that

As soon as the council had recovered itself from the surprise and confusion into which it had been thrown by the impetuosity of Muza, Abu Abdallah addressed it in a speech full of mild and soothing expressions. He endeavoured to convince them that it was not the want of valour or conduct which rendered submission imperative upon them, but the absolute failure of the means of defence ; that, in such a state of things, the boldest and most honourable man might be well content to save his life and possessions on the terms offered by the Castilian.

Glad to escape from the sensations of shame which consumed their hearts, the chiefs and counsellors of the monarch bowed complacently to his opinions. But it was not so with the people and some of their leaders : —the decision of the government was received with loud exclamations of contempt, and in the lapse of a few days the city was every where agitated with manifest signs of insurrection.

Abu Abdallah trembled at the consequences of this

he precipitated himself from the pinnacle of a rock into the sea ; and, another, that he passed the straits and became the founder of a new country and a race of heroes ; but the most popular and well-attested of all perhaps is, that on the night of that very day he was met riding towards the sea by a party of Christian horse, who, challenging him to stand, were attacked with the utmost impetuosity by the wandering Moor. Such was the desperation of his onset, that he slew and wounded several before they could surround and slay him. After a terrific struggle—when he had lost his steed, and fought on his knees with the blood rushing in streams down his armour, by a sudden effort he cast himself headlong into the waters of the Xenil.

turbulent disposition. He knew that if the surrender of the city were opposed by the populace, the Castilian troops would be instantly poured through all its quarters, and that while torrents of blood would be shed, he himself must forfeit the few means left him for supporting his humiliation and his exile. He now bitterly reproached himself as the author of his own calamities; for that criminal ambition which led him to usurp the throne of his sire,—a throne he must now resign amidst the execrations of a lost and enslaved people. If remorse and tears could expiate his errors and excesses, Abu Abdallah paid the bitter penalty; for in no instance does fallen royalty appear to have loosed its grasp upon the symbols of power with a keener sense of degradation and distress. In this exigency, the Moor had again recourse to the advice of his principal officers; and strengthened in his purpose by their opinion, he sent a messenger to Ferdinand charged with the intimation, that the city would be resigned into his hands as soon as he was prepared to enter it with his forces.

The intelligence which he thus received was as gratifying to Ferdinand as it was unexpected; and, in reply to his communication, he assured Abu Abdallah of his friendship and esteem, and gave him many promises of future protection and benefit. Nor did he delay to avail himself of the advantage thus afforded him. Scarcely had the light of the following morning broke, when he was on his way, at the head of a splendid retinue, to the devoted city. Restless in his afflictions, Abu Abdallah was equally early in his preparations for the day so fraught with sorrow to his people and humiliation to himself. His family, accompanied by a numerous train of attendants, bearing his treasures and most valuable effects, was already on the road to the Alpuxarras; and before the sun had long left the horizon, the sound of horns and cymbals announced to Granada the approach of the Christian monarch.

Mournful was the spectacle of that once free, warlike, and splendid city, now about to pass under the yoke of captivity. Throughout its whole extent, there was nothing to be heard but lamentations,—nothing to be seen but signs of despair and wrath. In the midst of these demonstrations of his people's feelings, the crownless monarch, who appeared to have lost the last remains of pride in the conflict of his passions, passed through a postern gate of the Alhambra, and proceeded to meet his Castilian victor. Upon the summit of the hill before him,* commanding the Gate of the Mills and the approach into the city, already gleamed the arms of Castile, and the troops destined to take instant possession of his Alhambra.

Abil Omixa was left to give up the keys of the city, and to surrender the grand fortress at the close of the royal interview. Having pursued his way by the mills into the plain, the humbled prince was received by Ferdinand with marked courtesy and attention. Preventing him from leaving his saddle, he expressed himself in terms calculated to soothe his feelings, and

* Called the Hill of the Martyrs.

diminish the pain which he saw in every line of his countenance.   The Moor felt even this kindness, and offering to kiss his extended hand, which Ferdinand prevented, exclaimed, " Glorious and puissant king, we are thy servants ; we resign into thy hands our city and kingdom, for such is the will of Allah ! "

Having thus addressed the conqueror, and declined his invitation to return towards Granada, he bade adieu to his unhappy capital, and continued his way to the Alpuxarras.*   From the mountain of Padul, he took a last and lingering view of Granada, that gradually disappeared in the misty distance.   " *Ala hu Akbar !*   Woe is me, great God ! " were the only words he uttered, but his eyes were full of tears, and his bosom seemed bursting with grief.   " Weep ! " was the bitter reproach of his noble mother ; " weep like a woman for thy kingdom, since thou couldst not keep it like a man ! "

Jusef Abil Omixa, his faithful attendant, gently sought to soothe the added pang thus inflicted ; but the fallen prince only replied, " No ! surely no calamities are like those I suffer ! " and melancholy the most oppressive continued to prey upon his heart and frame.   Time seemed to bring no relief; and at length his friends proposed his removal to a greater distance from scenes so painful to his recollection.   He mourn-

* As the Emperor Charles the Fifth gazed from the palace windows of the Alhambra towards the lofty heights of the Alpuxarras, " I had rather," he exclaimed, " have found a grave in a palace like this, than a little kingdom in yonder rugged mountains."

fully acceded, passed over into Africa, and soon
found the sole relief he coveted in an honourable
death, while engaged in the wars of his relative, the
King of Fez.*

Ferdinand and Isabella took possession of Granada
with all the pomp which could give splendour to their
conquest ; and thus expired, never again to rise, the
empire of the Moors in Spain.   But though the kingdom had perished, the native vigour of the Moorish
character still survived, and operated on the remnant
of the nation ; and, at the close of the eventful drama,
and when the curtain had fallen on the busy stage
where princes and nobles ended their blood-stained
career, a new scene of terror was commenced, in which
the actors seemed guided by a yet fiercer, sterner, and
more enduring spirit.

* By some of the Spanish writers it is stated, that the
Moorish king went forth to present the keys of the city to the
sovereigns on a cushion, in the most abject terms beseeching
their protection for his person.   The valley of Purchena, in
Murcia, was assigned him for his place of residence, and a
handsome revenue provided for himself and his family.   But
in a little while, "not having resolution," as Mariana ex-
presses it, " to endure a private life in the country where he
had so long reigned as king," he went over to Barbary.   The
royal entrance took place on the 6th of January, 1492.

THE FLIGHT FROM GRANADA.

There was crying in Granada, when the sun was going down,
Some calling on the Trinity, some calling on Mahoun :
Here passed away the Koran, there in the Cross was borne,
And here was heard the Christian bell, and there the Moorish horn.

Te Deum Laudamus was up the Alcala sung,
Down from the Alhamra's minarets were all the crescents flung :
The arms thereon of Arragon they with Castile display,
One king comes in in triumph, one weeping goes away.

Ferdinand and his consort, during their abode at Granada, beheld with disgust the freedom which the Jews enjoyed in the conquered city. In this feeling they were cheerfully met by many of their courtiers, who strongly partaking of the spirit of the age, rejoiced at the idea of subjecting the Israelites to the alternative of conversion or death. A decree was accordingly passed, by which the intended victims were commanded to submit without delay to the rite of baptism, or to be deprived of their wealth, as the forfeit of their blindness and obstinacy. The conse-

Thus cried the weeper, while his hands his old white beard did tear—
" Farewell, farewell Granada ! thou city without peer ;
Woe, woe, thou pride of heathendom, seven hundred years and more
Have gone since first the faithful thy royal sceptre bore.

Thou wert the happy mother of a high renowned race,
Within thee dwelt a haughty line that now go from this place ;
Within thee fearless knights did dwell, who fought with mickle glee,
The enemies of proud Castile, the bane of Christiantie.

The mother of fair dames wert thou, of truth and beauty rare,
Into whose arms did courteous knights for solace sweet repair ;
For whose dear sakes the gallants of Afric made display
Of might in joust and battle, in many a bloody day.

Here gallants held it little thing for ladies' sake to die,
Or for the Prophet's honour, and pride of soldanry ;
For here did valour flourish, and deeds of warlike might,
Ennobled lordly palaces, in which was our delight.

The gardens of thy Vega, its fields and blooming bowers—
Woe, woe ! I see their beauty gone, and scattered all their flowers ;
No reverence can he claim, the king, that such a land has lost,
On charger never can he ride, nor be heard among the host.

But in some dark and dismal place, where none his face might see,
There weeping and lamenting alone that king should be ;"
Thus spake Granada's king, as he was riding to the sea,
About to cross Gibraltar's strait away to Barbary.

*   *   *   *   *

" Unhappy king, whose craven soul can brook, (she 'gan reply),
To leave behind Granada—who hast not heart to die ;
Now for the love I bore thy youth, thee gladly could I slay,
For what is life to leave, when such a crown is cast away ! "

LOCKHART. Old Moorish Ballad.

quence of this ordinance was, the submission of the weak,——the exile and ruin of the more conscientious. In a short time, the pretended converts found that notwithstanding the sacrifice they had made, the same danger was hovering over them which had overwhelmed their brethren. An institution was erected which might claim the praise of novelty, even in the gloomiest annals of persecution. It was now for the first time that inquisitions were heard of, and that Christians assumed the ensigns of death, in order to act the part of guardians to divine charity. The miserable Jews who had subjected themselves to the Catholic law, could scarcely fail of falling into some offence against the doctrine or discipline of the church.

In the expectation of this result, the lynx eye of the holy office was ever directed towards them with all the vulture-like keenness of unpitying bigotry. Instances of a supposed relapse soon became frequent; the sword was drawn, the book of judgment opened in the secret vaults of the office, and crowds of victims were poured forth to lay their already mangled bodies on the heaped up faggots. While the persecuted Jews were thus suffering, the Moors looked on with a gloomy presage of coming ill. Nor were they mistaken in their apprehensions. The principle which had led to the persecution of the Jews, gathered strength from the victims on which it fed. When Ferdinand again held secret council with his bigoted ministers, they did not scruple to pour forth the most contemptuous expressions of hate against the enfeebled Moors. The ears of the sovereign drank in their words with evident delight; but to diminish the privileges which had been formally confirmed to the vanquished people was a dangerous experiment. It was to break the most solemn engagements,—to violate kingly honour, and overturn the foundations of all national confidence. How were the difficulties thus opposed to be overcome? The grand inquisitor and Ferdinand soon learnt the way of silencing the scruples which had hitherto kept him true to his treaty. First one, and then another instance of oppression occurred in the commerce of the Moors with his government. The laws which protected them were then repealed, and the insulted Moslem felt himself scourged on to madness. This was the state of mind in which the crafty politicians of the court desired to find them. Pretending to avenge the insult put upon his laws, Ferdinand gathered his forces about Granada, and by one exertion of power drove the hated people, like a flock of sheep destined for slaughter, from the city.

A portion, however, of the exiles as they looked back upon the scenes of their happy youth, sank into the hopelessness of heart-breaking grief; and in that moment of agony professed their desire to purchase a permission to return, by immediately adopting the faith of their conquerors. The offer was accepted, and several hundred Moors received the sign of the cross. But this only served to plunge them deeper in misery. No sooner had they adopted the name of Christians, than they were subjected to all the laws and enactments of the strictest ecclesiastical polity.

They committed numerous offences against the rule to which they were thus exposed; some from obstinacy, others from ignorance. But they were now bound to the church, and their offences, regarded as treason, were punished as such.

The inquisition spread wide the doors of its subterranean dungeons to receive them, and they now every where occupied the place of the unfortunate Jews. Dreadful was the rage with which the bands that had escaped to the mountains beheld this heartless persecution of their brethren. Secure amid the inaccessible rocks, in which they found shelter from the cruelty of the conqueror, they were now urged irresistibly forward to try their strength with so execrable an enemy. In vain, however, did these brave men shed their blood. Successive princes watched and laboured for their destruction. Their doom was written in the gloomiest vaults of the inquisition, and in the sanctuary of royalty; and a doom thus predetermined was not to be rescinded on any appeal. Hundreds after hundreds perished, either openly by the sword, or at the bidding of the inquisition. They had fought for a time, with the heroism of their fathers, but no impression was to be made on the serried ranks of the Castilian cohorts. Those who survived, retreated to their mountains; their souls still breathing vengeance, and their hands eagerly clenching their scymitars which yet remained,—the only sign of their early greatness and valour.

Years gave them strength, and renewed the spirit which had prompted them to such mighty deeds in their brighter and palmier days. Once more they descended the mountains, and the sound of their tread was like the rushing of a torrent newly replenished by the waters of the hills. But neither Charles the Fifth, nor his son Philip, was of a character to leave them unresisted. The provinces through which the Moors had to carry their operations, were summoned to arms; and in a brief period, even the remnant of the Moorish race was no longer to be seen.

Thus closed, in the two-fold darkness of a religious and political doom, the eventful career of this high-spirited and remarkable people. Distinguished above all of eastern, or even European descent, by their deep religious devotion, their brilliant valour, their unrivalled ingenuity, and their renown in arts and learning,—the influence they exercised on the mind of Europe roused her from the torpor and barbarism of ages to an energy, a spirit and glory of enterprise which we attribute too little to its primary source. But the poet still bewails their fall, because in the days of their prosperity they were great and heroic; the philosopher contemplates it as the result of necessary causes; the Christian, better and more truly, as one of the acts in the mighty scheme of a divine, mysterious Providence.

T

APPENDIX.

HAVING traced, in the preceding pages, a rapid out-
line of the decline and fall of Granada, with the
immediate causes and consequences connected with
that important event, it may not be uninteresting to
follow the fortunes of the unhappy Moors to their
final subjection and expatriation as a people. Their
ardent character, the mountainous nature of the
country, and the extreme pressure of tyranny upon
the spirits of the vanquished, rendered their very
existence a source of anxiety and alarm. To avoid
one of those terrible reactions which every where mark
the annals of political bondage, and to crown the
work of violated faith and religious persecution, nothing remained but wholly to eradicate the population,
root and branch, from the Castilian soil. Granada
threatened revolt; the surrounding districts were in
arms; and the singular decree went forth to deprive
a wealthy and prosperous community of an entire race
of industrious inhabitants,—the source of its rapidly
increasing energies and powers. Banishment, or the
still more dreaded rite of baptism, was the sole alternative; and recourse was had to the last extremes of

terror and compulsion, in place of the more prevailing pleadings of argument and truth.

In the human mind, as we see illustrated in all temporary creeds and doctrines, there dwells a powerful spring of resistance to injustice, which even in death finds its recompense in having triumphed over prescriptive authority, and feels a lofty pleasure as it inflicts a pang on the oppressor's soul and foils his object by removing beyond the reach of his self-consuming cruelty and malice. By their expulsion, the Moors had a more fearful and wide-spread vengeance, than if they had continued possessors of the soil, or re-assumed their lost dominion.

Among the inaccessible rocks and strong-holds of the Alpuxarras, the exterminating system was less easily executed, and the successive expeditions of the most celebrated Castilian generals were attended with fearful loss and sacrifice of life. In one of these, the chivalrous Alonzo d'Aguilar, so eminently successful in the last Moorish wars, met an untimely fate, deplored alike by his country and by his sovereigns.

The old Spanish ballad so admirably rendered by my friend, Mr. Lockhart, commemorates the fall of this last of the chiefs of a chivalrous age; his younger brother, Gonzalvo, the great captain though so near in point of time belonging to a new period, when war lost all the splendour conferred upon it by that spirit which expired under the keen lash of Cervantes.

The bold mountaineers met the troops, and the missionaries whom they escorted, with persevering hostility; nor was it till Ferdinand placed himself at the head of a powerful army, that they offered to purchase his clemency by the payment of fifty thousand ducats. But the same causes were at work, and, beyond the immediate sphere of the Spanish garrisons, the hollow truce thus afforded failed to exercise an influence upon either party. The monarch approached with fresh reinforcements, and for the first time the Moors craved permission for a free passage into Africa. They were answered by another ordonnance, imposing the rite of baptism within three months, or the penalty of quitting the country, leaving the whole of their property behind them.

While the Moors continued in possession of the coasts of Barbary, Ferdinand seemed to feel no security in his recent conquests; the vengeance of the Moriscoes only slept, prepared to seize the first occasion of retaliation, and to call to its aid the strength of its old allies. But a series of successful campaigns put the Castilians in possession of numerous sea-ports and towns of their enemy, exacting tribute even from the formidable Deys of Tunis, Tremecen, and Algiers. Hope itself then vanished from the eyes of the unhappy survivors of the downfal of Granada, and the waters of life were to them cut off at the fountain-head of their ancient strength and glory.

The dawn of Charles rose amidst storms and conflicts; his haughty nobles beheld in him the son of the stranger, eager to infringe their prerogatives, and re-model the customs and manners of their ancestors. Their murmurs, however, were soon stifled by the resolute spirit which made his favourite motto of

" plus outre," the active principle of his reign, and
silenced the voice of his subjects, like the threats of
his enemies, by the strong hand and will.   His lords
then sought to vent their disappointment by fresh
burthens and humiliations upon the heads of the
unresisting Moors ; and had once more recourse to
the terrors of the holy inquisition.   The sufferers
appealed to the justice of the emperor ; they sent deputies to lay the subject of their grievances at the
feet of the conqueror of Tunis and Algiers.   He referred them to another tribunal, composed of theolo-
gians, inquisitors, and bishops.   The great question
mooted was, whether the decree of conversion ought
to be enforced by the faggot ?   It was decided in the
affirmative.   The Archbishop of Seville issued forthwith
a royal ordonnance, which was placed in the hands of
the police to enforce, on a day appointed, a thorough
change in the government of the Moors of Granada.
It embraced customs, manners, language, and dress, as
if calculating that so sudden and radical a revolution
in exterior observances could not fail to obliterate all
traces of early associations, and the fixed opinions of
mature life.   Its execution was to be insured by heavy
penalties ; each Christian member of the state was
empowered to watch and lay informations before the
grand tribunal of the Inquisition established in the
heart of Granada.   This decree alone brought into the
treasury of Charles eight hundred thousand ducats
from the wretched Moors, as the price of some alleviation to its excessive severity, operating as a direct
tax upon the industry of this ingenious and intelligent

people. But in the provinces, and among the lower order, unable to meet the exaction, persecution continued to rage. Displeased with their reception, the Catholic priests accused them of horrible profanations which called for the signal vengeance of the people. The inhabitants of Valencia rose, and headed by lords and prelates, the cross in one hand, the sword in the other, they fell upon the peaceable Moors, drove them into the mountains, surrounded them in their last retreat, and put numbers to death; the rest they compelled to undergo baptism, but not one of the principal among them was spared.

Charles the Fifth extolled the zeal of the Valencians; the people of Andalusia, jealous of such eulogy, prepared to follow their example, and it was only the extreme penury and caution of the Moors which preserved them from the fires of the *autos-da-fé* kindled in the cities of Granada, Seville, and Cordova. The most trivial expression of complaint or suffering was sufficient to draw down on them the extreme penalty of the Catholic laws. Yet new modes of exaction and oppression were multiplied, till, goaded beyond endurance, the kingdom of Granada burst into sudden vengeance. They fought, and they also fell like martyrs, and the ruin of the survivors and their families was sealed. Nothing less than extermination,——the obliteration, if possible, of their memory,——could satisfy their persecutors, —— for Philip the Second reigned in Spain!

The archbishop conceived that it was no way orthodox that the Moorish women should appear veiled, or that the people should be allowed the use of baths. An ecclesiastical commission was appointed, — of priests, doctors, and inquisitors,—to whom veiled women, the luxury of the bath, and the Arabic tongue were among the enormities of the wicked. A learned doctor belonging to the University of Alcala satisfied them of this, by addressing his brother commissioners in the following singular and conclusive words :— " Are you not aware, that as regards enemies, we must leave as few of them alive as possible ?"

It was in vain the Moors appealed against the cruelty and absurdity of such regulations ; they were put in force with a precision which bore the appearance of making it at once a duty and a pleasure ; and when a woman stood veiled in the presence of the commissioners, she was instantly compelled to exhibit her features to their gaze. Did a Moor pronounce but a word in his own tongue, he was thrown into a dungeon ; his children, above the age of five, were torn from his side, and brought up in a public institution far from their home. Conspiracy after conspiracy was the result ; the support of Morocco and Algiers was secretly invoked, and the whole mountainous districts entered into the league. Suspicion was roused, the governor of Granada asked for farther reinforcements ; and this alone prevented the capital from falling into their hands. Unhappily also for them their communications with Africa were intercepted, the particulars of the plot transpired, the garrisons were augmented, detachments of cavalry scoured the adjacent country, and the spirit of resistance was crushed in its bud.

Still a number of the chief conspirators met in secret, and had the hardihood to elect a king—Mohammed Ben Omega — descended, it was believed, from the khaliphs of Cordova, and who had been forcibly baptized by the name of Fernando de Valor. After offering up prayers to their Prophet, each member swore to die for his religion, and each took an oath of fidelity to their new prince. The project was confided to the Moriscoes of the Albaycin, a quarter of the city assigned to the Moors; but instead of seconding it, they were suspected of having betrayed its authors, who betook themselves to the Alpuxarras. Here they were joined by the mountaineers, and repelled the attacks made upon them from the capital. Elated by this success, they demolished the convents and churches, slaying the priests, the authorities, and every Spanish soldier whom they found. Soon the insurrection reached the plains, and extended far along the coasts, and the governor, Mondejar, was unable to oppose its fury in the outset. Not till twenty desperate conflicts had taken place, was he in a condition to approach the Alpuxarras; there a more desperate struggle ensued, till the Moors were surrounded and cut to pieces by overwhelming numbers of the foe. Several of the towns were captured, but in a short space the insurgents re-appeared, more formidable than before, receiving succours from Africa and reducing their guerilla warfare to a more regular system.

It was then that Don John of Austria marched from Seville at the head of a large army, and the Moriscoes of the capital hurried to assure him of their allegiance, while the mountaineers made new efforts to resist him. Unfortunately, their leader was accused of betraying his trust, and perished by the hands of his own soldiers; but Muley Abdallah, who succeeded him, displayed talents which long held his enemies at bay. In the ensuing spring, Don John entered into negotiations, offering advantageous conditions and proclaiming a general amnesty. But the sole article of which the Moors availed themselves was to pass into Africa with their families, while Muley Abdallah, in an interview with the Castilian leader, undertook that the Moors of the Alpuxarras should be distributed throughout the different Spanish provinces. Secretly, however, he fomented the war, seeking only to gain time and means for fresh aggressions.

Enraged beyond endurance, Philip II. ordered the Alpuxarras to be ravaged from end to end, and its remaining inhabitants to be transported into Africa, or as slaves to the adjacent provinces. Muley Abdallah was assassinated like his predecessor, and in the reign of the third Philip, the Moors of Valencia and Murcia shared the fate of the mountaineers, and were removed by masses into the countries of Barbary. Two hundred thousand Moriscoes traversed France alone, destitute of property and means of support, to embark at the sea-ports of Guienne and of Languedoc.

Thus darkly disappeared this extraordinary people from the country they had conquered, animating with their brilliant qualities the dull, proud dynasty of the indolent Goths. Hospitable, full of compassion for the stranger and the destitute, attached in heart and action to the religion of his sires, and firm in his opinions and principles, the Spanish Moor long preserved unaltered the primitive features of the children of Ismael. As a patriarch and shepherd, as a warrior of tribes, as a worshipper of his prophet, he was faithful to his duties and resigned to the destiny appointed by Him, whose high will he sought to fulfil without a murmur. He united simplicity with luxury; but they were the luxuries of nature and of reason—not the grovelling appetites and excesses of the European vulgar,—of the northern wassailers in the Gothic halls of their drunken gods. Reposing under the shadows of his patriarchal dates and palms, in the mosque whose golden spires and minarets shone in the heavens above his head, he was still prompt and faithful in all the relations of life,—as at the sound of the holy Algihed, or the martial strain which invited him to the field of honour.

His dwelling, his court, and garden, like his religion and his country, evinced the active industrious spirit which insured success in his undertakings. The waters became tributary to his ingenuity and skill, enriching the lands he had won, and teaching the Gothic desert and the mountain height to blossom with the flowery verdure of an eastern summer, like the gardens of Irem or the sylvan beauties of Grand Cairo and Bagdad. As the merchant-prince and the mariner, he inspired the vanquished with a love and daring of discovery, which opened paths into new worlds, and conferred inestimable benefits on art and science, which Europe ceases not yet to enjoy.

But empires, like creeds, have their appointed seasons upon the earth. Were the promises of victory and glory more than the stability of a morning dream, the Moors might well have looked for enduring dominion over the minds and possessions of their fellow men. But they passed away like " shadows which come and go," and the solitary traveller, in tracking the desert plains and the crumbling palace-walls of that vanquished race which stretched their dominion from the Pyrenees to the rocks of Gibraltar, from the shores of the ocean to the banks of old Barcelona,—feels deeply the perishable tenure by which the greatest of nations enjoys all human power and possessions. The days of her Tarikhs, her Abderahmans, her Mohammed Alhamars, departed and left her, stealthily " as a thief in the night," and she found herself by degrees opposed to a world in arms, which swept from under her the very ground upon which she stood. All but the memory of her glory perished from the earth; and from the depth of her ancient desarts, the exile yet turns his eyes at sunrise towards the land of his early love, and offers up a prayer to Allah for the recovery of the terrestrial paradise which his fathers lost.

NOTES.

P. 7, l. 14.—" *The faith of the compassionate and the resigned.*"

Mohammed, the warrior-prophet, was far from being the monster of cruelty he has been represented by many writers. He often forgave personal injuries and insults, and spared the vanquished. In magnanimity he certainly surpassed King David or King Solomon, as his conduct in the Holy Temple evinced. Instead of slaying Kaab, the son of Zohair, at the sacred shrine, he embraced him, and taking off his own mantle, placed it upon the man who had been one of his bitterest enemies. He had the temerity to appear before the prophet, in the mosque at Medina, when he was engaged in exhorting the people. When he ceased, Kaab recited some verses he had composed in the chief's honour, and the mantle which they won him was afterwards purchased by one of the khaliphs from the poet's family at an immense price, and was borne in public only on the most solemn occasions. Nor was the prophet's death unworthy the character and authority which he had acquired by his splendid actions during his life.

P. 91, l. 22.—" *Unhallowed conflicts of the children of Allah.*"

Mariana, Garibai, Ferrerai, and Zurita, are among the Spanish chroniclers to whom most credit has been thought due. In eloquence and learning the first of these may be said to vie with the Roman Livy, but all are, less or more, influenced in their representations by the prejudices of their country. Thus the Arabic writers make no mention of the great battle of Tours. Hidjazi simply observes, that Charles Martel, beholding the Arabs in France, was unwilling to engage them in the hope that they would quarrel and destroy each other. " In short," he adds, " the Arabs of Damas and of Yemen, the Berbers, and the Modarites attacked each other, and thus lost the conquest of France." The princes of the dynasty of the Almoades, in the 12th century, forbade the annals of their reign to be written, under pain of death. Novari instances a case in which an author was put to death for making the attempt. The *Civil Wars of Granada*, by Perez de Hita, may be pronounced almost as much a romance as the well known *Romancero General* itself. His pictures of character and events are all highly coloured and extravagant, but convey a more vivid impression than do the more authentic historians.

P. 149, l. 9.—" *By the zealous Bishop of Jaen.*"

No less than three bishops fell in battle against the Muselmãns in the great fight of Albakara in 1010, namely Arnolfo, Bishop of Vic, Accio, Bishop of Barcelona, and Otho, Bishop of Girona.

Jaen, the capital of one of the four kingdoms of Andalusia, is six leagues from Anduxar. In the vicinity we find a great number of Roman inscriptions, which are a proof of its antiquity. The country between these two cities is extremely fertile, and has a fresh and beautiful appearance in seasons which are not too dry.

P. 163, l. 2.—" *The gallant English knight, Lord Scales.*"

Besides the Earl of Rivers, a number of English knights had, at different periods, sought the grand arena of the Moorish wars. Mariana informs us, that the city of Algesiras was taken from the Moors of Granada in 1344, and he especially mentions some Englishmen of distinction who came to assist at the siege in 1443, namely, the Counts of " Arbid" and of " Soluzber," most probably the Earls of Derby and Salisbury ; and Knighton expressly says, that the Earl of Derby was there. *X. Script.* 2583.

The father of English poets, Chaucer, alludes in his Prologue to the far-famed siege.

" In Gernade at the siege eke hadde he be
Of Algesir, and ridden in Belmaric."
Prol. p. 9, l. 57.

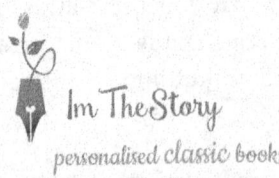
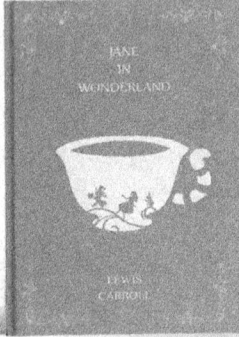

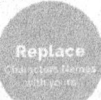
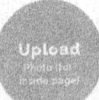

CPSIA information can be obtained
at www.ICGtesting.com
Printed in the USA
BVHW081809220819
556561BV00019B/4208/P